THE
DUNEDIN
AFFAIR

or

The Bishop who lost his See

Edited by Bob Simmonds

2024

writerbobsimmonds@gmail.com

ISBN 978-1-3999-7137-9

Front cover: Design for a Pastoral Staff by William Burges (Canterbury Cathedral Archives)

Back cover: Stained glass window in the South Chapel of St Mildred's Church, Preston-next-Wingham.

Photo by David Anstiss (djanstiss@googlemail.com)

Ordnance Survey Map (Sheet 117) Original survey 1878

Printed and bound by Biddles Ltd., in the United Kingdom

In regard to Otago and Dunedin, it was the intention of the founders to establish an especially Presbyterian settlement ... As to Dunedin we have lately heard more of its desire to have a Church of England bishop of its own than any other propensity. And it is going to have a bishop. I may say has got one, though when I was there the prelate had not yet arrived. A former bishop did indeed come out, but he was not approved of, and was returned, having never been installed.

It is marvelous to me that the Australian and New Zealand Sees can find English clergymen to go out to them. The pay is small, generally not exceeding £500 a year. That bishops do not become bishops for money we are all prepared to admit. But the power also is very limited, the patronage almost none at all, and the snubbing to which they are subjected is excessive.

Anthony Trollope
Australia & New Zealand
Chapman & Hall (1873)

Introduction

It says something about the richness and complexity of life that every so often connections and coincidences arise that change or challenge us in unexpected ways.

As a lad I was a member of the local crack platoon of Sea Scouts, and in the summer of 1966 we set up camp as far from the sea as our bikes would take us, on a farmer's field in the village of Preston-next-Wingham, Kent. That year turned out to be a rather good one for English football, and the farmer was kind enough to invite us all into his living room to watch the 1966 FIFA World Cup Final on his large screen TV. It was one of those moments to remember.

Twenty-two years later I was on the other side of the world, having swapped my job as Vicar of Grovehill, Hemel Hempstead with the Vicar of Oamaru in the Diocese of Dunedin, New Zealand for six months, and it was here that a connection was made.

Put simply, in 1868 the then Vicar of Preston-next-Wingham had arrived in Dunedin having been consecrated, and expecting to serve, as the first ever Anglican bishop of the newly carved-out Diocese of that southern region. He was the Rt. Rev. Henry Lascelles Jenner DD who, because of many diverse reasons, was not wanted by the church authorities in that land, and who had to return to Preston-near-Wingham where he remained as Vicar for the rest of his life.

A book called *Seeking a See,* describing Jenner's visit to New Zealand and his rejection by the Diocese of Dunedin, had recently been published by that diocese. This account of the way Jenner had been treated by both prelates and priests, and more importantly by the lay people of New Zealand, proved to be a good way to discover something of this country and of its version of the Church of England.

As I sat in the garden of the vicarage at Oamaru, where Bishop Jenner had visited on his tour of the diocese, I read the book with a growing sense of love and respect for the man, and anger and despair at the way he had been treated and the great loss to the life of the church that this had caused.

It would probably have been left there but, many years later, I found myself in a situation not dissimilar from that endured by Bishop Jenner. Despite my qualifications, training, and ordination – and years of experience as a parish priest – I found my ministry unwanted, my gifts and abilities ignored, and my priesthood wasted.

And I was not alone. Many gifted people were being left by the wayside, or badly treated, as the Church of England blundered on, both hidebound by its historic pomp and power, and at the same time turning its back on the richness and sanctity of the parish system, and losing its grip on a studied and grounded theology.

In light of this I felt that the 'Dunedin Affair' had much to say.

But if it was to be heard, then it needed to be more properly understood, and to be more scrupulously and objectively examined than it had in the few previous studies. Why, for example, was Jenner never offered another bishopric, or even a more demanding priestly ministry? How did it feel to be a 'spare' bishop in rural Kent?

And so I did a lot of research; scoured archives, libraries, websites and old newspapers, and then put together this book.

———————————————

In many TV crime dramas there is usually an episode where the solution to the mystery of who done it seems to be an 'open and shut case'. All the evidence points to one particular suspect. They have the motive, the means and the opportunity; and besides, they are generally disliked and have personal hygiene problems.

But the maverick detective in charge (with a failed marriage and an obsessive passion for real ale and macramé,) thinks differently. There is more evidence to be revealed, more complex personal ties and power struggles that are woven into the tapestry that surrounds the case, and whose unravelling leads to its inevitable drawing room denouement. And so it is with the Dunedin Affair.

If you look at any brief summary of Jenner's trip to New Zealand, it almost always states that he had to return to Preston because the people of the regions of Otago and Southland (which made up the new Diocese of Dunedin,) did not like his support of 'ritualism' and the new High Church practices that were challenging the church in England at that time. Which is, to a certain extent, true. In the same way as saying that Henry VIII founded the Church of England so that he could divorce his wives does hold a trace of truth.

The factors that lie behind, in, and through the whole of the Dunedin Affair – from the Bishop of New Zealand asking the Archbishop of Canterbury to find someone to be Bishop of Dunedin, to Jenner's final years of denied episcopacy – are many and complicated. They include elements as varied as the tensions that Catholic renewal was bringing to the Church of England at home; the problems that the Colonies posed for the Church of England abroad; the creation of an independent and authoritative synodical government for the Anglican church in New Zealand; the establishment of a completely new diocese; the cultural conflict between the English and Scottish settlers in Otago and Southland; and the social changes arising from the Otago gold rush.

That's not to forget the sensationalist or over-simplistic stories of the press of the time, and the manipulation of events by those who had power, and wanted to keep it.

And then there is, of course, the position of Jenner on developments like ritualism and the Gothic revival in England, in comparison with the ecclesiastical conservatism of the early immigrants to New Zealand.

In a way the Affair presents us with the problems that arise with any new and controversial development. In some cases it is possible, when reading a letter or a report, to just delete the word 'ritualistic' and replace it with feminist, gay, liberal, foreign, migrant, black, socialist, woke, capitalist, transgender, etc., etc., and for the sentence to still make sense. The ways in which we cope with or deny change have not themselves changed much over the years.

But perhaps the most destructive factors in the Affair were the views, positions, and decisions of the leading Bishops and the great and the good in both the Church of England, and in its New Zealand colony.

As the Rev. John Pearce wrote at the beginning of his Introduction to *Seeking a See* -

For those who cannot bear to read of Bishops who broke their bonds, and priests who posed and prattled, it would be best to omit this section and go straight to the Journal. But for those who are prepared to hear a squalid story, there is a tale of perfidy and treachery to tell.

CONTENTS

Pilgrimage to Preston-next-Wingham, Kent

Once it has left the ruins of St. Augustine's Abbey and passed the old Sessions House and Prison the road from Canterbury to Sandwich begins a very gentle, tree-lined climb.

As it passes the end of North Holmes Road there is a glimpse of the lychgate of St Martin's church – the oldest church building in Britain still in use as a church, and the oldest parish church in the English-speaking world.

At the top of the hill the road passes what had been the old Howe Army Barracks, now covered in new executive houses and called 'Royal Parade' and, further along on the right, the Canterbury Borough Asylum, built in 1903, and still offering mental health care as St. Martin's NHS Hospital.

From then on the A257 is a delight.

Following the comparatively straight course of the old Roman Road it is lined on either side by tall hedges, bushes, ferns, wild flowers and a variety of mature trees, broken only by a golf course, and the odd posh converted oast house.

Further along is Polo Field.

An exclusive collection of homes – designed to reflect the area's rich architectural heritage, retaining unique charm through the use of reclaimed brickwork and Cape Cod timber cladding – which will appeal to a range of buyers, including professionals, families, commuters and downsizers.

This is followed by Polo Farm Sports Club, which presumably gives the exclusive residents of Polo Field, and the many exclusive large, set-back, detached properties along this part of the road, something to do.

And then the woodland begins to thicken and the trees meet together above the road, forming a long, enchanted and refreshing tunnel of dappled leaves and branches of horse chestnut, beech, oak and field maple, which opens up again on leaving the straight line of the old

Roman Road. Here, fields spread out to the right, beyond the hedge of bushes and flowers, trees and ferns. Old oaks and hawthorn, dog-rose and hazel, cuckoo pint and blackthorn, together line the road as it makes its way to the pretty little village of Littlebourne.

Littlebourne contains sixty grade II listed buildings, over twenty of which line the A257, and, thanks to the flower troughs on the road and the parking spaces in-between, travellers will have time to admire as they drive slowly past.

After leaving the village, and crossing the Nail Bourne stream, the road continues in a near straight line through fruit fields and hedgerows, trees and farms; with huge clumps of ivy, paddocks with horses, and bridleway signs to places like *Half Acre* and *White Gate.*

After about a mile and a quarter there is another lovely tunnel of trees, signposted *Bramling*, followed by a few houses and a large, gracious building called *Bramling House,* home to a number of light industries with suggestive names like *Think One, Arto,* and *Thor.* This was designed in 1869 by Charles Barry Jnr - son of the designer of the Houses of Parliament. The Elizabethan-style chimneys are particularly fine.

The road makes a rare bend to the left as it passes the early nineteenth century *Haywain* pub, and then has another long and straight, field and hedgerow lined, stretch until a gentle, slow curve through open fields brings into view the tall fourteenth century spire of St Mary's, Wingham.

Wingham beats Littlebourne hands down for listed buildings, having ninety-eight within its boundaries, and over forty along the A257. It is also better for driving through as, once you have negotiated the left-hand bend by what used to be the *Red Lion,* it has a lovely wide, tree-lined High Street.

At the junction with Preston Hill are a pair of early sixteenth century thatched white cottages, and here, before the A257 returns to the route of the old Roman Road, our pilgrimage takes us left, off the beaten track to Sandwich, and towards our cherished goal of Preston.

Towards the top of the hill the straggle of houses thins out, and becomes architecturally more interesting. The hedgerow lessens, and there are now wide open skies, fields of wheat and orchards, serried rows of cabbages, and newly ploughed and seeded swathes of rich brown earth. The land here is over 100 feet above sea level and fairly flat - a sort of East Kent version of the Great Plains of North America.

And then there are, not one, not two, but three signs for Preston, the one on the right side of the road having the old cast-iron shield of *Invicta*, the white horse of Kent.

Here the pilgrimage makes its final turn, left, into the wide funnel-like entrance of Court Lane. Although signposted as being a 'dead end' this narrow lane leads to the site of the beginning of, what will become for us, the *Dunedin Affair*.

With a tall hedge to the right, and broad wheat-fields to the left, the lane keeps its height with views across the valley of the Little Stour, past a bend with a park bench and a row of modern houses, before entering a lovely long, narrow avenue of trees. To the right glimpses of grazing horses can be seen, before a large pond – from a natural spring, and edged with huge broad-leaved *Gunnera* plants – marks the presence of *Preston Court*. (Early nineteenth century, Grade II listed, and the site of an ancient manor, where Juliana, "Infanta" of Kent, died in 1367. Now popular for weddings.)

To the left appears the central focus of our pilgrimage, and background to the 'Affair', the church of St. Mildred, Preston-next-Wingham, Kent.

The road leads through to the large car park of Preston Court, surrounded by several old steam engines lying peacefully in the grass, a reminder the great fun-packed steam rallies that used to be held here.

The Right Reverend Henry Lascelles Jenner DD

On the south side of St Mildred's church, tucked up against the east wall of the south chapel, is a somewhat lichen-infested and weather-worn Celtic cross, decorated with a typical Celtic endless-knot, and a dotted chevron design around the circle. The top of the cross has been badly chipped.

In only just visible engraved lettering is written -

✝ HENRY
LASCELLES JENNER
FIRST BISHOP OF
DUNEDIN AND FOR XLIV
YEARS VICAR OF THIS
PARISH HE WAS BORN AT
CHISLEHURST JUNE VI
MDCCCXX AND DIED AT
PRESTON SEPT XVIII
MDCCCXCVIII
✝ GRANT HIM O LORD
ETERNAL REST AND LET
PERPETUAL LIGHT SHINE
UPON HIM AND UPON
MARY ISABEL HIS WIFE
WHO FELL ASLEEP JULY MCM
R I P
HAVE MERCY ✝

✝ MILDRED ISABEL JENNER
BORN JANY III MDCCCLV DIED
MAY V MCMXXII
FOR XLI YEARS SHE GAVE
HER SERVICES AS
ORGANIST IN THIS CHURCH
R I P

In just one sentence of this simple inscription are contained the two ingredients that provide the basis for the whole Dunedin Affair – *First Bishop of Dunedin and for forty-four years Vicar of this Parish.*

On first reading there doesn't seem to be that much of a problem. After all, Bishop Selwyn, the first Bishop of New Zealand, had been both Primate of New Zealand and Bishop of Lichfield at the same time, and many clergy of that era held more than one living, often many miles apart.

However, the issue under question here is whether Henry Lascelles Jenner was ever actually the First Bishop of Dunedin.

The story of the Dunedin Affair is a complex, disgraceful and, for some, a very controversial interweaving of several unappealing traits in humanity, including ignorance, power, dominion, weakness, misrepresentation and folly.

And it all happened to a quite remarkable, creative and loving man, who deserved far better treatment from the church that he loved, and to which he offered his life.

Henry Lascelles Jenner could trace his ancestry back to Sir Thomas Jenner of Petersham, Surrey (1638–1707) - a barrister, King's Sergeant, and member of parliament for Rye.

Thomas's grandson was Charles Jenner (1707–1770) - Archdeacon of Huntingdon, Rector of Buckworth, and Chaplain in Ordinary to King George II; and his son was Robert Jenner of Chislehurst, Kent (1743–1810), who married Ann Birt, daughter and co-heiress of businessman Peter Birt, who had made a fortune out of the Aire and Calder Canal.

Robert and Ann had three boys and two girls. The eldest son, another Robert, (1776-1824) married Frances, the first daughter of Major-General Francis Lascelles, whilst the eldest daughter, Anne, retained the Kentish link by marrying the man who was to become Sir Percival Hart Dyke, Fifth Baronet of Lullingstone – forebear of the present Tom Hart Dyke, the creator of Lullingstone's fantastic World Garden.

Robert and Ann's second son was Herbert, later to become Sir Herbert Jenner-Fust (1778-1852), who married Elizabeth, the fourth daughter Major-General Francis Lascelles. They begat eight sons, one of whom was our Henry Lascelles Jenner, and three daughters – one of whom kept things in the family by marrying Francis Hart Dyke, Sir Percival's fourth son.

There is a vague connection between Henry Jenner's ancestors and those of Edward Jenner, who pioneered the concept of vaccines and created the smallpox vaccine, although this is very tenuous.
Where there is absolutely no link is between Henry's ancestors and those of the Kardashian–Jenner family, the American celebrities.

The Lascelles connection

Whilst two of the Jenners married "daughters" of the Major-General, there is a strong likelihood that all of his children were actually illegitimate.

Their mother was a very beautiful, rich and famous actress and singer, who by various means had risen from being the daughter of a hackney coachman and washerwoman in Tower Hill, to become a great celebrity of her time. It was she who provided the wealthy lifestyle and property that she shared with Lascelles, but there was no record of a marriage between them.

At her death she left all her estate to her children, made no mention of a 'husband', and signed the will in her maiden name *Anne Cately*. Her only reference to the Major-General is as the children's father, although as she had ten children – many of whom married into high society – and had a very scandalous lifestyle, they were perhaps not all his. The National Portrait Gallery has an etching of each of them which appeared in the *Early Diary of Frances Burney* 1768-1778 – illustrations of people, events and places described by Fanny Burney in her account of society and court life at the end of the eigteenth century. They are labelled *Miss C-tl-y* and *Col L-s-ll-s*.

Furthermore, Richard Atkinson, who swore the affidavit to her will, refers to Anne as a *'spinster'*. This, and the fact that before the Married Women's Property Act of 1882 a married woman could not, by law, own property in her own right, strongly suggests that Anne and Francis Lascelles may not have been legally married.

Before launching into the early life of Henry Lascelles Jenner, it is worth taking a look at the achievements and social standing of his dad, Sir Herbert Jenner-Fust, as these had an inevitable bearing on the kind of life that was open to him.

Sir Herbert was a Doctor, or Advocate, of Doctors' Commons, becoming King's Advocate in 1828. He was knighted, sworn of the Privy Council, and appointed Vicar-General of the Province of Canterbury. In 1834 he became Dean of Arches and Judge of the Prerogative Court of Canterbury, and in 1843 was appointed Master of his old college, Trinity Hall, Cambridge.

Doctors' Commons, also called the College of Civilians, was a society of lawyers practising ecclesiastical and admiralty law in a series of buildings near the south west corner of St. Paul's Cathedral Churchyard. Had it not been for Charles Dickens, who in his youth had worked there as a shorthand writer for the proctors in the Consistory Court, we would know little about it, nor about Sir Herbert's character. In his *Sketches by Boz*, Dickens describes a visit to the court.

Crossing a quiet and shady court-yard, paved with stone, and frowned upon by old red brick houses, on the doors of which were painted the names of sundry learned civilians, we paused before a small, green-baized, brass-headed-nailed door, which yielding to our gentle push, at once admitted us into an old quaint-looking apartment, with sunken windows, and black carved wainscoting, at the upper end of which, seated on a raised platform of semicircular shape, were about a dozen solemn-looking gentlemen, in crimson gowns and wigs.
At a more elevated desk in the centre, sat a very fat and red-faced gentleman, in tortoise-shell spectacles, whose dignified appearance

announced the judge; and round a long green-baized table below, something like a billiard-table without the cushions and pockets, were a number of very self-important-looking personages, in stiff neckcloths, and black gowns with white fur collars, whom we at once set down as proctors. The red-faced gentleman in the tortoise-shell spectacles had got all the talk to himself just then, and very well he was doing it, too, only he spoke very fast, but that was habit; and rather thick, but that was good living.

By his own exertions plus a certain amount of privilege, (in those days considered quite proper,) Sir Henry gained a large professional income, and spent it quite freely. It is a tribute to his memory that Bishop Jenner, (so records his son,) could never to the end of his life speak of his father without a break in his voice. Reverently he adopted his father's immortalised tortoise-shell spectacles.

However Sir Henry did not always put his judgments into private practice. Bishop Jenner recalled that once, when his father arrived home from the Court from a case where he had ruled that prayers for the departed were legal in the Church of England, he had said, "Well, I have given my judgment in favour of prayer for the dead, but it won't make me pray for them."

Whilst Sir Henry's other sons went to Eton, for some unknown reason Henry was sent to Harrow. The headmaster at the time was Charles Longley, who was to become Archbishop of Canterbury and the most significant player in the Dunedin Affair. Almost inevitably Jenner went up to Trinity Hall, Cambridge and read law. He took a second-class honours degree with a first class compliment on his "Act" which he composed, read and defended in Latin. It was his father's intention that he should go into Doctors' Commons, but instead he chose to take Holy Orders and left Cambridge a Bachelor of Law.

It was in Cambridge that there was to be a significant encounter that was to shape many of Jenner's future beliefs about the nature of the church – beliefs that were to be a major factor in the course of his career, and particularly in the Affair.

For it was here that he came under the influence of fellow Trinity undergraduates John Mason Neale and Benjamin Webb, founders of the *Cambridge Camden Society* – later to become *The Ecclesiological Society* (ES) - whose aim was to promote "the study of Gothic Architecture, and of Ecclesiastical Antiques," and to return the Church and churches of England to the religious splendour it saw in the Middle Ages. Jenner became a life-long member of the ES, serving on its committee from 1851 to 66, and being its secretary for music between 1856 and 62.

Through its members, its journal *The Ecclesiologist*, and country-wide research, the Society influenced virtually every aspect of the life of the Anglican Church, and almost single-handedly reinvented the layout and design of the parish church.

Henry Lascelles Jenner was ordained Deacon in June 1843, and Priest in June, 1844. He served his title at Chevening, near Sevenoaks in Kent.

In 1846 Jenner left Chevening and became Curate to the Rev. S. E. Walker, Rector of St Columb Major in Cornwall. Walker was the only son of a wealthy London barrister, and when he came down from Trinity College, Cambridge his father purchased the living of St Columb for him. He moved to the parish in March, 1841 and immediately set about reforming it. He had the ancient Rectory restored by William White, FSA (1825–1900) at a cost to himself of £7,000, in the hope that it would be the Bishop's Palace for the new diocese of Cornwall. White was an established London architect working in the Gothic Revival style, and adhered closely to its views on the moral dimension of architectural fixtures and fittings, expounded by Pugin and Ruskin:

That there should be no features about a building which are not necessary for convenience, construction or propriety; and that all ornament should consist of enrichment of the essential construction of the building ... the smallest detail should have a meaning or serve a purpose; and even the construction itself should vary with the material employed.
(A. W. N. Pugin, *The True Principles of Pointed or Christian architecture*, 1841)

In 1860 plans for the church were drawn up by another Gothic Revivalist, William Butterfield, in the hope of St Columb church becoming the new cathedral. [It was eventually established in Truro, which gave its name to the diocese.]

Jenner married Mary Finlaison at St Columb in August, 1847. She was the daughter of Commander William Finlaison RN, who had sailed on the *Beagle,* been in command at St Helena during the exile of Napoleon there in 1817, and had also been the Commander of Ascension Island.

While at St Columb Jenner wrote an article for *The Ecclesiologist* called *Of Flowers as Employed in the Adornment of Churches,* which contained lists of flowers of the liturgically correct colour for all the festivals of the Book of Common Prayer, usefully commenting that, *"Flowers of the proper colours might be forced on purpose at almost any time in the hothouses of a rich parishioner."*

He also saw the use of colour as an important contribution of the Catholic movement, against the drab black and grey of Protestantism, and asserted that:

The same tone of mind which would lead to the loathing of white or grey walls in churches, 'Anglican simplicity', and the like, would lead us to the overthrow of a vast quantity of Puritanism that hangs about us, in our observances on Sundays, in our usual ritual. Quiet colours were never thought of by our ancestors for anything, except (with manifest propriety), for the every-day habit of ecclesiastical personages. A grey Protestantism hue still however opposes us.

In May, 1849, Jenner became Curate to the Rev. John Francis Kitson at Maryfield near the Torpoint in Cornwall. Kitson was of the Gothic renewal movement as was the squire, Mr. William Pole-Carew, father of the celebrated Lieutenant-General Sir Reginald Pole-Carew, KCB, CVC, and one of a long line of the Pole-Carew family, who still live at the nearby Anthony Estate.

Mr Pole-Carew had built an L-shaped building in Maryfield, designed by William White, with one wing serving as a house for the Curate – its bedrooms having open roofs and dark stained rafters in the best Gothic-revival manner – and the other as a church and, (with a curtain drawn across the sanctuary,) as a school on weekdays. With the building in 1870 of the Church of St Philip and St James – also designed by White – the house became used as the Vicarage.

Jenner, although nominally a curate of Kitson's, was given a free hand in his 'district'. He could be as advanced as he pleased. Accordingly he adopted the wearing of stoles, and monotoned his prayers. He placed a cross and candles on his altar, and stood before it in the Eastward Position. There was a daily service.

Jenner was a born teacher and a faithful pastor and, although backed by squire and parson in his innovations, he introduced them only after careful public instruction from his pulpit, and private tuition in the peoples' houses, every one of which he visited for the purpose. It is reported that there was universal consent for the revival at Maryfield.

There were a number of intelligent young men in the parish whose adult education was taken up by Jenner. One of them, who cleaned the boots and knives at Antony House, was sent to St Augustine's College at Canterbury, and eventually became an Archdeacon in India.

[There was another link here with the Cambridge Camden Society as St Augustine's College had been founded by A. J. B. Beresford Hope MP, a Trinity man and generous provider of funds for the Society, who had purchased the ruins of St Augustine's Abbey in 1844, and, with designs by William Butterfield, built the college to train clergy for the newly established church in the colonies.]

In 1851 came the sad news that Sir Herbert's health was rapidly declining, and he asked his son to be near him. Jenner and his young family now moved to Leigh, near Southend, in Essex. The Rector, Dr. Eden, had been consecrated Bishop of Moray and Ross, but did not resign the Essex living for some time. Instead he appointed Henry Jenner as Curate-in-Charge. Towards the end of his life Sir Herbert was living at his house in Chesterfield Street, Mayfair, and in those days it was apparently a fairly convenient journey for Henry to take a steamer up the Thames from Southend to go and visit him.

Jenner stayed at Leigh for only six months as, Sir Herbert Jenner-Fust having died in February 1852, he felt that there was nothing to keep him there.

The Revd. Dr. William Hodge Mill invited him to take the curacy at Brasted, near Sevenoaks. His church, St Martin's, had recently been restored. Its walls had been 'very successfully cleared of whitewash and its cumbrous and unsightly western gallery removed'.

Mill was another Trinity Cambridge graduate, an expert in oriental languages, and the first principal of Bishop's College, Calcutta. In 1848 he became Regius Professor of Hebrew at Cambridge and given a canonry at Ely Cathedral.

In his various ministries Jenner had shown a great musical ability, both in reading and writing music, singing and playing various instruments. These abilities were to be of great value when, in the autumn of 1852, a vacancy for a minor canon at Canterbury Cathedral arose. He applied for the appointment and got it.

There is no doubt that he deserved it, and that his own merits more than justified the Dean and Chapter in taking him. However, the fact that his father had been the senior lay official in the Diocese, and had a worldwide reputation in church circles, might have been helpful.

Also, one of the examining canons was Francis Dawson who, as Rector of Chislehurst, had baptised Jenner and had known him all his life.

Another examining canon was Roger Moore, who was the son of Archbishop John Moore (1783-1805). It was suggested in *The Dictionary of National Biography* that the Archbishop, in his distribution of patronage, had paid more attention to his own family than was usual at that time. That was certainly true for son Roger as, when *The Star* did a little arithmetic about Canon Moore on his death, discovered that:

The rectory of Hollingbourne, with the salary of £787, was enjoyed by Mr. Moore for sixty-three years. The rectory of Hunton, with an income of £1,057 was enjoyed for sixty-three years also. The rectory of Eynsford, at

£600 a year for sixty-three years, amounts to £37,800, and the rectory of
Latchingdon, at an income of £955 for sixty-one years, amounts to £58,255.
The Canonry of Canterbury Cathedral, at £1,000 a year for sixty-one years,
amounts to £61,000. The registrarship of Wills at £8,000 a year for fifty-
three years to 1858, yields £424,000, and the compensation allowance of
£7,990 for seven years amounts to £5,930. ...Personally, Mr Moore was,
doubtless, a most estimable man. [Quoted in *The Guardian*, 13 Sept 1865].

So it was all settled and the Jenners moved into the precincts of
Canterbury Cathedral in October 1852. They lived in a house in the
north east corner of the Green Court, opposite the *Dark Entry* of
Ingoldsby fame.

English society at this time was divided into sets, the dividing lines
being more obvious and clearly defined than in the charade of a
'classless society' that we pretend exists now. However, at Canterbury
there were two sets that really counted. First there were the Cathedral
dignitaries, the officers of the Calvary Depot, the neighbouring county
gentry and a few professional men. Jenner was in this set. Below him he
saw another set, clergy, doctors and solicitors for the most part. He
suspected that below them there was another set made up chiefly of
tradespeople. From reading literature of that period it seems to be that
this seemed right and proper, and that there was no overt snobbishness
on the one side or aggressive jealousy on the other come in later and
more democratic days– all that was to. Jenner was popular among his
fellow minor canons, in part because they felt that he had raised their
status.

One achievement of Jenner's at this time was to found and conduct the
Canterbury Amateur Musical Society. When Henry Alford became Dean
he joined it and, since it met chiefly in private houses and called itself
the C.A.M.S., the Dean promptly labelled it the *Cake and Muffin Society*.
However, it served its day and provided a good deal of entertainment for
vocalists and instrumentalists in the district. Among them was Thomas
Sidney Cooper the landscape painter, famous for his images of gloomy
looking cows standing water-logged in the River Stour. The concerts had

the effect of bringing a wider public into touch with the Cathedral. Jenner also founded the Canterbury Diocesan Choral Society, and was its Precentor from 1861 to 1866.

In 1854, the Cathedral Chapter living of Preston-next-Wingham fell vacant. Jenner was thirty-four years of age and felt that it was time that he had a living of his own, and as the senior minor canon he stated his claim to the parish. He was duly instituted and held this tiny isolated parish, with its population of a mere 500 persons, for the next forty four years.

The Parish of Saint Mildred's, Preston-next-Wingham

If it wasn't for the golf course, the sports club, and the executive housing developments, the road that Henry Jenner and his family took to their new home in Preston would not have been very different from how it looks today. There were lots of trees and fields and cows, but not so much traffic, and the few properties that lined the rutted road at that time are probably now listed under the Planning (Listed Building and Conservation Areas) Act of 1990.

It was and is a fairly quiet, sparsely inhabited, rural part of Kent, with little of any housing or commercial development to have marred the landscape over the last two centuries.

Preston-next-Wingham is so called to distinguish it from Preston-next-Faversham, which was once an ancient parish but is now part of the ever more sprawling town of Faversham. It was significant enough in 1086 to be listed in the *Domesday Book,* where it is recorded as having 25 villagers with 17 smallholders.

In 1849, five years before Henry Jenner became the Vicar of Preston, a new edition of Samuel Lewis' *Topographical Dictionary of England* had been published. The entry for Preston read -

PRESTON (St. Mildred), a parish, in the union of Eastry, hundred of Preston, lathe of St. Augustine, E. division of Kent, 2 miles (N.) from Wingham; containing 515 inhabitants. The parish is situated upon a tributary of the river Stour, and near the high road between Canterbury and Sandwich. It comprises 1471 acres 38 perch, of which 819 acres are arable, 494 meadow, 57 in orchards, gardens, and homesteads, 27 woodland, 5 hop-grounds, 6 river, and 27 in roads. The living is a discharged vicarage, valued in the king's books at £9. 15., net income, £399; patrons and appropriators, the Dean and Chapter of Canterbury.

The 2021 cencus revealed a near doubling of the population to 920 inhabitants, although the increase in numbers can be attributed to the fact that the area involved now included the neighbouring parishes of Elmstone and East Stourmouth.

However the number of parishioners under Jenner's care in 1854 involved a very different kind of workload for a parish priest than the parish structures of today. St Mildred's, Preston is now part of the *Canonry Benefice*, and the Vicar in charge of that has seven parish churches to run, including that of Ash, a large village with a population of over 3,300 people.

The role of the local Vicar would have been very different in the 1800s, given the lack of social services, schools, doctors, supermarkets and tarmacked roads that we enjoy today.

And St Mildred's wasn't the only church in the district. In 1825 a Congregational Church had been built in the centre of the village and this was enlarged in 1836.

One of the more obvious differences between nineteenth and twenty-first century vicars concerns the buildings they are given to live in. Today houses called 'The Vicarage' or 'The Rectory' can find themselves on the mailing list of an imaginative dealer in expensive luxury cars, on the basis that they are often now inhabited by the kind of person who could actually afford a new Bentley or a Porsche. Usually these ex-homes of the clergy have the word 'Old' in the title, and the modern Vicarage can be anything from a converted council house, to a large new detached property that its over-ambitious builder couldn't afford to complete. The present home of the Vicar of Preston is in Ash, and is a fairly modern detached house in a row of similar properties not far from the village church.

But Henry Jenner was instituted as Vicar of Preston at a time when Vicarages were of a size and structure that were appropriate for gentlemen with an Oxbridge education, social skills of a high order, and a large family whose history stretched back generations to titled ancestors with their own coat of arms. Such architectural gems provided not just a place for the priest to live but a base and workshop for his role in society. They were big, not just to be a useful place for the Bishop to stay on his Diocesan visitations, but for social gatherings, political debates, parties in the grounds, and articulate literary discussions. Their many rooms provided shelter for the temporarily dispossessed, a rest for the traveller, and a place for confession, counsel, creativity, and home-grown entertainment.

Preston's was a good example of this kind of Vicarage, and Henry Jenner was not adverse to making as much use of it as he could.

Edward Hasted in his description of Preston in *The History and Topographical Survey of the County of Kent: Vol. 9* (1800) wrote:

The vicarage-house having been burnt down, Robert Wyborne, gentleman of this parish, in order to replace it, gave by his will in 1711, his dwelling house, with thirty-two acres of land adjoining to it, (then worth about forty pounds per annum,) to the Vicar and his successors, on condition that they lived in it, and performed divine service twice every Sunday in St. Mildred's.

Whilst it is a long time since Preston had its own Vicar, the Vicarage is still very much as the Jenner family would have known it. Historic England has it registered as a Grade II Listed Building and call it, inevitably, *The Old Vicarage and Attached Garden Walls*. This is how it is described:

Early C18. Red brick and plain tiled roof. Two storeys and an attic on a plinth, with a moulded projecting stone string, and a parapet to the roof. There are chimney stacks to rear left, centre left and end right, and four flat-roofed dormer windows. Four glazing bar sashes on first floor, and six on the ground floor. A central canted bay window on the first floor is supported by fluted Doric columns, forming a porch to the panelled front door with fluted surround. There are extensive wings to the rear. The garden walls are to the left and right, about eight feet high – the lower section being of early C18 brick, and the upper section of later C18 – projecting about twenty yards to the front of house.

It is a beautifully proportioned and attractive building, with plenty of parking space for the Porsche.

However, one of the problems about inheriting a hand-me-down Vicarage from the laity, rather than getting a new model 'off the peg' from the Church Commissioners, is that it may not be quite fit-for-purpose. Whilst it was no doubt very kind of Mr. Wyborne to leave his house to the Vicar of Preston, its position, on the very eastern edge of the parish, made it as far away from the church as it could be, and nowhere near the centre of village life.

This problem became a source of levity in the mid-1800s when an equally grand and exquisitely designed residence for the Rector of the neighbouring parish of Elmstone was built just across the road. This is now the 'Old Rectory', and the two buildings could be said to stare at each other across the lane, if it wasn't for the eight foot high wall that the Old Vicarage hides behind. [The difference between a Vicar and a Rector is too complicated to bother with, and besides, now seems rather lost in the shrouds of history and Church of England power structures.]

It is not known whether the Jenners found living next to another clergy family a good thing or not. Presumably it came in handy when they ran out of communion wine or sermon ideas. But they probably found their own house very good for their life as a family.

When they first arrived it consisted of the Rev. Henry Lascelles Jenner (aged 33), his wife Mary, Isabel (33), Henry (5), Mary (3), and Herbert (1). Over the next two years Mary was to give birth to Mildred Isabel in 1855 and Katherine Amabel in 1856.

A glimpse of the kind of life that was led in Preston Vicarage can be obtained from occasional, unrelated articles and memoires in different publications. For example, in an article called 'A Bishop without a See' by Robert Douglas in *Bygone Kent* Vol. 24 he describes the experience of various schoolchildren, and in particular a Gladys Harrison, in the parish.

Throughout his incumbency at Preston Henry Jenner actively encouraged the schoolchildren to share his love of music, and if possible to learn to play a musical instrument. Not all the children came up to his expectations. Gladys Harrison could play the piano with only moderate ability. It was gently and tactfully suggested to Gladys that perhaps her talents could be more usefully employed pumping the bellows for the church organ, a task she performed almost every Sunday until she left the village school ...

Free elementary French lessons were given at the Vicarage in the evening by one of the Jenner daughters to several interested pupils of the village school on a one-to-one basis. Gladys looked forward to this course of instruction, for when the lesson was completed she would be invited to share the family meal and play card games together with them afterwards. Mrs. Jenner always insisted that Gladys stayed over-night; she would not allow her to make the return journey to Lodge Farm at Elmstone unaccompanied in the dark.

The Vicarage also provided a home for other members of the Jenner family. In 1861 Mary's sister, Marion Finlaison (sub-editor of Charlotte Younge's *Monthly Package,*) lived there with their aged mother – her father, Commander William Finlaison, having passed away in 1852. Many years later Younge was to put in a letter to a friend:

Miss Finlaison is at Preston for her holidays with her nieces, the Jenners, whose mother died this spring. They are in the same house, Preston Vicarage, Sandwich.

Unless, like Francis Kilvert or James Woodforde, their diaries are so interesting that they get published, the things that Vicars get up to in their parishes are not usually very well known. Bishops keep hidden 'blue books' on their clergy to keep them under control, but if you are not an 'offering-envelope carrying' churchgoer who arranges the flowers or reads the lessons then what goes on under the dog-collar is often a mystery.

For the people of Dunedin, however, it was important to know these things as they decided whether to have him as their Bishop or not. Hence this unusual letter published in the *Southland Times* of March 1869.

Dear Sir,
I am sorry I have been unable to answer your letter of the 12ᵗʰ inst. before,

When a Minor Canon at Canterbury he founded and conducted the Canterbury Amateur Musical Society, and also founded the Canterbury Diocesan Choral Society. When he arrived in Preston he set about forming a church choir out of the rural congregation that he found there, and installed a proper organ in the church. When in New Zealand he was much welcomed as a teacher and encourager of choirs in the newly formed churches that he visited.

However, Jenner's most creative musical work lay in his writing of words and music for hymns, and his translation of ancient texts, which were to become significant in hymnals and the anthem repertoire. Like others in the Ecclesiological Society, of which for some time he was Musical Secretary, he was keen on the restoration of plainsong and ancient hymnody in church worship, although he was also able to see the value of simple music, and, with his daughter, versified the Church Catechism as hymns for children. *The Musical Times* for April 1896 has the following advertisement:

JENNER, RIGHT REVEREND BISHOP and Amabel Jenner – The Church Catechism in Metrical Form, for singing as Hymns (Novello) 1d.; in packets of 50, 3s. 6d.

Henry Jenner's most familiar hymn tune is *Quam Dilecta*, written in 1861 for *We love the place, O God*, written by William Bullock in 1854. However, he also produced a great number of other pieces of music, and words for hymns, which are not so familiar, but which can still be found in various hymn books.

For example his tune *Preston*, also written in 1861, has been set to the hymns *Lord of the harvest once again* written by Joseph Anstice in 1836, and *The Lord my pasture shall prepare, And feed me with a shepherd's care* written by Joseph Addison in 1712.

Jenner's hymn in the 1889 *Supplemental Hymns* to *Hymns Ancient & Modern, Christians, sing out with exultation*, was his translation of *Faisons éclater notre joie* by Benedict Pictet in 1705, whilst *A Child Is Born In Bethlehem*, for which he wrote the tune, is his translation of *Puer natus in Bethlehem* a fourteenth century Benedictine Processional hymn.

Whilst this letter plays down the more 'ritualistic' aspects of Jenner's ministry, it would not be surprising to discover that he carried with him the passions and hopes of the Cambridge Camden Society, and the burgeoning influences that were coming from the Catholic Revival. The changes and innovations that he had made whilst a curate in Cornwall and Essex he now sought to implement in Preston-next-Wingham, Kent.

As Pearce writes in his Introduction to *Seeking a See:*

Jenner was sensitive of the feelings of others. Whatever some contemporaries of his own school might do, and they did a number of stupid and irritating things, Jenner was a thoughtful, cultivated, gentleman. In the Dunedin controversy his friends would say that his virtue leaned to failing's side. 'Whoever came back from New Zealand it would not have been I', said Bishop Wilberforce to him in conversation. He could not change his nature, and the reforming measures he took at Preston, as at Maryfield, were taken slowly and after the most careful teaching and preparation.

It took two years' hard work to educate the parishioners to the acceptance of the proper Camden principles for the restoration of their church. But at the end of the period they had raised the necessary money and they were with him all the way. The restoration began in September 1856. The church was of the thirteenth and fourteenth centuries in origin, and beautified in the seventeenth and eighteenth centuries. Jenner did away with the three-decker pulpit, the reading desk and the clerk's desk, the square box-pews in the chancel and nave, and the west gallery. Perhaps the greatest enhancement came from his un-bricking of the original windows in the aisles. These consisted of two lights each and had been blocked up earlier in the century on account of the draught. Dormer windows had been cut in the roofs to supply the light thus lost below!

The altar was enlarged and raised on steps, oak choir stalls were introduced, a light screen with a cross on it divided the chancel from the nave, and a carved oak eagle was introduced as a lectern. The nave and aisles were reseated, and the parishioners were not sure whether they or the parson had thought of all these things. Dr. Mill's successor at Brasted having no use for popish furniture, the churchwardens presented Jenner with a very fine pair of altar candlesticks of Cambridge Camden Society design and a set of choir surplices.

The single objection to all that was done came from a gentleman farmer who, seeing the surplices for the first time, picked up his top hat and walked out. The only result of this protest was that other leading members of the congregation called on him the next day to ask after his health, and wish him a speedy recovery!

It is important to know exactly what constituted the ideal that Jenner held before him as it reflected the stage of development of the Catholic Revival at that time. Again it helps us to understand his thinking in the events which were to follow. His first move towards the ideal was the introduction of daily services. These were at nine a.m., and on Saints' Days there would be evensong at seven.

A choir was started of boys and girls drawn largely from the village school, but very soon men joined the choir and for some reason the girls were dropped. There were ten men and ten boys. Jenner was infinitely patient as a choir master and soon their voices, which were rather rough at first, improved under his guidance. They were taught plainsong chants for the psalms and canticles, and some simple anthems for festivals.

At first there was a barrel organ, but Jenner had the barrel removed and keyboards added to the instrument. The instrument was new, and it says a lot for his powers of persuasion that the improvement was accepted in good faith. A little later a splendid organ was given to the church by the Revd. Samuel Stephenson Greatheed, another member of the Trinity set, and a composer of sacred music. This organ, splendid as it was, had no swell, for the Society variously described the device as mechanical or meretricious.

Greatheed designed the organ himself and insisted that the pipes should be arranged in their proper order which meant that it nearly filled the chancel aisle.

However the Society didn't seem to mind that, wanting to be 'correct', and being so relieved to get rid of the hautboys, clarionets, and serpents that made up the bands in the west galleries.

On Sundays there was Matins, the Litany, and Holy Communion with a sermon at 10.30. Evensong was at 3 in the winter months and at 6.30 in the summer. After the second lesson at evensong there was catechising of the school children at first, and later a sermon was preached instead. If there was a baptism it was taken before the sermon in strict accordance with the Prayer Book rubrics.

The canticles, and at evensong the Psalms, were sung by the choir to plainsong, but at Matins the Psalms were said, alternate verses by the Vicar and congregation, and the Glorias sung. The congregation liked it that way and in deference to their wishes it always remained the practice until Jenner's death in 1898.

A celebration of Holy Communion was introduced at 8 o'clock on Sundays, except on the first Sunday in the month, on Saints Days, and on the greater festivals and also after Matins. Coloured stoles, with altar frontals and pulpit hangings to match, were used towards the end of the fifties. Apparently Jenner's son first saw a chasuble worn in 1858, but not by his father, and many years later he adopted the use of a white linen vestment, made by his wife with a Y cross, cross-stitched in red. From the nave it was hard to distinguish from a surplice.

Jenner had run his village school himself for six months when he had been unable to get a master, and this had made him very popular with the children. Above all his practice, after the evening service, of gathering the boys and young men around him on the lawn, and telling them stories and drawing morals from them was amazingly popular. His worst enemies always said that he was a warm-hearted, sensitive man, and that 'he had all the pastoral gifts in large measure'.

The restoration of St Mildred's by William White (1825–1900), who Jenner had met in Cornwall, was probably the most obvious and lasting change that Jenner was to make during his time there. The *Ecclesiologist* of February 1857 in its Church Restoration section wrote

St. Mildred, Preston, Kent. - *This interesting specimen of a Kentish church has been excellently and unpretendingly restored by Mr. White. The plan comprises chancel, nave and aisles, west tower, and a large chantry –*

on the north of the chancel – of somewhat better architecture than the rest of the church. This chancel is Middle-Pointed, while the chancel was originally First-Pointed, and the nave a little earlier.

The great feature in the new works is their simplicity and reality. It is a real restoration, and not a needless obliteration of ancient features. The architect has done little more than to clean, and to renew when necessary; and the result is that, with some rudeness, the old character of the building is thoroughly preserved.

A new triplet has been inserted in the east end of the chancel, and appropriate windows in its south wall.

The area has been opened, laid with rough tiles, and the arrangements made quite correct, with a light screen, longitudinal benches in the chancel, and a lectern and pulpit in the nave on the south side.

The most noticeable thing, however, is the treatment of the nave roof. All the windows of the aisles – which were small, and mutilated, and inconvenient – have been blocked, and two large dormers, of simple detail in wood, inserted in the roof on each side.

The effect is extremely picturesque externally, and internally the light is abundant and very agreeably diffused – as if from a clerestory. Had the funds allowed the complete opening of the cradle roof, the effect inside would have been still better.

A pyramidal capping of tiles with bands of colour has been added to the tower, with a thoroughly satisfactory result.

Upon the whole we have seldom seen a better restoration than that of this church, in which, from our connection with its vicar, we take a special interest.

A corona lucis (a circle or hoop of lights or candles, either suspended or supported on a stand) in the chancel, the handiwork (we are told) of a member of our society, struck us as being remarkable for vigour and practicality.

Although *The Ecclesiologist* reported that White's restoration included the blocking of the 'small, and mutilated, and inconvenient' windows of the aisles, a watercolour of 1807 by Henry Petrie FSA (1768-1842) - noted topographical artist, antiquary, and Keeper of the Records in the Tower of London - shows that this had been done before then, and that three small conventional dormers had been inserted on the north side, which were then replaced with White's dormers on both sides.

White also wanted to improve the often cold and hard floor of a church, and in February 1857 he had asked for the sanction of the Incorporated Church Building Society to an alteration in the specification for his restoration of St Mildred's. His request was to replace the boarded floor and joists under the seats with 'wood blocks laid herring bone fashion in lime and hair upon a properly prepared bed.' There was no objection to White's proposal, and in March it was followed by a sketch showing that blocks, 13½×4½×1½ ins, were to be laid in a herringbone pattern on 4 ins of concrete.

In 1890 White claimed that 'not far from 40 years ago' he had 'first invented the flat wood-block paving'. White's niece later reported that he refused to take out a patent on this system of flooring that was 'strong ... pleasant to the foot and comparatively noiseless, for he said that it was far too useful for anyone to be debarred from using it'.

Unfortunately wooden blocks no longer grace the floor of St Mildred's, Preston, but a fine example of White's work can still be seen in his St Michael's church, Wandsworth Common, London SW11 6SP.

It was not just dormer windows and wood-block flooring, however, that White introduced into St Mildred's under Henry Jenner's direction. The *Ecclesiologist* of 1858 included this high praise for White's work on the organ:

In the parish church of S. Mildred, Preston near Wingham, Kent there has been erected a new organ of two Manuals, which appears to deserve description in these pages. The drawings for the case have been supplied by Mr. William White ...
Among the features for which credit is specially due to Mr White, we may mention the corbelling out of the upper part of the west front, as a happy idea. There are several improvements of detail which, as far as we are aware, have never been thought of previously, since the revival of Christian architecture. The stopper-handles of the stopt pipes, instead of being made in the usual plain form, have, as is desirable when these pipes are exposed

to view, been carved (in mahogany) according to designs furnished by the architect, the patterns being different for different stops. The front extremities of the keys, which are usually faced with bits of wood, in this organ honestly show the lime-wood of which the body of the key is made, and are simply chamfered on their vertical edges, total effect of which is very satisfactory ... (continues for several paragraphs).

Perhaps this is what kept his daughter Mildred going for those 41 years of playing the organ.

Renaissance man

Readers who picked up this book in the hope of enjoying a tale of ecclesiastical erotic excesses, or an antipodean version of Anglican paedophilia, will no doubt be disappointed by now at the purely historical and factual nature of the content.

However, before launching into the account of 'Bishops who broke their bonds, and priests who posed and prattled', and the mistreatment of the Rt. Rev. Henry Lascelles Jenner, it is perhaps important to complete the list of the man's valuable gifts and abilities, in order to fully understand what was lost to the Anglican church through the machinations of the Dunedin Affair.

During the Renaissance period – a cultural movement that spanned roughly the fourteenth through to the seventeenth century, that began in Italy and later spread to the rest of Europe – a gentleman was expected to speak several languages, play a musical instrument, write poetry, and wear a wig, thus fulfilling the Renaissance ideal. (Wikipedia)

It could be said that there are few people around today who fulfil that ideal. On the whole the present school curriculum doesn't perhaps lend itself to the creation of many Leonardo Da Vincis or Jonathan Millers.

However, it might be argued that Henry Jenner was himself a bit of a 'Renaissance man'. His musical abilities, knowledge of languages, sporting prowess and passion for art have all been mentioned, and there are yet other gifts and abilities that can be revealed.

Early on in his introduction to *Seeking a See* John Pearce wrote that:

Henry Lascelles Jenner was possessed of a singularly fine tenor voice, and he had great taste in music which he read with ease at sight. He was accomplished in making music by keyboard and by reed, and was a reasonably good performer in the developing field of brass instruments.

But perhaps, more importantly, he was passionate about sharing this love of music with others.

When a Minor Canon at Canterbury he founded and conducted the Canterbury Amateur Musical Society, and also founded the Canterbury Diocesan Choral Society. When he arrived in Preston he set about forming a church choir out of the rural congregation that he found there, and installed a proper organ in the church. When in New Zealand he was much welcomed as a teacher and encourager of choirs in the newly formed churches that he visited.

However, Jenner's most creative musical work lay in his writing of words and music for hymns, and his translation of ancient texts, which were to become significant in hymnals and the anthem repertoire. Like others in the Ecclesiological Society, of which for some time he was Musical Secretary, he was keen on the restoration of plainsong and ancient hymnody in church worship, although he was also able to see the value of simple music, and, with his daughter, versified the Church Catechism as hymns for children. *The Musical Times* for April 1896 has the following advertisement:

JENNER, RIGHT REVEREND BISHOP and Amabel Jenner – The Church Catechism in Metrical Form, for singing as Hymns (Novello) 1d.; in packets of 50, 3s. 6d.

Henry Jenner's most familiar hymn tune is *Quam Dilecta*, written in 1861 for *We love the place, O God*, written by William Bullock in 1854. However, he also produced a great number of other pieces of music, and words for hymns, which are not so familiar, but which can still be found in various hymn books.

For example his tune *Preston*, also written in 1861, has been set to the hymns *Lord of the harvest once again* written by Joseph Anstice in 1836, and *The Lord my pasture shall prepare, And feed me with a shepherd's care* written by Joseph Addison in 1712.

Jenner's hymn in the 1889 *Supplemental Hymns* to *Hymns Ancient & Modern, Christians, sing out with exultation*, was his translation of *Faisons éclater notre joie* by Benedict Pictet in 1705, whilst *A Child Is Born In Bethlehem*, for which he wrote the tune, is his translation of *Puer natus in Bethlehem* a fourteenth century Benedictine Processional hymn.

Although he only obtained a Cambridge second-class honours law degree, Henry Jenner did receive a first class compliment on his Legal Act - 'The Inviolability of Ambassadors, from the field of international law' - which he both composed, read and defended in Latin. This ability with foreign languages was an important ingredient in his various writings, sometimes to the point of making him difficult to read.

For example, between 1851 and 1899 Charlotte Mary Yonge edited a magazine targeted at middle and upper-class Anglican girls, with the aim of providing instruction, entertainment and improvement in the spirit of the Catholic revival. It was called *The Monthly Packet*, and was the first periodical to publish Lewis Carroll's short stories, which were later compiled into *A Tangled Tale*.

Henry Jenner wrote a regular item for it called "The Monthly Packet Botanical Society", under the name *Vertumnus I,* (a Roman god of gardens, orchards, and seasonal change). The following example gives some idea of the linguistic hurdles that the young ladies were given to surmount.

BOTANICAL SOCIETY

The subject for April consists of four genera (Adoxa, Lathræa, Narcissus, Paris) two of which belong to the Monocotyledonous class. The careful student will not fail to observe that whereas Adoxa and Paris are, naturally, poles asunder, the former being Dicotyledonous, the latter Monocotyledonous, the Linnæan arrangement places them in the same class and order, Octandria tetragynia – a good illustration of the artificiality of the latter system.
Any specimens of Narcissus sent must be unquestionably wild. Vertumnus hopes that many members will be able to light upon the very curious Lathrœa squamaria or toothwort. It is not uncommon in hazel copses and, like the Broomrape tribe, will turn black in drying.
Vacancies in the list of members have occurred and been filled up. It will be well for candidates for admission to keep the Secretary (Preston Vicarage, Sandwich) informed from time to time of their wish to join the Society.

It was not just his readers in the *Monthly Packet* who needed a fair knowledge of foreign languages. Pearce writes of Jenner's son Henry:

Although young Jenner was not yet four years of age he could repeat a good deal of Longfellow by heart, could compare the fairy tales of Anderson and Grimm, which were just coming out, where they overlapped, and mirabile dicto *could repeat an ode of Anacreon in Greek without knowing what a word of it meant.*

It is hard to believe that a mind like Jenner's would be content with just the day-to-day parochial events of Preston-next-Wingham, and, although we do not have diaries of his life other than in New Zealand, we can catch glimpses from other documents.

Certainly Henry Jenner would have travelled to London on many occasions, if for nothing other than his involvement with the Ecclesiological Society. Some of his letters during the Dunedin Affair were written on the headed notepaper of the Temple Club, Arundel Street, Strand. This no longer exists, but in *Old and New London: Volume 3* of 1878 it was described as follows:

The Temple Club, which was erected at a cost of more than £20,000, contains above thirty rooms. What was formerly the hall, a magnificent apartment, capable of seating 1,000 persons, is now the dining-room. One of the principal objects which the founders had in view was to "create the nucleus of a community whose members, uninfluenced by any political bias and unconfined to any literary or scientific pursuit, might enjoy the possession of a neutral ground whereon to reciprocate their ideas with regard to art, literature, and science." The Temple Club already numbers about 3,000 members.

Another intriguing snapshot of Jenner's social life comes from the creative art-work of Georgiana Louisa Berkeley. As the great-granddaughter of the 4th Earl of Berkeley, Georgina occupied the lower echelon of aristocratic society and, despite her lack of title or inheritance, maintained the sophisticated lifestyle that her ancestry provided. Georgiana and her older sister, Alice, participated in the country-house party circuit, enjoying the hospitality of their many landed and titled relatives, whilst their home in London's prestigious Belgravia offered them access to the city's cultural amenities and the proximity of people of power.

One thing that came out of this lifestyle was her creation of collages that were made up of social scenes, or pieces of furniture, or animals etc. onto which she pasted photographs of the faces of her family and friends.

These are now held in the Musée d'Orsay, Paris, who, in a recent exhibition called *Whose afraid of female photographers,* gave this introduction:

The show tells us these women photographers were fulfilling their roles as custodians of family memory, but there is also something subversive about, for instance, Georgiana Louisa Berkeley's family collages (1866–71): graphic yet decorative, they feature family members cut out of their original settings, then re-placed into watercolours of a salon, or the family porcelain, as if reflecting on the reduction, once again, of people to things.

It says something of the social life of Henry Jenner that he appears in at least two of these collages. In an albumen print photocollage titled *View of a living room with eight portraits of men and women* he is shown entering a large, lavishly decorated living room in which, along with others, are placed Lady Emily Dundas, the Hon Richard Cavendish, and Admiral of the Fleet, Sir George Francis Seymour — no mere minor celebrities.

Another of Berkley's photocollages places Jenner's head and shoulders in the watercolour of a stained glass window. His is in a central position, bordered with blue and gold, and with him wearing a surplice and stole. The only other known person included in the window is the Rev. Hugh Smith Marriot, Rector of Horsmonden and a relative of the artist, although all of them look like clergymen.

These people would have been part of Georgiana Louisa Berkley's world, and so it is perhaps a sign of Jenner's place in society that she included him in these scenes, and in such commanding positions.

So far an attempt has been made to give an, albeit rather limited, picture of the Rev. Henry Lascelles Jenner and his various gifts and abilities. It is now possible to look at what the *United Church of England and Ireland, including the colony of New Zealand* made of him.

Meanwhile, on the other side of the world ...

The Church of England's colonisation of New Zealand had begun rather badly.

The first Anglicans to arrive were the evangelical missionaries of the Church Missionary Society, landing on the North Island in 1814, and led by Samuel Marsden – who had met Maori chiefs whilst being chaplain to a penal colony in Australia. Marsden believed that the first missionaries should be mechanics rather than clergy, and so it was – a carpenter, a shoe-maker, and a schoolteacher.

Unfortunately the people who followed them lacked something in the way of demonstrating Christian leadership. They fell out with each other, selfishly pursued their own interests, and bickered over how to proceed with their missionary work. Within twenty years three had been dismissed, one for adultery with a Maori, one for drunkenness, and the other for something which was not a rarity in the early mission days, arms trading with the native tribal leaders.

They did not find the Maoris an easy people to convert, and progress in spreading the Gospel was somewhat slow. For example, there were no Maori baptisms before 1830. The Maoris had their own perfectly good beliefs and customs, and from a spiritual perspective the missionaries had very little to offer. They were seen largely as another trading opportunity to be manipulated, and the missionaries could do little about this, as their economic and physical welfare were dependent on the goodwill and patience of the Maori elders.

The situation changed with the signing of the Treaty of Waitangi in 1840, when the colony of New Zealand was annexed to the British Empire, and became a safer and more fertile ground for the Church of England to operate in. George Augustus Selwyn arrived in 1842 as its first Anglican bishop, and set about the traditional Anglican task of creating Dioceses and appointing Bishops. These were established in the parts of New Zealand that had been settled by British immigrants through the work of groups like the New Zealand Company and the

Canterbury Association. As such these people did not need converting, but could have their religious needs met by being provided with a church just like the one they were used to back home.

By 1858 Bishop Selwyn's original Diocese of New Zealand had been divided into the dioceses of Auckland, Christchurch, Waiapu, Wellington and Nelson.

The Diocese of Christchurch was very much a Church of England creation. The town of Christchurch itself had grown with the arrival of settlers attracted by the offers of the Canterbury Association, and being set in the Province of Canterbury in the middle of New Zealand's South Island.

The Association had been formed in 1848 by members of parliament, peers, and Anglican church leaders, with the purpose of establishing a Church of England settlement in New Zealand. It received a royal charter of incorporation in 1849 but was wound up in 1852, when the New Zealand Constitution Act provided the Canterbury settlers with a provincial government. In its short existence the association sent out twenty-three ships and nearly 3,500 migrants.

However, the Diocese of Christchurch covered nearly two thirds of the South Island, with the population and terrain of the bottom half – the Provinces of Otago and Southland – being rather different from that of the Province of Canterbury itself. This was partly due to the fact that the settlers in the south were mainly from Scotland, and not just that, but were adherents of the newly formed Free Church of Scotland.

A Scottish settlement in New Zealand had first been thought of in 1842 when Scottish architect and politician George Rennie, concerned at English dominance over the first New Zealand Company settlements, hoped to establish 'a new Edinburgh' in the southern hemisphere. To establish a colony around the port of Dunedin (the Gaelic form of 'Edinburgh') became possible once the New Zealand Company had purchased the large Otago block of land from its Maori owners in 1844.

However, divisions within the Church of Scotland transformed Rennie's original plan. The great upheaval in that church, which resulted in the emergence of the Free Church of Scotland in 1843, was largely caused by a dispute about establishment. When nearly 400 ministers and professors signed the *Act of Separation and Deed of Demission* they voluntarily surrendered an income amounting to over £100,000 a year. These people were indeed in earnest. In such a community anything that savoured of state control, and particularly of English control, and in religious matters anything which suggested of episcopacy or priest-craft, would be viewed with the gravest suspicion. Some of these dissenters saw Otago as a home for a new 'Free Church', and so two-thirds of the original Otago settlers were Free Church Presbyterians.

As Pearce wrote,

When men care enough about their own form of religion to settle in colonies where liberty of worship is to be upheld, it is their own form of liberty they usually have in mind.

In Otago the early colonists created an atmosphere which coloured both the life and beliefs of the whole community.

A second ingredient to change the nature of the region was the gold rush there in 1861.

When gold was first discovered in Otago it had an inevitably profound effect on the economy of, and immigration to, the then tiny colony. Dunedin soon became the largest city in New Zealand, and transport networks and townships expanded into the interior.

By the end of 1861, 14,000 prospectors were working the goldfields, and within a year the region's population swelled immensely, growing by 400 per cent between 1861 and 1864, with prospectors swarming in from Australia and America, and later from China and other parts of the world. The number of miners reached its maximum of over 18,000 in February 1864.

The goldfields gave rise to mining towns, and communities of temporary shops, hotels and miners' huts made from canvas or calico fabric covered timber frames. As the scope of the goldfields developed, communities became more permanent, with buildings constructed in timber and concrete, and eventually large towns with grand architecture, like Queenstown, were established.

Alongside the gold-rush was the expansion of land ownership and growth in sheep farming. This was achieved with ruthless determination and heroic effort in a revolution that converted 51% of New Zealand's surface area into grassland through bush clearance, the introduction of vigorous strains of European grasses, the application of vast quantities of minerals, and the use of artificial fertilisers and herbicides. This allowed the introduction of huge herds of sheep and dairy cattle that had been bred out of British and Australian stock. In Otago most of the sheep rearing land had been bought from the Maoris by 1857, and all of it was in use by about 1866, mainly for the export of fine wools to England and the Continent.

In the face of this development it was clear to the hierarchy of the Church of England and Ireland in New Zealand that the Provinces of Otago and Southland needed more ecclesiastical involvement than they had enjoyed so far. Its General Synod had already responded to the situation in 1860 when it passed a statute allowing the setting up of the Rural Deanery Board of Otago, to take over the local management of the church in that region. In 1862 Selwyn could announce to the second General Synod, meeting at Nelson that:

A Rural Deanery Board has been organized in Otago, which, under the present circumstances of that province, we hope will expand itself into the Synod of a new Diocese.

This hope was taken up by the Board itself which, at their Annual Meeting in January 1863, passed a resolution which read:

That this Board, endorsing the views expressed by the Primate, the Bishop of Christchurch, the Diocesan Synod of Christchurch, and the Rural Deanery Board, is of opinion that the time has arrived when it is desirable that there should be a Bishop of Dunedin, who should have the spiritual superintendence of the Church of England in the Provinces of Otago and Southland.

It was later agreed that an attempt should be made to find 'a hundred contributors' willing to guarantee the collection of £50 each within two years to set up an Endowment Fund and to pay and house the new Bishop.

The Bishop of Christchurch, Dr. H. J. C. Harper, then wrote to the Deanery Board:

Every visit which I have paid to the Southern Provinces since the discovery of the gold fields, has convinced me more and more that the spiritual wants of the members of our communion, who are now spreading themselves in rapidly increasing numbers throughout the Provinces, cannot be effectually supplied except by efforts which require more personal and unremitting direction than can be given by a Bishop resident at Christchurch. It must be borne in mind that the duty of a Bishop in these Provinces is not limited to the oversight of already formed Parishes or Churches. He must follow the population into the Agricultural, Pastoral, and Gold Mining Districts, and ascertain by personal observation where congregations are to be gathered, Churches built, and Ministers sent, and by his repeated visits and exhortations, stir up the people to make the necessary provision for their spiritual wants; and such duties, it is evident, cannot be fully discharged during the visitation of a few weeks once a year; nor, if due time and attention be given to the parts of the Diocese situated in Canterbury, can such visits be prolonged or made more frequently.

In writing this Harper had the necessary support of the other dioceses. At the General Synod in Nelson Dr. Selwyn had been pressed to take steps to find a Bishop for Dunedin, and in the next General Synod, meeting at Christchurch on the 27 April 1865, they did so again. To reinforce the point it was resolved that the next Synod, in 1868, should be held at Dunedin, provided a Bishop had been appointed by that date.

And so it was that on 26 May 1865, at a meeting of the Standing Committee of the Rural Deanery Board of Otago and Southland, Bishop Selwyn suggested that:

At the next meeting of the Board resolutions should be passed to request him to write to the Archbishop of Canterbury [the Rt. Rev. Charles

Thomas Longley,] *to know if his Grace could name an eligible person as Bishop of Otago and Southland.*

The next meeting of the Board was a month later and, after looking at various issues like the amount of money that had been raised to support the new Bishop (the Endowment Fund) a resolution was duly proposed that:

The Primate of New Zealand be asked to communicate the above facts to the Archbishop of Canterbury, and to request that his Grace will be pleased to recommend a clergyman whom he may deem fit to be consecrated for the proposed See.

However, this was not passed by the majority of the board. Many thought that, for financial reasons, it was premature to make an approach to the Archbishop of Canterbury, although they did not raise an objection to this happening at a later time. Then there were those who regarded the 'Historic Episcopate' as probably useful for the church's well-being but not essential to its existence, and others who could see no need for a Bishop at all.

Unfortunately Bishop Selwyn did not take any notice of this decision, and wrote asking Archbishop Longley to recommend a new Bishop of Dunedin anyway. As Pearce was to write:

Dr. Selwyn had not built up the Church in New Zealand on democratic principles, or by allowing events to take their natural course.

The Promptitude of a Prelate

After having travelled half-way around the world Bishop Selwyn's letter to the Archbishop of Canterbury, Charles Longley, asking for someone to be the Bishop of Dunedin, eventually arrived, around July or August of 1865, at Addington Park (later to be called Addington Palace,) in Croydon. This was the summer residence of the Archbishops of Canterbury between 1807 and 1897 - having replaced the nearby Croydon Palace, which had provided the prelates with a useful break between Lambeth and Canterbury for over 500 years, and which had become somewhat dilapidated and inconvenient.

On 14 October 1865 Archbishop Longley summoned Henry Jenner to Addington Park, and told him that he had received a letter from the Metropolitan of New Zealand asking him to nominate a Bishop for Dunedin, and that Dr. Selwyn had asked for:

A clergyman able and willing to undertake the work of hewing a statue out of a very rough block of stone; a vigorous man, with some power of speech, and real earnestness of purpose, able to walk and ride, and not afraid of the weather!

The Archbishop had known Jenner at Harrow, and he now knew him to be one of the most successful parish priests in his diocese. He could not only walk and ride, but could swim powerfully, and was a wizard at handling a boat. He was exceptionally strong and robust, and a dab hand with an umbrella. And so he thought him an ideal candidate for Dunedin.

No record of this interview appears to have been preserved, but at a later date Longley was to write to Jenner, "I knew all the while perfectly well that you were a great advocate for Choral Services and surpliced choirs; but all this did not weigh with me in prevention of your appointment to that See".

Jenner accepted the offer on 17 October, and the Archbishop then wrote to Selwyn notifying him that Jenner had accepted the nomination. He also sent him the declaration of adherence to the Constitution of the New Zealand Church, which Jenner had duly signed.

My dear Bishop of New Zealand,

In compliance with the wish expressed in your last letter that I would fix upon some clergyman to occupy the proposed See of Dunedin, my choice has fallen on the Revd. Henry Lascelles Jenner, Vicar of Preston, in my Diocese. I think he possesses, in the main, the qualifications which you mention, and I pray that a Blessing may rest upon this choice made.

He is a very sound Churchman, and has been the chief Manager of the Choral Society of Canterbury Diocese. He is in the prime of life, active in mind and body, of a fine presence, and in dealing with his people has shown himself conciliatory without compromise. I enclose his declaration of adherence to the Constitution of the Church in New Zealand.

He is very anxious to be consecrated in this country – and I see that since the last judgment of the Judicial Committee of the Privy Council this will be a strong feeling in the minds of those who leave this country to undertake Episcopal Functions in the Colonies. They earnestly desire to feel this link with the Mother Church. I think this desire is a very natural one, and I shall be ready to act upon it, should the Colonial Metropolitans consent to me doing so.

Yours sincerely

C. T. Cantuar

He wrote to Jenner on the same day, asking, "May it please God to prosper your work, and bless your labours in spreading the Tidings of the Gospel among the Heathen." Which is interesting, given that at that time the majority of the population of Otago and Southland were Scottish Presbyterians, and that there were hardly any Maoris in the region.

Selwyn replied from Auckland in a letter dated 4 January 1866 -

My dear Lord Archbishop,

You could not have presented me with a more acceptable New Year's gift than the two letters which I have received today. The delay in the arrival of the Mail obliges me to answer them at once, and to thank you most cordially for the promptitude with which you have carried out my wishes by the recommendation of a Bishop for Dunedin, and for procuring his written acceptance of the Constitution ... On the subject of Consecration I need only to say that in requesting your Grace to act for General Synod, we intended to leave it entirely to your discretion whether to Consecrate the Bishop in England, or to leave the Consecration to us. If you can clear up the business with the judgement of the Judicial Committee of the Privy Council, and reduce the Royal Mandate to its true dimensions, you cannot confer a greater obligation upon us than by Consecrating our two Bishops without further delay. [Andrew Suter was to be consecrated the Bishop of Nelson.]

The following day Selwyn wrote to Bishop Harper in Christchurch to tell him what had happened:

I have received a letter from the Archbishop of Canterbury informing me that he had selected the Rev. Henry Lascelles Jenner, Vicar of Preston, Kent, to occupy the new see of Dunedin. His Grace gives a very high character of Mr. Jenner. The promptitude with which the Archbishop has acted upon my request that he would recommend some clergyman for the office makes it necessary to take immediate steps for raising the Endowment Fund, and also for ascertaining that the Diocese of Christchurch is satisfied with the Archbishop's choice.

Resolutions concerning a new Bishop have already been passed by the Otago Otago and Southland Rural Deanery Board, but our Constitution provides no mode of election or nomination of a bishop for a newly-constituted diocese.
In all former instances I have suggested the person, and the Church members in the district proposed for the new diocese have given their

formal consent, without which I should not have proceeded further. In this
instance, having exhausted my stock of personal friends, I applied to the
Archbishop, and, through his kindness, I am now enabled to mention the
name of the Rev. H. L. Jenner, and to certify that he has formerly accepted
the Church Constitution, by an instrument in writing, and will be ready to
come out as Bishop of Dunedin if he is assured of the willingness of the
members of the Church to welcome him as their chief pastor.

This is a fascinating letter for a variety of reasons, the most revealing being Selwyn's confirmation that preferment in the Church of England was then, just as now, a matter of nepotism and partiality - "having exhausted my stock of personal friends". This otherworldliness also comes through in his bland assumption that the Church members in the district would feel themselves experienced or knowledgable enough to question the Bishop's decision.

What it hints at, but doesn't actually spell out, is Selwyn's concern about the speed and manner in which Longley had responded to his request. This can be seen in his concern to make some progress, both in raising the Endowment Fund, and in ensuring that the situation would be according to the constitution and the will of the Diocese (i.e. Synod).

From various other letters written at this time it is clear that the Bishop of New Zealand had not expected the response to be so quick, and to be so particularly related to just one choice. The problem is that we do not have that original letter to know what exactly was requested.

In 1870, as Bishop of Lichfield, Selwyn was to write to the then Archbishop of Canterbury, Archibald Campbell Tait, giving him an account of his memory of 'Bishop Jenner's Case', which included:

When I wrote to Archbishop Longley asking him to select a suitable
Clergyman, I did not anticipate a settlement of the question so speedy as
that which was announced to me by His Grace within a very short time.

In *A History of the English Church in New Zealand* H. T. Purchas offers an interesting explanation of what had happened:

When Selwyn wrote the letter to Longley he was fresh from the great General Synod of 1865, where the whole constitution had been revised, and the procedure on the election of a bishop made more clear and precise. How could he violate a law to which he himself had just subscribed? The only answer is that he did not violate it. His letter can have contained no such request as the Archbishop imagined. Selwyn himself was as much startled as anyone, when he found what his letter had led to. But obedience to authority was the ruling principle of his life, and he determined to take upon himself the whole responsibility for what was done. It was doubtless an act of heroism, but a simple insistence upon the plain truth would have prevented much misunderstanding, and saved the New Zealand Church some years of trouble.

But Bishop Selwyn may not have been the only one to be caught in a dilemma. The reasons for Archbishop Longley's speed and decisiveness of action in choosing Jenner may have been in response to issues arising in other areas of his domain. The letter upon which he acted had arrived in England not long after the news from New Zealand's North Island of the murder by a Maori tribe of the Rev. Volkner, an Anglian priest.

It was perhaps difficult for those who had never left England to realise the social and political difference between the Hauhau-ridden natives of the north and the law-abiding people of the south in such a distant country as New Zealand. The archbishop might well have thought that his best course was to send out another bishop as soon as possible, without waiting for compliance with constitutional formalities.

Also, he was going to consecrate Bishop Neville Suter for the Diocese of Nelson in New Zealand, and it would be much easier, and save a lot of time, to do both at once.

In January 1866 Dr. Selwyn wrote to Jenner expressing his satisfaction at the nomination and accepting it. On 13 February Dr. Harper, Bishop of Christchurch, wrote to Jenner:

I am most thankful to hear by a letter from your sister, Mrs. Dyke, that you have expressed your willingness to undertake the office.

[Bishop Harper knew the Jenner family fairly well, and had been at Eton with several of the brothers. Charlotte Dyke was the wife of Francis Hart Dyke, the Registrar of the Province of Canterbury.]

If Jenner had any doubts about Selwyn's satisfaction they were probably laid to rest when he received another letter from the Metropolitan on 16 April, which began:

My dear Bishop of Dunedin,
I thus address you in the hope that my letter to the Archbishop will have removed all doubts, and that you and Dr. Suter are already consecrated.

By 2 May he is getting a little anxious.

My dear Bishop of Dunedin,

On my return from the South I found your letter of 25 January which had not been forwarded to me, as I was expected at home a month earlier than I actually returned. It is very gratifying to me to find that you have so heartily given yourself to our work: and I hope that you will not be disappointed. My late tour through the Province of Otago has convinced me that you have a very hopeful field of work before you. May an abundant blessing be granted to you. I very much regret the delay in your Consecration; because you might have made good use of your time in England in raising funds and engaging Clergymen. We shall not expect you much before the end of the year.

You seem to have been told that your subscription to the New Zealand Church constitution was premature, if not unnecessary. On the contrary, the General Synod expressly requested the Archbishop of Canterbury to place our Constitution in the hands of any Clergyman whom he might select, and obtain his written assent to it, before he recognised him as Bishop Designate.

The result showed how calculated these words were to mislead the person to whom they were written, since from them Dr. Jenner not unreasonably drew the conclusions stated by him in a later publication. *If language has any meaning at all, the above extract proves that the Archbishop was authorised by the General Synod to do three things: -*

1. To select a clergyman;
2. To obtain his written assent to the Constitution;
3. To recognise him as bishop-designate.
And all these several steps did Archbishop Longley take in regard to myself.

If there was any doubt about Jenner's consecration in Bishop Harper's mind, there was little sign of it in his Charge to the Christchurch Diocesan Synod on 22 November 1866.

My Reverend Bretheren and Bretheren of the Laity -
Intelligence has recently reached us from England of the consecration of the Rev. Henry Lascelles Jenner as Bishop of Dunedin.
This is an event for which our thanks are due to Him who ordereth all things in heaven and earth. It is the accomplishment of an object suggested by ourselves, and earnestly desired by our brethren in Otago and Southland, who for some time past have felt the need of the spiritual oversight and pastoral ministrations of a resident bishop. You will, I am sure, join me in the prayer that he, who has been called to this office, may have strength and power to fulfil the same, and in that portion of the Church which is now to be entrusted to his charge, may faithfully serve God to the glory of His name. (Lyttleton Times.)

The Constitution of the Church in New Zealand

Reference has here been made to a 'Constitution', which the Archbishop was to place into the hands of any clergyman he thought would make a good Bishop. The existence of such a Constitution meant that the Church in New Zealand was now independent of the Crown, which itself was then independent of New Zealand. This meant that Bishops chosen to serve in that country could no longer rely upon the Queen's Letters Patent to give them authority, but only a Queen's Mandate or License. Instead the authority would come from the General Synod of the Church in New Zealand. Which is why it was necessary for the new Bishop to declare his asset to it. However, unlike the Queen's Letters Patent, the authority of the Constitution cut two ways – it affirmed the status of the Bishop given to him by Synod, and also the status of the General Synod in relation to the Bishop.

This is Jenner's declaration of assent, mentioned in Selwyn's letter of 5 January, 1866. (His consecration was on 24 August, 1866).

I, Henry Lascelles Jenner, Clerk, LL B, do declare my submission to the authority of the General Synod of the Branch of the United Church of England and Ireland in New Zealand established by a Constitution agreed to on the 13 day of June 1857, and to all the provisions of the Constitution.

And I further consent to be bound by all the regulations which may from time to time be issued by the authority of said General Synod; and I hereby undertake, in consideration of being appointed Bishop of Dunedin, immediately to resign my appointment, together with all the rights and emoluments appertaining thereto, whenever I shall be called on so to do by the General Synod, or by any person or persons lawfully acting under the authority of the General Synod in that behalf.

Jenner is to reinforce his intention of resigning if he causes any offence in future letters to his opponents, and it is useful to remember that he made this declaration.

When he heard that the consecration was shortly to take place, the Bishop of Christchurch wrote to Jenner:

The last mail brought us the intelligence of your proposed consecration on 24 August, an event which I trust has been realised, though it is not yet clear to us how it has been brought about inasmuch as no formal resignation of that part of my diocese, which lies in the provinces of Otago and Southland, has been sent in by me.

His lordship then presumes, correctly, that the authorities in England intended to leave it to the New Zealand General Synod to settle the question of territorial jurisdiction; hence the wording of the mandate included '*a bishop in New Zealand*' rather than '*of Dunedin*'.

Henry Lascelles Jenner was duly consecrated Bishop of the *United Church of England and Ireland in the colony of New Zealand* on St Bartholomew's Day, 24 August, 1866, in Canterbury Cathedral.

In the Library of Lambeth Palace there are several copies, in lovely flowing italic handwriting, of the following document associated with the event.

The Queen's Mandate to consecrate the Revd H. L. Jenner LLB as Bishop

Victoria by the Grace of God of the United Kingdom of Great Britain and Ireland Queen, Defender of the Faith, to the Most Reverend Father in God, Charles Thomas by Divine Providence Lord Archbishop of Canterbury, Primate of All England and Metropolitan, Greeting.

Whereas you the said Archbishop have humbly applied to Us for Our License by Warrant under Our Sign Manual and Signet Authorizing and Empowering you to Consecrate Our Trusty and Well-beloved Henry Lascelles Jenner, Clerk, Bachelor of Laws, Bishop of the United Church of England and Ireland in Our Colony of New Zealand. Now it is Our Will and Pleasure and We do by this Our License under the Sign Manual and Signet, Authorize and Empower you the said Archbishop to Consecrate the said Henry Lascelles Jenner to be a Bishop of the United Church of England and Ireland in Our Colony of New Zealand.

Given at Our Court at Osbourne House, Isle of Wight this Fourteenth Day of August 1866, in the Thirtieth Year of Our Reign.

By Her Majesties Command,

Carnarvon

[This was Henry Herbert Carnarvon, 4th Earl of Carnarvon who was secretary of state for the colonies from 1866-67.]

To which Archbishop Longley responds :

Know all Men by these Presents That We the Charles Thomas Lord Archbishop of Canterbury having obtained Her Majesty's license by Warrant under the Royal Sign Manual and Signet and called to our assistance the Bishops whose names are hereunto subscribed did on Friday the 24th day of August in the year of our Lord 1866 being St. Bartholomew's day in our Cathedral and Metropolitan Church of Christ Canterbury admit Our beloved in Christ The Revd. Henry Lascelles Jenner Clerk, Bachelor of Laws into the office of a Bishop of the United Church of England and Ireland in the Colony of New Zealand.

Consecrations usually took place at Westminster Abbey, for the convenience of the Archbishop, and the Dean of Canterbury had to give his consent for this particular ceremony to be held in his cathedral. After all, Jenner had been connected with the Cathedral as priest-vicar, he loved it dearly and had an intimate knowledge of the building, he had greatly improved its music, and now he held a chapter living.

The cathedral congregation was very large, there were a great many communicants, and the service was very long.

Six of Bishop Jenner's brothers were present (Arthur was in Canada) and all were over six feet tall and particularly broad and handsome. They were doing well in their chosen professions – the Law, the Navy, the Army and the Civil Service. His sister Charlotte was there with her husband Francis Hart Dyke, Queen's Proctor and Registrar of the Province, whose job it was to read the Licence, and his sister Anne came along with her husband Evan Nepean, Canon of Westminster.

Icebergs

On a beautiful headland that projects from Dunedin out into the South Pacific Ocean is a stretch of cliff that is home to some elegant and fascinating examples of marine wildlife. Visited at the right time of day it is possible to see *Yellow Eyed Penguins* and *Little Blue Penguins* as they waddle in from the sea to their homes on dry land. They are both a fairly rare species, and found only in certain parts of the southern hemisphere. It is almost certain that they would have been there in the nineteenth century as British settlers sailed close by on their way to a new home in Otago and Southland.

It would perhaps have surprised them to see penguins so far away from the frozen Antarctic, with which they were usually associated. It can surprise us, and then delight us, to find these aquatic flightless birds in places that are warm and easy to visit, as it is one of those commonplace myths that penguins only exist on the icy wastes of the south pole. However, of the seventeen penguin species that exist, only seven are actually found in Antarctica, and those that live on the Otago Peninsular are only found in New Zealand. This is not true, however, for icebergs. Icebergs need lots of freezing cold sea to fall into when they break off from glaciers. There is little of this around New Zealand.

The iceberg, however, makes a useful metaphor when describing the experiences of the Rt. Rev. Henry Jenner as he enjoyed being a bishop waiting for his See. For icebergs have marked similarities to the damaging words and actions that floated about in the articles and the committees of those who wanted to bar his way. Like icebergs they were to a large part hidden, in the muddled facts of history or the details of stories wrongly told. Like icebergs they had a certain attractiveness and allurement that veiled their ability to damage and destroy. Like icebergs they were destined to exist for a relatively brief time, to ultimately melt into the ever moving waves of present reality. Like icebergs they did a huge amount of irreparable damage.

During the passage of the Dunedin affair three particularly large and damaging 'icebergs' were to be the cause of Jenner's rejection as its Bishop. They were 'Colonial assertions', 'The elusive Endowment', and 'Ritual misperceived'.

Colonial assertions

The mid 1800s were not a good time to be seeking a See in the newly founded British colonies. For over the two hundred years since the English Reformation there had been no Anglican bishops outside of the British Isles. It was only after the American Declaration of Independence in 1776 that this began to change, and even then reluctantly. Sixty years later there were thirty-seven overseas bishops (twenty-seven of them in North America), but by the mid nineteenth century this number had doubled.

One particular issue that this raised, and which took a century to resolve, was the question of accountability. By whose authority did the rapidly growing number of Anglican bishops hold their position, and to whom were they accountable? A train of events that helped to bring the issue into sharp focus was the so-called 'Colenso affair', involving the Rt. Rev. John William Colenso, the Bishop of Natal.

As a result of his work interpreting the scriptures into the Zulu language Colenso began to question the Pentateuch (the first five books of the Old Testament,) as being a faithful contemporary account of Jewish life. He also maintained that the numerical discrepancies found in Genesis raised doubts concerning the historical accuracy of the Bible, and his study of St Paul's letter to the church in Rome led him to the conclusion that salvation didn't need to be through a subjective response to Christ's act of atonement on the cross – the need to 'accept Jesus as your personal Saviour'. It was, he believed, sufficient to proclaim Christ's love as a model for all to follow, and that there should be no doctrine of eternal punishment for sinners and unbelievers.

In this he was simply moving in the same direction as many liberal theologians in England, who were formulating new forms of biblical criticism and theological thought in response to scientific and philosophical advances resulting from the works of Darwin etc. Because of this however, and because of his toleration of polygamy among the Zulus, Colenso was summoned in 1863 by his superior, Bishop Robert Gray of Cape Town, to appear before him on a charge of heresy. Colenso was convicted the next year, but in 1865 was acquitted on appeal by the Judicial Committee of the Church Privy Council in England, which held that, because the Crown was powerless to appoint a bishop in a colony possessing its own independent legislature, the royal courts could not uphold the legality of Gray's authority.

This would mean that, in newly settled countries where they had established their own Constitution and legal framework, Bishops could no longer be appointed to a particular diocese with the power and status of a Crown appointment and Letters Patent, but rather with a rather gentler 'it's OK by me' kind of permission of the Queen's Mandate or Licence.

The church in New Zealand had by this time effectively 'disestablished' itself by producing a Constitution, and so new bishops like Jenner were consecrated as Bishops of the United Church of England and Ireland in the colony of New Zealand as a whole.

As the church in New Zealand found its own identity, with Dioceses, Bishops and Synods, a certain amount of tension and discord developed between the Mother Church of England and its colonial offspring. Whilst Anglicans in New Zealand wanted to keep strong links with the church authorities back home, they also wanted the freedom and power to operate in new and independent ways and not be tied to the shackles of tradition. After all, they had left Britain to establish a new life in a new land.

This feeling about the church in England was perhaps most clearly presented in this extract from the minutes of the General Synod for 1865 in which the New Zealand Synod had been described as being guilty of 'unripeness' in the way that it operated.

In its defence the Rev. J. Wilson thought that there had been much more freedom of action and independence of feeling in the Colonial Bishops than in those of England. The English Bishops had been for a long time so fettered and trammelled by the absolute rules laid down for their guidance that they hardly possessed any freedom of action. For his own part, he would rather trust himself to the opinions of the six Bishops of New Zealand than to that of the six-and-twenty in England.

This rising tension had been exacerbated by the treatment of New Zealand in relation to the church in Australia. Bishop Selwyn had been appointed Bishop of New Zealand in 1842, subject to the Archbishop and Metropolitan See of Canterbury. In 1847 Bishop Broughton was appointed to the See of Sydney and made Metropolitan of Australasia (not just Australia), himself being subject to the Archiepiscopal See of Canterbury. This had the effect, as Bishop Selwyn pointed out, of giving him two Metropolitans, and it was rightly regarded in New Zealand as a slight on his position. When Broughton died in 1853 his successor was made Metropolitan of just Australia, so that Selwyn was once more directly under Canterbury.

When Dr. Harper was appointed the first Bishop of Christchurch, the Letters Patent made him subject not to Selwyn but to the Metropolitan See of Sydney. The Church in New Zealand wrote to the Crown pointing out that by the arrangement then in force all future bishoprics would also be subject to Sydney. They were righteously indignant that Selwyn should be so slighted and cut off from his Episcopal colleagues. The matter was righted in 1858 when the *Gazette* of 5 October gave notice that:

The Queen has been pleased to direct that letters patent be issued under the great seal for reconstituting the Bishopric of New Zealand and for appointing the Right Rev. George Augustus Selwyn, D.D. to be Bishop of the said See and Metropolitan of New Zealand ... and for placing under the jurisdiction of the Metropolitan of New Zealand the See of Christchurch now under the jurisdiction of the Metropolitan of Australia.

In future negotiations with Canterbury the Church in New Zealand would not forget these vacillations and would work for 'sturdy independence'.

By the 1850s the creation of, and adherence to, legislation and constitutions – and the resulting voting power of ecclesiastical committees – had become of immense importance in the affairs of the New Zealand church. Indeed this process of creation and appraisal was going on in their General Synod at precisely the same time as Jenner was being made their bishop back in Canterbury.

Probably because they were operating in totally new circumstances – without the traditions of the past, and the knowledge and academic ability of many of the leaders of the Church back in England – whether a motion was passed or rejected by just one vote, or ruined by a failed amendment, gave the result a significance that might have been different if the broad feelings of the meeting were taken into consideration, and the views of others obtained, rather than just the often biased opinions of a limited group of men, sometimes, as we shall see, after a long night of tedious debate.

Whilst New Zealand and its population can now be experienced as one of the most beautiful and intelligent countries in the world, in the early days of the colony things might have been a little different, as John Pearce suggested:

When the British establishment talked about New Zealand being closest to the Mother Country, and New Zealand Society being English Society transferred to the antipodes, they were very far off the mark. New Zealand did not attract the aristocrat, the country gentleman, the artist or the intellectual, nor could those below the poverty line afford to go there. We are left therefore with 'the less well-to-do' and the less 'intellectual' sections of the middle classes, the better paid and better housed sections of the working classes ... New Zealand was not, as some observers thought it, the paradise of the working man, but rather the paradise of the petit bourgeois. How did they suppose the colonies were won and run? Waterloo may have been won on the playing fields of Eton but it took considerably more than that to eliminate and despoil native populations. And in New Zealand, where they boasted that Jack was better than his master, one had to be tough and crafty.

Against such a background it is not surprising that Henry Jenner entered the scene with something of a disadvantage. This is clear from his very first introduction to the world of colonial bishops – his selection and appointment by the Archbishop of Canterbury.

As has been mentioned, the problem started with the difference between Selwyn and Longley in their understanding of the needs of Dunedin. Selwyn had asked for someone from England to be suggested as a possible Bishop for a new future diocese, whereas Longley acted as if the need was for someone to be chosen by himself and as soon as possible. The result being that the choice of Henry Jenner was sent to Selwyn as a *fait accompli.*

This was in marked contrast to the selection of the Rev. Andrew Suter as Bishop of Nelson at about the same time – although this did admittedly start out with the advantage of being an already existing Diocese with retiring Bishop attached.

When the first Bishop of Nelson, the Rt. Rev. Edmund Hobhouse, decided to retire through ill health, the Diocesan Synod had difficulty in coming up with a successor and, following guidance from Hobhouse, decided to seek help from the Bishop of London in obtaining a replacement. The Synod Standing Committee then drew up a signed legal document delegating Bishop Tait *"to nominate a fit and proper Clergyman to be appointed to succeed the Right Reverend Edmund Hobhouse..."*

From collections in Lambeth Palace Library it is clear that Tait devoted a great deal of time and energy to this task. There are letters from clergy in various parts of the country suggesting colleagues they knew who would make excellent colonial bishops, and Tait requests more information about four of these, finally making the choice of Andrew Suter, Vicar of All Saints, Mile End.

As well as being formally chosen and appointed by a Bishop legally delegated to the task, Suter also benefited from regular communications with both Tait and the Diocese of Nelson. He had been told by Bishop Hobhouse of the need for clergy in the new parishes that had formed around the gold diggings, and for teaching to the indigenous population. This meant that, by the time he set sail for New Zealand, he had accomplished a great deal towards his new job. As the *Taranaki Herald* of 3 August 1867 was to report -

On the morning of May 25th the Right Rev. Dr. A. B. Suter, Bishop of Nelson, New Zealand received a large number of visitors on board the Cissy, which is now lying in St Katharine's Docks, London. The Right Rev. prelate stated that he intends to leave England on the 1st of June, that he has nearly raised funds sufficient to guarantee the stipends of three clergy for two years, while one will join at his own cost. He added that he will take out with him 45 young women, 14 married couples as artisans, farm labourers, &c, and six single men — in all about 120.

On his arrival in New Zealand the *Nelson Examiner and New Zealand Chronicle*, of 28 September ran this article:

On the 12th September, on board the Cissy, *at sea, to the wife of the Rev. Richard. J. Thorpe, the birth of a daughter.*

ARRIVAL OF THE BISHOP OF NELSON

The arrival of the ship Cissy, *on Thursday morning last, with Bishop Suter, several clergymen, and a more numerous body of immigrants than have reached our port in a single ship for many years, was an event that appeared to afford a considerable amount of satisfaction throughout the city. The voyage of the* Cissy *was not quite so rapid as had been anticipated, it having occupied 110 days from the Downs, but the passage, on the whole, was a highly pleasant one.*

By comparison Henry Jenner arrived at Dunedin without any fellow clergymen, immigrants, or newly born babies, and, rather than affording any satisfaction to the city, was seen by many as an unwanted arrival.

There are no records of Archbishop Longley being involved in any way with the preparation of Jenner for his new role, and without having any creative communication with the Christchurch Diocesan Synod there was little chance that he could work at fulfilling some of the diocesan needs. Indeed, being stuck out in the relative obscurity of Preston-next-Wingham, he had none of the contacts and networking that would have existed in the Mile End region of London – although it has to be said that he did do a lot of travelling and preaching in order to raise funds for his Endowment.

Without the constitutional backing to his appointment, and because of the rather confused way in which it had happened, Jenner's appointment was seen by the church in Dunedin as an example of the Mother Church imposing its will on the colony. More importantly it was held to be against the decision by the General Synod of 1865 to incorporate a new Article into their constitution.

The nomination of a Bishop shall proceed from the Diocesan Synod, and if such nomination be sanctioned by the General Synod, or if the General Synod be not in session, by the majority of the Standing Committee of the several Dioceses, the senior Bishop shall take the necessary steps for giving effect to the nomination.

As Otago and Southland didn't actually have a Diocesan Synod, nor even a Diocese, the appeal to such legislation was perhaps a little premature, but the Rural Deanery Board gallantly took on the role of a synod and at its meeting in February 1866 passed the following resolutions:

That as a sufficient provision has not been made for the support of a Bishop, it is not expedient to take any action at present with a view to confirming the conditional appointment of the Rev. H. L. Jenner, more specially as that appointment has been made without the authority or concurrence of the board. That this Board is desirous to record its extreme regret that through misconception the Rev. H. L. Jenner should have been led to suppose that the time has arrived for the appointment of a bishop for Otago and Southland, there being at present no sufficient endowment raised, and that this Board continues to be decidedly opposed to the appointment of a bishop without a sufficient endowment having been provided, and that the honorary secretary be requested to forward this resolution, together with the minutes of the last meeting of the Rural Deanery Board, to the Rev. H. L. Jenner, through the President of the Board.

Jenner was not told about these resolutions because the President of the Board, the Bishop of Christchurch, vetoed them. In fact he first learned of the meeting and its resolutions four months after his consecration. In his letter of welcome to Jenner, dated 13 February 1866, Bishop Harper had added a postscript; *"I will write again by the next mail if I have anything fresh to communicate"*. He does not, however, write to Jenner again until 14 May, when he gives details of the improvement in the prospects of the endowment since he last wrote, but makes no mention of the adverse resolutions.

As Jenner was to write to the Harper in 1873:
Had I been allowed to receive these resolutions, you may be very sure I should not have presented myself for consecration, and thus I should have

escaped the tremendous injury, which, to the eternal disgrace of the New Zealand Church, has been inflicted upon me.

In England an early understanding that all was not well came in the publication by *The Guardian* of 11 September 1867 of parts of a Memorial said to have been signed by 'A large number of members of the Church of England, residing in the new diocese of Dunedin.' It was in fact the work of the Revd W. F. Oldham, the Vicar of Riverton, Southland, and was addressed to the Archbishop of Canterbury, complaining that an appointment had been made in direct opposition to their wishes.

The Memorial of the undersigned Members and Office-bearers of the United Church of England and Ireland, in the Provinces of Otago and Southland, New Zealand.

Sheweth –

That a Clergyman, the Rev. H. Lascelles Jenner, has been consecrated by your Grace as Bishop in New Zealand, with a view to his taking charge of the Provinces of Otago and Southland.

That the said Bishop was not in any sense elected by the Members of the Church, but the appointment made in direct opposition to their wishes, expressed during the Session of the Rural Deanery Board held in February, 1866, and acquiesced in only when it appeared too late to raise objections.

That Dr. Jenner, having identified himself publicly with the Ritualistic Party, the peace and harmony of the proposed new diocese would be destroyed, and great numbers of most earnest members alienated from the Church by the presence of such a chief pastor, and that the work of the Church in these provinces would be hindered if not utterly brought to a standstill.

Leaving aside the issue of Ritualism, the concerns about the way in which Jenner had been appointed were expressed by a small number of leading members of the 'new Diocese of Dunedin'.

In April 1868 a William Carr Young wrote in the *Otago Witness* to 'The Members of the Church of England in Otago and Southland,' complaining that the Rural Deanery Board of Otago and Southland had:

Ignored his expressed intention that the opinion of every Church member in the diocese, respecting Bishop Jenner as our diocesan, should be faithfully ascertained. But the Board appears to have considered themselves entitled to hold the conscience of the people in their own hands, and while affecting to be your representatives, have come to a decision without offering to consult your wishes on the subject.

For example, the Goldfields were not represented at all, Invercargill's supposed representatives voted in direct opposition to the wishes of their constituents, and the congregational meetings to discuss the question were held after the meeting of the Board. Would the latter have been necessary if the Board had previously consulted your wishes as they ought to have done? And does not the result of these congregational meetings prove also that the majority of the Board did not possess the confidence of the people upon the question at issue?

The constitutional concerns of the General Synod in New Zealand, about the way Jenner was chosen, were put clearly in a response to a criticism of their actions by the Archbishop of Canterbury in 1871.

That His Grace having no jurisdiction in New Zealand, and the matter not having been referred to him by the Church in New Zealand, the pronouncing of any (so called) judgement is an infringement of the liberty of that section of the church to which we belong.

That the late Rural Deanery Board of Otago and Southland had no legal authority to nominate or accept the nomination of a Bishop, but also that there was no authority whatever for any nomination to the See of Dunedin, and in fact, that no such Diocese then existed or was constituted before 1ˢᵗ January 1869.

That Bishop Jenner has no claim, pecuniary or otherwise, upon this Diocese, and that the painful position in which he finds himself placed is due alone to his own injudicious conduct.

Which was rather unfair on Jenner. As he himself often said, he was selected and consecrated as a Bishop by others. He did not put himself forward for the job, but did feel that, having been through the sacred right of consecration, he could hardly deny it all and go back to being a Parish Priest.

The elusive Endowment

It doesn't seem to matter which period of history is chosen, but any study of the Church of England always gives the impression that it was, and is, both very powerful and very wealthy. After all, it has immense investments, huge property portfolios, some of the best heritage sites in the country, and a power base that stretches from bishops in the House of Lords to a national network of parish priests who have the cure of souls of everyone in their patch.

And so it comes as a bit of a surprise to discover that, in Jenner's time, bishops who had been chosen to take their mitres to a foreign land were required to organise their own financing, or to go somewhere rich enough to provide the salary, the house, and the working expenses in order for them to survive. For the future Diocese of Dunedin the difficulty in building an adequate Endowment Fund for its new bishop was a constant source of anxiety, and was to be one of the main reasons for Bishop Jenner's return to Preston.

The first mention of the Fund was as early as 1861 when the Rural Deanery Board of Otago and Southland passed the following resolution:

The Board, on the recommendation of its President (Dr. H. J. C. Harper, Bishop of Christchurch) and the Diocesan Synod, has taken into consideration the great importance of Endowing a Bishopric for Otago and Southland, but no plan of action has yet been decided on.

By its meeting in January 1863 this had become:

That this Board, endorsing the views expressed by the Primate, the Bishop of Christchurch, the Diocesan Synod of Christchurch, and the late Rural Deanery Board, is of the opinion that the time has arrived when it is desirable that there should be a Bishop of Dunedin, who should have the spiritual superintendence of the Church of England in the Provinces of Otago and Southland, and that an attempt should be made to find 'a hundred contributors' willing to guarantee the collection of £50 each within two years.

However, this turned out to be a bit optimistic, and the following year the Board passed a reduced resolution:

*That this Board, recognising the desirability of completing the subscription
to the Bishopric Fund for the proposed Diocese of Otago and Southland,
recommends his Lordship to receive guarantees of sums of £20 and
upwards.*

Whether this worked or not doesn't appear in future minutes, but by
June 1865 the Board was able to produce an itemised picture of how the
fundraising was progressing.

*That whereas £1,000 has been set apart from the Colonial Bishopric's Fund
towards the Endowment of the Bishopric of Otago and Southland, on the
condition that £5,000 be raised from other sources, and whereas £1,000 has
been given by the Society for Promoting Christian Knowledge in Aid of the
Endowment, and 75 acres of land (value £1,000) situated in the province of
Canterbury, have been allocated to the same object, and whereas
subscriptions to the amount of £1,000 had been promised in the Rural
Deanery, it is expected that the sum now required to complete the
Endowment of £6,000 will, in the course of another year, be contributed.*

The significant words here of course were '*in the course of another year*',
which didn't quite fit in with the estimated time of arrival that Bishop
Selwyn, the Primate, had envisaged for a new Bishop in the new diocese.
His rising anxiety can be detected in his grateful acceptance of
Archbishop Longley's choice, written on 4 January 1866.

*We must now go to work in earnest and complete the Endowment Fund,
towards which I hope something more may be done in England, over and
above the £2,000 promised by the SPCK and Colonial Bishop's Fund. I made
a beginning last year, but the time at which I went to Dunedin was
unfavourable, as the place was then passing through one of those fits of
depression which occur in all gold producing countries. Now that I have
your authority for saying that a good man is ready to come out, I can
renew the effort with more hope of success.*

When Dr. Harper wrote on 13 February he was also a little cautious
about the possibility of raising the necessary endowment:
*We have at present towards the £6,000 which is needed for the endowment
of the See about £4,200, and I shall be much disappointed if the remaining
£1,800 be not speedily raised. At the same time it is right that I should add,*

that I am not very sanguine about this. The gold fields which formed the chief source of wealth in that part of my Diocese are now comparatively deserted and the sheep and cattle station holders are suffering with the rest of the Province in the prevailing monetary depression.

He goes on to say that, *The knowledge that there is a Clergyman highly recommended by the Archbishop of Canterbury willing to undertake the office of a Bishop amongst them, will stir up their zeal and liberality.*

Having heard the news about Jenner's appointment, the Rural Deanery Board met on 22 February 1866, and passed two resolutions:

That as a sufficient provision has not yet been made for the support of a Bishop, it is not expedient to take any action at present with a view to confirming the conditional appointment of the Rev. H. L. Jenner, more especially as that appointment has been made without the authority or concurrence of the Board ...

and

That this Board desires to record their extreme regret that through a misconception the Rev. H. L. Jenner should have been led to suppose that the time has arrived for the appointment of a Bishop, and this Board continuing to be decidedly opposed to the appointment without a sufficient endowment having been raised, request that the Secretary be requested to forward this resolution, together with the Minutes this meeting, to the Rev. H. L. Jenner, through the President of the Board.

As seen earlier, Harper chose not to pass this information on to Jenner in Preston.

In his defence Harper was to say, in a letter to the *Otago Witness* of July 1867:

This resolution of the Board was virtually, though not formally, withdrawn by the acquiescence of the Board in the endeavours of the Bishop of New Zealand to collect subscriptions for the endowment of the Bishopric*, and by the contributions for this purpose by several of the members of the Board who had voted for the resolution. This was subsequent to the appointment of Dr. Jenner, and when it was generally understood that he was to be the Bishop of Dunedin.

*In March 1866 the Bishop of New Zealand, much disturbed by the passing of these resolutions, hastened to visit the southern provinces for the purpose of raising funds by his own personal exertions. Calling at Christchurch on his way down he expressed his extreme surprise at the unwonted promptitude with which his suggestion had been acted upon by the Archbishop, as contrasted with the proverbial "slowness" of Church work.

A fascinating account of Selwyn's visit to the southern provinces is contained in the *Memoir of the Life and Episcopate of George Augustus Selwyn, DD* by H. W. Tucker, published in 1879.

The bishop found himself placed in a position of very great difficulty, and came to the conclusion that the only thing for him to do was to go to the Southern Island and 'make a raid on Dunedin itself' and raise what funds he could towards the endowment of the See. The prospect was not encouraging, for trade was depressed and money scarce. On his arrival at Dunedin he found nothing had been done; and at Christchurch he had been met by a series of resolutions throwing cold water on the scheme, 'not for any wish to oppose it, but from fear of having to pay.'

Seeing no hope of a speedy accomplishment of the purpose which had brought him away from his own diocese, where his presence could be ill spared, he yet resolved to spend a month in visiting the 'Runholders', that it might not be said that the endowment had failed for want of effort on his part.

The ride through the province of Otago gave to the bishop an opportunity of ministering to the diggers who in large numbers had been attracted to the goldfields. While thus engaged he wrote:

'The change of climate and country is complete; open hills without a tree and covered with yellow grass; sheep runs without a visible sheep; accommodation houses every three or four miles; tilted waggons going up and down between Dunedin and the Diggings; horsemen rushing along as if they had not a moment to lose; horses feeding out of mangers made of sacking stretched between the shafts of the waggons, and eating as if they too had not a moment to lose. The traffic seems to go on Sundays and week-days alike, and a Scotsman, whom I invited in vain to church, admitted that all the lessons of the old country were forgotten on this road ...

Upon the whole, as the thing was to be done, I am not sorry to have had to go over this province. Part of my object is to visit as many diggers as I can, and to hold services wherever I find them disposed to attend. There was a large party of them on board the Phœbe, *returning from Hoikitika, who assured me that it was a mistake to suppose that there were not many among them who cared for better things than digging gold. They have the character of being a manly and independent body of men, for the most part orderly and honest ...*

It is a comfort to think that this is the last work of bishop-making in which it will be necessary for me to engage; and when this is done I may break my wand.

In the course of his visit Bishop Selwyn managed to raise £1,300 – not enough to complete the endowment.

Meanwhile, back at the Rural Deanery Board, a meeting was held on the 21 February 1867, at which the Bishop of Christchurch got them 'up to speed' as far as the Endowment was concerned.

Since the last Meeting of the Rural Deanery Board, a step has been taken which has an important bearing on the welfare of our Church in these parts. It may be remembered that in 1863 an address was presented to me in which the Board strongly expressed its opinion that the Rural Deanery of Otago and Southland should be formed into a separate Diocese, and I was requested to bring this matter before the different Parishes and districts of the Deanery, and to urge upon the members of the Church the exercise of an abundant liberality in contributing to the endowment of the proposed Bishopric.
The opinion of the Board was so entirely in accordance with my own views, that I did not hesitate to act upon it, and the effort which I made for this proposal was responded to by the offer of subscriptions to the amount of £950. This was at a time when the resources of the Province of Otago appeared to be daily increasing, and we had every reason to hope that the amount required would be speedily raised. A check, however, in the prosperity of the Province occurred, and the efforts to obtain additional subscriptions were attended with little success.
In the meanwhile, a clergyman in England was nominated to the Bishopric

of Dunedin by the Archbishop of Canterbury; and in the prospect of this consecration the Bishop of New Zealand visited the Rural Deanery, and by his personal exertions added considerably to the contributions for the endowment; and he also announced his intention of appropriating to the same purpose the several sections near Invercargill, originally purchased for Church purposes from funds at his disposal.

It must be obvious that the necessities of the Church have not diminished since the resolution of the Board in 1863. The number of Church members since then has been steadily increasing in this city and its suburbs. Extensive portions of the agricultural districts of the Provinces of Otago and Southland have been permanently occupied, and large townships have been established in the immediate neighbourhood of the older goldfields, and though something has been done in these districts by the zeal and activity of ordained clergymen and laymen, yet much more is needed, and can scarcely be adequately and efficiently supplied except under the superintendence of a resident Bishop.

If a Bishop were needed in 1862, it must be admitted that he is still more needed at the present moment. This I am persuaded is well understood, by those who are acquainted with the real state of the Provinces of Otago and Southland, and who desire to maintain for themselves and others the blessings to which they have been called as members of the Church of England. And thereby, perhaps, we hardly expected so speedy a fulfilment of our wishes, and our preparations for the reception of a Bishop are still very incomplete, yet we cannot but recognise in his consecration to his office the hand of God working for our good and think that no exertion on our parts will be wanting to show that we are truly grateful for this. On hearing of the consecration of Dr. Jenner, I lost no time in communicating with the Church Societies in England, whose aid had been promised for the endowment of the Bishopric.

[The Bishop went on to give a figure of £4,336.7.10 as available, leaving a gap of £1,663 to make up the necessary £6,000, and urged the local people to do more.]

The Revd H. Jenner is prepared, no doubt, to serve in his office with a very limited income, but, still the Church should provide a sufficiency for his support, and for those unavoidable expenses which are incidental to his office.

The *Otago Daily Times* of 25 February 1867 included a report of this meeting of the Rural Deanery.

The Rural Dean (Rev. E. G. Edwards) moved – 'that this Board consider what steps should be taken towards augmenting the Otago and Southland Bishopric Fund, and providing the Bishop with a house.' He considered that, among the steps which it might be agreed to take, it would be proper to send an address to the Primate suggesting that he should ask the other Bishops to join with him in calling upon the lay members of the Church throughout New Zealand to contribute. The Rev. Mr Gifford thought it highly important that the public should be reached, and that it should be suggested to the clergy to call meetings of their parishioners. It would probably be the last Bishopric that would be formed in New Zealand for a very long time, and that it was desirous that every publicity should be given to the effort that was being made; and that, through the Primate, substantial cooperation should be invited.

For some reason this clerical campaign didn't prove to be as fruitful as they had hoped. It is always interesting to see how often we attribute to others the interests and passions that are in essence solely ours.

The whole debate about Bishop Jenner and the Endowment came to a head at the meeting of the General Synod in 1868.

Because of the many conflicting accounts and heated debate surrounding the matter, a committee was appointed to look at it rationally, although it included none of the members from Otago and Southland. This was his account of proceedings:

Your committee, having carefully considered the subject submitted to them, and having taken such evidence, and examined such documents, bearing thereupon, as were within their reach, including a statement by Dr. Jenner, beg to report as follows:-
They have ascertained that the endowment fund for the proposed diocese is, in its present state, insufficient for the support of a bishop. They have further ascertained that the objections entertained in the contemplated diocese to the alleged opinions and practices of Bishop Jenner preclude the probability of the speedy completion of this fund. At the same time they are led to believe that the pecuniary circumstances of Bishop Jenner*, so far as

they are able to form an opinion upon them, are such as would cause him to be wholly dependant on the fund.

*[Jenner's income at Preston that year was £400 and, unlike many of his brother clergy, he did not have any other livings adding to his funds. For some reason – probably the size of the family – he seems to have had little in the way of money from the Bank of Mum and Dad.]

In coming to a decision they have not thought themselves to take into consideration the alleged ritualistic practices of Bishop Jenner, but they consider that the state and prospect of the Endowment Fund, and the circumstances above referred to, constitute sufficient reasons for the following decision, namely:- That they are not prepared to recommend the Synod to confirm the appointment of Bishop Jenner.

On the following day the Bishop of Christchurch moved, on behalf of the committee; *That the appointment of Bishop Jenner to the See of Dunedin be not confirmed by the Synod.*

Jacobs continues:

The debate which ensued was prolonged and exceedingly animated, the Synod being almost equally divided. There was no little heat, and much barely suppressed excitement on both sides ... the position was becoming a painfully strained one, when it was agreed to adjourn the sitting for half an hour to give an opportunity for free discussion. On resuming Archdeacon Harper (the Bishop's son) moved, seconded by the Dean of Christchurch, 'That, whereas the General Synod is of the opinion that it is better for the peace of the Church that Bishop Jenner should not take charge of the Bishopric of Dunedin, this Synod hereby requests him to withdraw his claim to that position.' After some debate this motion was adopted without a division. If it appears a somewhat 'lame and impotent conclusion', the cause must be attributed to the extreme unwillingness of the members of Synod to come to an open breach with their President (Selwyn), whom they unfeignedly admired and revered, whose splendid hospitality they had enjoyed, and from whom they were on the eve of parting.

John Evans gives a good analysis of the situation.

The great disappointment about all this was the report of the committee. The real issue was the opinions and practices of Bishop Jenner, and the fears of a minority in Otago and Southland, whose objections had caused all the trouble. This was the very question that the committee explicitly declined to consider. Instead they based their recommendation on the incompleteness of the Endowment Fund and Jenner's poverty which would compel him to depend on it for his maintenance. Compared with the essential justice of his claim and his integrity in promising not to make innovations that would offend his people, this was an unimportant consideration. It is comforting to read that Jenner's cause had strong support. It is a pity that it was not stronger. Of course the Synod had the right legally to withhold confirmation of the appointment. Whether it had the moral right to do so on this occasion is another question.

Meanwhile, back in England, the church authorities were taking Jenner's departure to Dunedin as a done deal, as can be seen from this announcement in *The Record* of 26 October 1866.

The Rev Henry E T Cruse, BA of Worcester College, Oxford, a young gentleman just ordained, is about to be married to the daughter of the Very Rev. Dr. Alford, Dean of Canterbury. Mr. Cruse is also to be presented by the Dean to the vicarage of Preston-with-Wingham (sic), *near Sandwich, worth about £500 a year, in the room of the Rev. Henry Lascelles Jenner L.L.D., lately consecrated Bishop of Dunedin, New Zealand, who will resign it at the close of the present year.*

Jenner was well aware that, if he was to make a proper start of his ministry in New Zealand, he would have to encourage people in England to make a contribution. This he did by preaching in different parishes across the country, often in those whose incumbent was known to him through the Ecclesiological Society and the movement for Catholic renewal.

Many of these were in churches that were celebrating a re-dedication after having had structural alterations, and therefore laid on very elaborate and celebratory worship, which usually caught the attention of the local press (and which then ended up in the local papers of Dunedin.)

In December 1866 the *Otago Daily Times* reported a meeting at the Church of St John the Evangelist, Rotherham to hear the Lord Bishop of Dunedin talk about his future work in New Zealand. (Originally contained in *The Rotherham and Masbro' Advertiser*.)

The meeting was opened by prayer, intoned by the Chairman and chanted by the choir ... The Lord Bishop of Dunedin began by giving a description of the country where his work would lie. He said that he did that more for his own satisfaction than for their instruction, for he could hardly believe that in a town like Rotherham any one could need information with regard to New Zealand. Of course, since his study of the country, he had learned to look with supreme contempt upon those who were not so well informed upon the subject as himself - (Laughter) ... After a brief description of the country his lordship proceeded to point out the wants of the new diocese of Dunedin. They should require more churches, and his desire was that the churches that were built under his auspices should be worthy of the great object of their erection. He desired also that the worship of God should be worthily conducted – (Cheers). Then he should require clergy. The church – the mere fabric – was useless without the living voice, the priest who should administer the sacraments and perform the offices of religion. And the clergy he should require should be superior men. The notion prevailed that anything would do for the Colonies; but that was a great mistake. As to the population to whom he should be called upon to minister, they were chiefly European emigrants – either sheep-farmers, tradespeople or gold-finders. There were not more than a few hundred Maoris in his diocese. He ended by hoping that the Mother Church would be generous towards the Colonial Church in its contribution of funds and its prayers.

The meeting continued with various clergy telling stories about their visits to the Colonies. It doesn't say whether slides were shown.

There were many other places where Bishop Jenner exercised his ministry, some only receiving a couple of lines in the local paper.

LAVENHAM

On Sunday afternoon the Lord Bishop of Dunedin, New Zealand, the Right Rev. H. L. Jenner, LL.B, preached a very eloquent sermon in Lavenham

Church, before a good and attentive congregation. A collection, which amounted to £4 8s., was made at the close of the service in aid of the Dunedin Diocesan Fund. (Bury and Norwich Post 9 October 1866)

ST MARY'S, WENVOE

On Sunday afternoon a most earnest and impressive sermon was preached in this church by the Lord Bishop of Dunedin, the Right Rev. Henry Jenner, in behalf of various church objects in the diocese, to which he has been consecrated by the Archbishop of Canterbury ... Long will it be ere the sentiments that he expressed in such a life-giving manner on the promotion of God's glory by prayer, self-denial, and almsgiving, be forgotten. His lordship also preached the same evening at Newcastle Church, Bridgend. A collection was made for diocesan purposes, which amounted to £ 33 14s." (Cardiff Times Nov 1866)

There was a family connection here, as the Rector was one of three generations of Jenners to hold the position, the Jenner family having inherited Wenvoe Castle through marriage in 1801.

In December 1866 the *Norfolk Chronicle* descibed this interesting audiovisual presentation.

A meeting was held at the Corn Hall, on Tuesday evening, when the Right Rev. Dr. H. L. Jenner, Lord Bishop of Dunedin, gave an interesting account of the missionary work in New Zealand. About fifty coloured engravings, illustrative of the various places of heathen worship and life were exhibited, which gave additional interest to the bishop's address. The collection amounted to £5 12s. 6d.

In February 1867 the local newspaper for Somerset published the following encouraging account of Jenner's preaching abilities.

MISSIONARY SERVICE – As announced by us last week, on Sunday evening a service was held in the church to further the objects of the Mission Church in the diocese of Dunedin, New Zealand. The sermon was preached by the Right Rev. H. L. Jenner D.D., Bishop of Dunedin. So masterly was the discourse, and so musical the voice that delivered it, that the only regret expressed by the unusually large congregation was that, though the sermon was not short, it would have been delightful had it been double the length. The collection was highly satisfactory, and altogether the service was a refreshing spiritual treat.

Despite the fundraising efforts in both England and New Zealand, however, the full amount necessary for the Bishops Endowment never seems to have been reached. However, the lack of a full endowment paled into insignificance when Jenner's ritualistic tendencies came to be seen as a much more significant problem. Indeed, it could be argued that the problem of the lack of an endowment was an early ploy by Jenner's opponents to sow the seeds of anxiety and dissent amongst the churchgoers of Dunedin. Certainly the issue of his ritualism was anticipated as providing a reason why people would not feel happy about paying his wages and running expenses if he were enthroned. The fact that Jenner's lack of funds, and therefore the need to raise an endowment, made him an undesirable candidate for the fairly poor provinces of Otago and Southland, stands in marked contrast to the financial situation of the man who would be accepted in his place.

George Selwyn, who in 1868 had become the Bishop of Lichfield, suggested the name of the Rev. Samuel Tarratt Nevill, Rector of Shelton, Staffordshire, for the vacant diocese of Wellington, New Zealand. Nevill wasn't keen, but accepted Selwyn's suggestion that he at least visit New Zealand, where his wife had brothers living in the North Island.

He duly arrived in New Zealand – having brought letters of introduction from Selwyn – and after an extended family visit, journeyed south and made himself known to the clergy of Dunedin. They were now a fully fledged Diocese, and so were eager to appoint a new bishop who wasn't like Jenner, and, by coincidence, Nevill proved to be the ideal man. Not only did he have the support of Selwyn, but he was most certainly not from a ritualistic background. His church, St Mark's, Shelton, although having been built in 1833 to a perpendicular/gothic design, is shown in a watercolour painted in the 1850s as having wall-to-wall box pews, balconies on all sides, and a huge three-decker pulpit that obscured most of the east window. More importantly, his financial security was beyond doubt, his wife having acquired a vast inheritance from her grandmother, whose wealth had come from her father James Penny's business as a very successful slave trader. He was one of several Liverpool traders who were delegated to speak in favour of the practice at a parliamentary inquiry into the slave trade in 1788, and he continued to maintain the trade, even when other Liverpool merchants had caught the nation's mood and had ceased to do so.

JAMES PENNY'S FAMILY TREE

James Penny (c.1741 - 1799) Slave trader
(See Liverpool Record Office - *Logs on board H.M.S. Agamemnon, the Count du Nord and the Mampookata, with related papers* Ref 387 MD 62)
There is a good account of his trade in the following website -
https://www.cumbria.gov.uk/eLibrary/Content/Internet/542/795/41053132 443.pdf

Father of

James (Stubbington) Penny (1772-1861)
Record of his Baptism in St. Peter's, Church Street, Liverpool on 13 November 1772

Father of

James Parker Penny (1803-1884)

Father of

Mary Susanna Nevill (née Cook-Penny) (1834-1905)
Married *Samuel Tarratt Nevill* 1863

When approached, Nevill indicated that if Dunedin were to nominate him as its first bishop he would accept, and so he was duly nominated, he accepted, and was consecrated on 4 June 1871. It proved to be a most rewarding episcopate.

As the diocese was still unable to afford to build a bishop's palace Nevill built his own, which the diocese then rented from him, often being in arrears on the amount agreed. Other projects that he helped to fund were a theological college, a girls school, and a third of a new Cathedral. A slight irony about his appointment was that, as the Rev Michael Blain points out in his *Biographical Directory of Anglican clergy in the South Pacific* (1991), Nevill was an Anglo-Catholic.

My own reading of the 200 clergy of his episcopate suggests that there were a higher proportion of markedly high church priests in Nevill's Dunedin than elsewhere in the contemporary New Zealand church. Yet Nevill came to Dunedin after the noisy rejection of the Ritualist Jenner.
To sedate the ghosts, he had distanced himself very carefully from comment or action that might arouse similar resentment against himself. Thus he shows a particularly hostile unease about minor ceremonial gestures when Hubert Carlyon, a priest in Christchurch diocese, was put on trial for such offences. Among the judging bishops of New Zealand Nevill took a strong stand and ensured Carlyon's admonition and suspension in 1877.
A high church prelate thus had used his position and undoubted intelligence to destroy the ministry of a high church priest. Yet, as the decades calmed prejudices, even a few years ahead and certainly by the end of his reign, his diocese was taken to be the most high church diocese of New Zealand.

By 1919, when Nevill retired, the golden years of the later nineteenth century had long closed. Otago was no longer the financial heartland of New Zealand. The close of his episcopate also meant the end of those generous subsidies which Nevill had provided for half a century – which, given the source of the wealth, was perhaps no bad thing.

Now, church institutions brought into existence by a determined prelate, but set up with inadequate financial bases, put greater strain on the diocesan budget. The diocese needed to start again in reduced circumstances, and to own its own issues for the first time on its own terms. The frustrating disappointments known by Bishop Harper, way back in the 1860s, squeezing blood from the stones of the Rural Deanery Board's penury, were fully present and now undisguised. Not two years into his retirement, Bishop Nevill died, still wealthy despite his munificence. His estate was valued at £38,000.

So, what happened to the money raised for Jenner's Endowment?

In June 1871 Bishop Selwyn wrote to the Archbishop of Canterbury.

I think that your Grace will not be sorry to hear that Bishop Jenner has placed in my hands his written resignation of all claims to the Bishopric of Dunedin. The Dunedin Bishopric Endowment Fund stands in my name in the New Zealand Bank, Dunedin, to the amount of about £1,300, chiefly collected by me for Bishop Jenner, but some of the contributors have refused to allow their donations to be applied to his benefit unless he enters into possession of the Bishopric, with the consent of the Synod. I have paid to him two hundred pounds (£200) on account of interest which has accrued upon the Endowment Fund collected by me ... I hope that the sum of four hundred pounds (£400) which he has now received in all will have covered his expenses, and thus we may consider that your Grace's written opinion upon his case has now been carried out.

Henry Lascelles Jenner D. D.
Bishop of Dunedin 1866 – 1871

The Right Reverend Henry Lascelles Jenner D.D.

National Portrait Gallery

Photograph taken by Martin Jacolette, sometime after he had established himself as an international portrait photographer, in both Dover and London, sometime in the late 1880s.

A light screen with a cross on it divided the chancel from the nave, and a carved oak eagle was introduced as a lectern. Dr. Mill's successor at Brasted, having no use for popish furniture, the churchwardens presented Jenner with a very fine pair of altar candlesticks of Cambridge Camden Society design. (Page 20)

Watercolour painted by H. Petrie FSA in 1807, showing that the aisle windows at St. Mildred's had already been blocked and replaced by three gabled dormers. (From the Ecclesiologist *of 1874)*

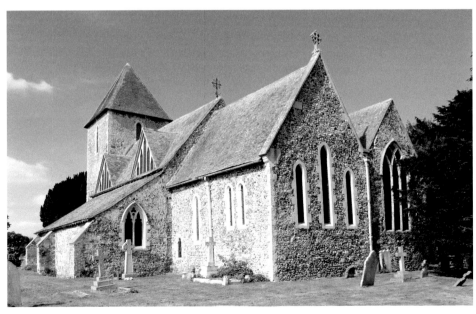

St. Mildred's today
The Jenner family grave can be seen just in front of the south chapel window

Jenner's 'Snug Vicarage'

The view of a living room with eight portraits of men and women: Miss Dormer, Lady Emily Dundas, The Bishop of Dunedin, Miss Julia Cavendish & dog, Reverend I. Cavendish Taylor, Honorable Richard Cavendish, Maud White, Admiral Seymour. Created by Georgiana Berkeley. (Orsay Museum, Paris)

ADDINGTON PARK.
His Grace THE ARCHBISHOP OF CANTERBURY

ADDINGTON PARK.
CROYDON.

Decr. 19. 1867.

My dear Lord.

The whole Bench of
Bishops had been
& postulating, remonstrating
against the deep of Ritual
which was impelling
the Church of England, & you,
but just consecrated throw
the weight of your influence &
example, into the Scale of these
scrapes. Such conduct was felt
to be embarrassing, and offensive.

very truly Yours.

G. T. Cantuar:

(Edited extract from a letter in Lambeth Palace Library. See page 102)

Charles Thomas Longley
Archbishop of Canterbury
(1862 – 1868)
(Photo taken by Lewis Carroll)

Bishop Jenner with Burges' Crozier.
Taken at the First Lambeth Conference
by Mason and Co of London.

Section of the The First Lambeth Conference group photo 1867

St. Mark's, Shelton, whose Vicar became the second Bishop of Dunedin.
Note the three-decker pulpit, galleries and box-pews. (1860)

J. Wright's, 'By piety's due rites 'tis given/To hold communion with Heaven', *print (c.1800).*
Although clearly a caricature of a church interior and service, it is an interesting record of the
style of worship that the Ritualists wanted to replace.

The City of Boston
Liverpool to New York

Cathedral of St Finn Bar - Cork
W. Burgess, Architect.

Saint Fin Barre's Cathedral, Cork
as designed by William Burges,
and below being built around the time
of Jenner's visit.

Ritualism - a different groove, or 'leaning the other way'

The rise of 'popularism' in recent times, in religion just as much as in politics and the media, means that the fastest growing churches tend to be those with a drum kit, guitar stands, and a row of microphones at their east end – where the altar or pulpit used to be – and a large sound-mixing console somewhere towards the back. Nearly all churches now seem to have a large screen propped up at the front somewhere – often on the pulpit – for displaying the words of the hymns and readings.

However, in the past, and still for many today, the common image of a church was of an ornate building with an altar and candles, choir stalls and pews, pillars and a pulpit, and a Mother's Union banner in the corner. Beams of dusty sunlight would shine through richly coloured stained glass windows to glance off a much polished brass eagle or list of past Vicars, and small piles of hymn books would litter a table by the door, where you might also find a brief description of the church, some tatty postcards, or a copy of the church newsletter. On a notice board at the back would be a poster about some missionary society working in Umbutuland, a plaintive little card showing the cost of running the church, and this month's rota of flower arrangers.

To visit the church on a Sunday morning would – in a vast number of churches, even some with music groups and OHP screens – reveal a ceremony involving organ music, an order of service, singing, kneeling, processions, candles, and people wearing white hooded gowns and brightly coloured robes. There may even be a bunch of boys and girls, or adults, dressed in cassocks and surplices, who sat together at the front and sang louder than everyone else.

It may therefore come as a surprise to discover that this apparently ubiquitous form of church and worship is, on the whole, the nineteenth century product of the 'Ritualists', of whom Henry Jenner was a passionate member. Indeed, it was his ritualistic tendencies that were to be the major factor in his being rejected as the First Bishop of Dunedin.

So, if they were to have such a great effect on the life of the Church of England, why were their views unacceptable in Dunedin? And was it only that particular part of the far-flung British Empire that had this feeling of revulsion towards them? What was Ritualism, and why did it become a cause of controversy in nineteenth century Britain?

The rich tapestry that is the history of Ritualism, or Anglo-Catholic Renewal, is one made up of many threads, some good, some bad, some just plain silly, but all woven to form a complex pattern, which, like their church designs and acts of worship, is full of light and colour and meaning.

All that can be done here is to give a very rough and simple sketch of some of the threads involved. There are many books, far better than this, that can more fully bring to light the whole picture of Ritualism. If you already know it then skip to the next chapter.

In medieval times the English Church had been part of the Western Roman Catholic Church, presided over by the papacy in Rome. Therefore the country's church life had been characterized by a good deal of ritual – centred on the mass and the sacraments – and church order and regulation – administered by the priests and the church hierarchy. In addition there were many religious houses, with their daily rounds of processional services and sung offices, times of silence and meditation, pools of discovery and study, and often service to the poor outside their gates.

Much of this heritage was eradicated by the sixteenth century Protestant Reformers in their desire to recover a simpler way of religious life, and a kind of worship more in keeping with the New Testament and early church practices. Protestantism at that time was about a 'protest for' the Reformed biblical faith, and not a 'protest against' Romanism. Protestantism emerged in England under Henry VIII, and for the most part English church worship became and remained plain and unadorned until the middle years of the nineteenth century. This was when a series of events combined to create a renewed desire to recover medieval ritual in the Church of England.

The move towards ritualism came from the second generation of the Oxford Movement (or the Tractarians, after their publishing of tracts to convey their beliefs). The first phase of Tractarianism, from 1833-41, had primarily been concerned with doctrinal issues. In particular, Tractarians had been concerned to argue that the Church of England was part of the one true Catholic Church and that, through the hands of an unbroken line of bishops, the apostolic succession could trace its roots back to the original apostolic community. Despite this strong doctrine of the church as the divine society, the Oxford leaders did not themselves adopt advanced ceremonial. In fact, until the time he left the Church of England in 1845, Newman wore a plain black gown for preaching, and celebrated Holy Communion standing at the north end of the communion table. Pusey likewise was, in this early phase, against what he termed 'provocative trappings' and 'popish toys', but did eventually come to see the logic of Ritualist development - "We, the clergy, taught the truth: the people said, 'Set it before our eyes'. I do think that it is scarcely philosophical to regard this so-called 'ritualistic movement' otherwise other than an eminently lay movement."

As early as 1844 Francis Close had linked the ideology of Oxford with the artistry of Cambridge.

Romanism is taught analytically at Oxford, [and] it is taught artistically at Cambridge. That it is inculcated theoretically, in Tracts, at the one University, and it is sculptured, painted and graven at the other. The Cambridge Camdenians build churches and furnish symbolic vessels, by which the Oxford Tractarians may carry out their principles.

Most ceremonial began in Oxford in the late 1830s and 1840s, and consisted of intoning services, having lighted candles on the altar, wearing stoles, and preaching in a surplice rather than in the traditional black gown. But even these innovations were considered to be popish, and were sufficient to cause riots in churches in Exeter in 1845 and 1848, in East Grinstead between 1848 and 1857, and in the London churches of St Barnabas', Pimlico in 1850-51 and St George's in the East in 1859-60. In other parts of the country, however, the innovations were quietly accepted and greatly extended. Some clergy went out of their way to proceed cautiously, beginning with doctrinal teaching and only proceeding to greater ceremonial when they were sure it would be accepted. By the mid 1860s ritualist clergy were recognised by their use of what were known as the 'six points': the celebrant standing on the east side of the communion table, the wearing of Eucharistic vestments like a stole and alb, having candles burning in daylight, the use of wafers instead of bread, water mixed with the wine, and the use of incense.

Several factors led the second generation of the Oxford Movement to be concerned about ritual.

First and most basic was their emphasis on the undivided Catholic Church of the first five centuries. The first generation leaders of the Movement, and Newman in particular, had looked back to what they termed the via media or middle position which had characterized the undivided Catholic Church of these first Christian centuries.

As the Tractarians studied the life and worship of this period of church history they found many doctrines and practices which Protestant bishops had removed on biblical grounds at the time of the Reformation. These included, for example, regular fasting, prayers for the dead, prayers to the saints, the veneration of Mary, an emphasis on celibacy, religious communities, a belief in the real presence of Christ in the Eucharist, and the idea that the bread and wine changed in substance when the priest called the Holy Spirit down on them.

Secondly, there was a missionary motive behind the desire to change the style and meaning of worship. How worship was presented – with movement, ceremonial, light and colour; enhanced by music, singing, and silence; and in a building of beauty, space and form – was seen to be of vital importance if the Church was to be welcoming and comprehensible to the people of nineteenth century England. Bishop Blomfield (Bishop of London 1828 –1856,) described the average church service of the 1850s as being:

Blank, dismal, oppressive and dreary. Matins and the litany, with a sermon lasting the best part of an hour, in a cold and gloomy church, was not the kind of worship to appeal to a man or woman with no education or little imagination.

Such a church would have had a tall three-decker pulpit, from which a wordy service was offered to those wealthy enough to own or rent one of its many box pews, and to others who stood at the back or sat in the gallery where it was free, and where there may have been a small music group. [Church organs were a rarity. For example in 1750, only half the churches in London had organs, and in 1800 only three churches in Dorset had one.] A small wooden table would be at the east end where Communion was celebrated perhaps once a month, or just on Holy Days like Easter and Christmas.

The Ritualist's desire for colour, movement and design was mirrored by the developing Romantic Movement which had captivated Victorian England. Romanticism can be seen as a rejection of the precepts of order, calm, harmony, balance, idealization, and rationality, that typified Classicism in general, and late eighteenth century Neoclassicism in particular. It was also to some extent a reaction against the Enlightenment, and against rationalism and physical materialism in general. Romanticism emphasized the individual, the subjective, the irrational, the imaginative, the personal, the spontaneous, the emotional, the visionary, and the transcendental. It looked back with warmth and admiration to the 'Merrie England' of the medieval period. It could also be seen as a reaction to the growing emphasis on nationalism, scientific discovery and cold logic of the early 1800s.

In literature it was seen in the poetry of Blake, Coleridge, Shelley, and Keats, and in the writings of Scott, Hazlitt, Austin, and the Brontë sisters. In art it was most visible in the Pre-Raphaelite School which, like the Ritualists, sought to recover the insights of the medieval period – in their case before the time of Raphael – and in the paintings of Blake, Constable, and Turner.

However, the influence of the Romantic Movement was probably most visible in the use of a neo-Gothic style of architecture, to be found in public buildings like the Houses of Parliament, and St. Pancras Station; in country mansions like Woodchester Mansion, Gloucestershire; and in a large variety of suburban houses. Many of the designs were the creation of architects such as Pugin, Barry, Ruskin, Burgess and Gilbert Scott, who were also active in the Arts and Crafts movement. Along with designers like William Morris and Edward Burne-Jones they applied the neo-Gothic style, not just to the buildings, but also to their internal features, their furniture, staircases, ceilings and wallpaper. In the fashionable suburbs which were springing up on the outskirts of many towns and cities there was a growing taste for more elaborate housing. Doorsteps and hallways were frequently laid with brightly coloured tiles, and small windows would be of stained glass.

So it can be seen that the Ritualists were not some small group of rebellious oddballs, trying to make Roman Catholicism the leading religion in England, but part of a very broad, national – indeed international – movement of ideas and creativity that was transforming our whole society. From the point of view of the Church of England this development was seen most clearly and forcefully in the work of the Camden Society.

Already mentioned as being formative in Henry Jenner's beliefs, and an organisation that he was committed to throughout his adult life, the Cambridge Camden Society was named after the antiquarian William Camden (1551-1623). It began in 1839 as a university club for people interested in Gothic churches, and was started by John Mason Neale and a small circle of associates, most of whom were undergraduates. It was formally founded with the aim 'to promote the study of Gothic Architecture and Ritual Arts and the restoration of mutilated architectural remains'. To this end it sought to ensure that all new churches were erected in the Gothic style, and that all restorations were carried out after the pattern of medieval buildings. They kept lists of specially approved architects, among them being Sir Gilbert Scott, William Butterfield and Augustus Pugin.

In 1845 it moved to London and became known as the Ecclesiological Society. Its activities would come to include publishing a monthly journal, *The Ecclesiologist*, advising church builders on their blueprints, and describing new church buildings and restorations when done in the neo-Gothic style. At the peak of its influence in the 1840s, the society counted over 700 members, including bishops of the Church of England, deans at Cambridge University, and Members of Parliament.

So what were the main concerns of the Ritualists?

The Real Presence

When they started to apply their theology of the sacraments to the life of the church the Tractarians found that the Eucharist had become a widely neglected act of worship. In fact for many churches it was almost an optional complement to normal parish worship. Their study of the early Catholic Fathers of the undivided church however, revealed the Eucharist to have been a much more central form of Christian worship. For example, there was a clear doctrine of a 'real presence' taught by Cyril of Jerusalem in his *Catechetical Lectures* in the middle of the fourth century. In a celebrated sermon preached in 1843 entitled 'The Holy Eucharist a Comfort to the Penitent', Pusey spoke of *'That bread which is his flesh,'* and of *'Touching with our very lips the cleansing blood'*.

Religious Orders

In the later years of the nineteenth century the second generation of the Oxford Movement encouraged the re-founding of religious orders, and the need arose for devotional offices which were beyond the scope of the Prayer Book services. Monks and nuns and other members of religious communities felt the need for stillness, quiet and places for contemplation, and it was perhaps in the context of the newly formed religious houses that many Catholic practices and styles of worship began to develop.

The Ornaments' Rubric

The Ritualists were further encouraged by the 'Ornaments' Rubric'. This was printed with the Preface to the 1559 prayer book and was retained in the front of the 1662 Book of Common Prayer. The rubric stated explicitly that:

Such Ornaments of the Church, and of the ministers thereof, at all Times of their ministration shall be retained, and be in use, as were in this Church of England, by the Authority of Parliament, in the Second Year of the Reign of King Edward the Sixth.

They sought to maintain that they were simply adhering to the original regulations, and that it was perfectly legal to wear *'a white alb plain with vestment or cope,'* and to celebrate, not at the north end of the table, but *'afore the midst of the altar'* as specified in the Book of Common Prayer immediately before the Prayer of Consecration. At this level it was quite hard to take action against the Ritualists. They argued that their vestments, far from being illegal, were the only legal form of dress at Communion.

Reservation and Adoration

The custom of retaining and storing some of the bread and wine from the Holy Communion was re-introduced by the Ritualists. Reservation had been a common practice in medieval times but was halted by Cranmer and the Protestant Reformers. This is made clear by the sixth rubric at the end of the 1662 Prayer Book order of service which stated categorically:

If any remain of that which was consecrated ... the Priest and such other of the Communicants as he shall then call unto him, shall, immediately after the Blessing, reverently eat and drink the same.

Reservation was viewed with disfavour because it could lead on to the associated practices of adoration and benediction. As the opposition saw it, adoration was nothing short of idolatry. They held the practice to be explicitly condemned by Article XXV which stated that:

The Sacraments were not ordained of Christ to be gazed upon, or to be carried about, but that we should duly use them.

However, these practices became an increasingly popular ingredient in ritualistic spirituality, particularly where the reserved sacrament was used when visiting the sick, and meeting the needs of those unable to attend the church service.

Vestments and the Eastward Position of the Celebrant

The eastward position of the celebrant at Holy Communion and the use of Roman Catholic mass vestments including the alb, chasuble and stole, were further prominent aspects of ritualism. Many Ritualists adopted the custom of standing in the middle of the west side of the communion table or 'altar' with their back to the people. In such a position the priest was held to be in a mediating position between the people and the altar, implying that the priest was offering a sacrifice on behalf of his people. Ritualists attempted to justify this position on the basis of the rubric in the 1662 service which speaks of 'the Priest standing before the Table' rather than 'at the end of' the altar as per the north end position.

Vestments began to appear in the 1850s. For example, the Rev Brian King first used them in 1857 at St George's Mission in London's dockland when a group of his parishioners offered him a gift of two silk chasubles. Liturgical colours to indicate the changing seasons and festivals of the Church's year became a growing feature.

It is helpful to remember that the alb, chasuble and stole were all originally everyday dress items in the early Roman Empire, and had no religious significance whatsoever. Later, when the Christian Empire was overrun by the pagan Goths, many Christians retained Roman dress as part of their Christian witness. With the passing of time only the priests retained the old Roman dress and that during divine service. The alb (or basic garment), the chasuble (over-cloak) and stole (badge of profession) thus became linked with the offering of the mass during the high Middle Ages. This quite rational use of such garments was severely rebuked by the Ritualist's opponents.

For example Lloyd George described it as 'salvation by haberdashery', whilst Bishop Samuel Waldegrave had described wearing the surplice in the pulpit as *in many cases but the first of a series of Romeward movements.*

So big an issue was it that in March 1867 Lord Shaftesbury introduced a bill, *The Sacrificial Vestments Bill*, into the House of Lords:

For better enforcing Uniformity in the Vestment and Ornaments to be worn by Ministers of the United Church of England and Ireland in the performance of Public Worship.

There were many other aspects of ritualism which gave offence. These included the use of incense in worship, the singing of the *Agnus Dei* (Lamb of God) during the reception of the bread and wine at communion, and the bowing at the name of Jesus. Nothing, however, provoked a stronger reaction than the introduction of the confessional and the practice of priestly absolution.

The Confessional and Priestly Absolution

The Ritualist's encouragement of the use of personal confession to, and absolution by, a priest was perhaps an inevitable attachment to the concept of priesthood and sacrament from the medieval past. In their understanding of confession one sees a characteristic appreciation for mystery and reserve.

It could be said that the practice of confession in the Church of England dates from Pusey's two sermons on *The Entire Absolution of the Penitent*, in 1846, in which he argued that the revival of the importance of the sacrament should be complemented by the revival of an opportunity for confession and forgiveness, as in the medieval traditions. He made reference to the Prayer Book order for the visiting of the sick as a moment for personalized confession and absolution.

Of the ingredients that made up the Ritualist pudding this was to create some of the greatest controversies, and it has perhaps never found a place in the broad scheme of Anglicanism in the way that, say, vestments and church interior design have done.

Whilst the Ritualists in England seem, in hindsight, to have had a lot going for them, and to be part of a much greater social and artistic movement, they were fiercely opposed, particularly after the restoration of the Roman Catholic hierarchy in 1851, when the view was held that Ritualism was in reality Romanism in disguise. A good example of such opposition was the *Church Association*, whose views can be seen in this extract from a tract entitled, 'Address of the Lay Members of the Council of the Church Association to the People of England'. It gives advice on how to recognize whether your parish clergyman is a ritualist or has ritualist sympathies.

The test by which the laity may detect such a man is easily applied. If the clergyman.calls himself a priest [a note here indicated that by priest was meant one who performs sacrifice]; *if he tells his people that by his priestly power he can absolve them from sin; if he says that by his priestly act he can turn the bread and wine of the Lord's Supper into the body and blood of Christ – the case is clear, we can see what he is; he is not a pastor of the Reformed Church of England; he is a priest of the Church of Rome. He must be treated as such ... such persons must be treated as men having the plague. They must be put in quarantine, lest they infect us.*

A major aspect of the Church Association's campaign was the attempt to take ritualist clergymen to the Church Courts. In 1867 they lodged a protest against Alexander MacKonochie for his ritualistic practices at St Alban the Martyr's, Holborn. His belief in the doctrine of the Real Presence and his introduction of daily communion was controversial and divisive, as were the elevation of the host, having lit candles on the altar, and the cleansing of the Eucharistic vessels at the altar. They also didn't like his *'use of the mixed chalice, incense, chasubles of coloured silk, confessionals, stations of the cross and other popish toys'*. St Alban's was the first Anglican Church to hold the three-hour devotion on Good Friday (in 1864) and one of the first to celebrate a Harvest Festival. MacKonochie also openly heard confessions.

It is also worth noting that attacks against Ritualists were not just against how they took church services, but also their very integrity. As those writing critically about Jenner in the 1867 *Memorial* put it:

Your memorialists have no confidence in the disclaimers of Bishop Jenner, for the party to which he belongs is well known to be singularly aggressive, pertinaciously carrying out their particular views to the extreme limit of the law, and even beyond it.

However, the Ritualists did infect the Church of England and brought about changes in almost every part of its life. This was particularly so where the interior design of churches was concerned. The symbolism and ritual of the eucharist, and the use of colour and music, meant that the three-decker pulpit, galleries and box pews, where the focal point of the services were the spoken word and the sermon, were rapidly removed and replace with chancels, pews, altars and aisles. The introduction of music and song required a place for the choir to sit, and a vestry where the robing could take place, and where the books and worship vessels were stored. Before the 1830s, apparently, no ordinary parish church had a choir sitting up in the chancel.

Having said that, it is perhaps worth noting that for much of the 1800s the number of ritualistic churches in England was not large. The main concentration was in the south, and in London in particular. In 1882, out of 903 churches in London, 37 had vestments, 10 used incense, 45 had candles on the 'altar', and 270 used the eastward position for the celebrant at communion.

Another contribution that the Ritualists made to the life of the church was the publication of a hymn book. In the churches of the eighteenth century hymns were not widely sung, and even in the early days of the 1800s the music was often in the form of chants and plainsong, particularly as there were few organs around. *Hymns Ancient and Modern* was an avowedly Anglo-Catholic collection which was edited by John Mason Neale and first published in 1861. Of a total of 273 hymns in the first edition 187 were, according to the Church Association, 'taken from Roman Catholic Breviaries, Missals and other Roman Catholic sources'.

Perhaps a lesser known but very important influence of the Ritualists was their support for the abolition of privately owned or rented pews. In the early nineteeth century churches supported by the Church Commissioners were only required to offer 20% free seating, and most churches had box pews that were owned by the local gentry, with lesser mortals being relegated to standing at the back or sitting on benches in the galleries. However, the Catholic Reform movement's desire for the worship of God to be, not just glorious and colourful and musical, but also free and available for everyone, began to change attitudes. In his seminal pamphlet of 1844 *Church Pews, their origin and legal incidents, with some observations of the propriety of abolishing them,* John Fowler describes how the Cambridge Camden Society had made an inquiry into the comparative advantages of box pews and open benches in churches around Cambridge. The grounds for the calculations included the need for pews to allow certain postures in worship – kneeling, standing and sitting – and the most comfortable position that each provided. Box pews were found to be cramped, and took up a lot more space.

By the 1860s and 1870s that view had become quite orthodox, and many of the new Anglo-Catholic parishes were founded at this time as "free and open churches" characterized by their lack of pew rentals. Members of the *Free and Open Church Association* - founded in1866 by Samuel Mayer to work for this change through publications and meetings - are often found in the list of dignitaries at the kind of celebrations and inaugurations that Jenner attended.

The passage of the *Public Worship Regulation Act* in 1874, was one response to the changes that the Ritualists were making. Secured by Archbishop Tait, and having the support of the then prime minister Benjamin Disraeli, it was designed to restrict the growing ritualist movement. One of the most famous attempts at prosecution under the 1874 act began in 1888. It was aimed against the Bishop of Lincoln, Edward King, but the Archbishop of Canterbury Edward Benson revived his own archiepiscopal court (inactive since 1699) to avoid the prosecution of the saintly King in a lay court.

Such prosecutions ended in 1906 after a Royal Commission recognized pluralism in worship, but the act was not repealed until the Ecclesiastical Jurisdiction Measure 1963.

Early Signs of Opposition

When Bishop Jenner's appointment was announced some of the English newspapers quickly seized upon the fact that he was closely associated with the Cambridge Movement, and delighted to label him as a *Ritualist*. What was said in the English papers was copied into the papers in New Zealand, and inevitably led to a good deal of heart-searching amongst the Anglicans there, particularly in the south.

As has been stated earlier, in contrast to Canterbury, which was an Anglican Settlement, Otago was fostered by the New Zealand Company as a Scottish Presbyterian Settlement, with the result that anything that savoured of state control, and particularly of English control – and in religious matters anything which suggested episcopacy or priestcraft – would be viewed with the gravest suspicion. The use of the word Ritualist in the press, however it was understood, was bound to create some opposition.

This became public in the *Memorial*, from 'a large number of members of the Church of England, residing in the new diocese of Dunedin,' published in *The Guardian* of 11 September 1867.

It was addressed to the Archbishop of Canterbury, and complained that an appointment had been made in direct opposition to their wishes, and that as Dr. Jenner had identified himself publicly with the Ritualistic Party:

The peace and harmony of the proposed new diocese would be destroyed, and great numbers of its most earnest members alienated from the Church by the presence of such a chief pastor, and that the work of the Church in these provinces would be hindered if not utterly brought to a standstill.

As said earlier, the *Memorial* was actually the work of the Revd. W. F. Oldham, the Incumbent of Riverton, New Zealand. Which is odd, as on 27 February 1867 he had written to Bishop Jenner:

I am anxious, if possible, to express to you the pleasure with which I, in common with all the clergy, I think, look forward to your arrival among us.

I look upon it as likely to be an era in the history of our Church out here, and I hope to work with you for many years, with all my energies, in her much loved service.

But by September that had become -

To the Editor of the Guardian,

Allow me to draw attention, through your columns, to a Memorial to the Archbishop of Canterbury from Churchmen in the province of Southland, New Zealand, part of the proposed new diocese of Dunedin. Its object, you will see, is to pray his Grace to represent to Dr. Jenner, the Bishop consecrated with a view to his taking charge of this southern portion of the colony, the strong feeling of Church-people against the new developments of doctrine and ritual. We are a set of very good moderate Churchmen, and are anxious for the future peace and welfare of the Church of England in New Zealand. A few remarks only need be made upon the petition to render it clear to those ignorant of all the circumstances of the case.

The Bishop of New Zealand, without any authority to do so at that time, wrote to the Archbishop of Canterbury to nominate a clergyman suitable for a new see he was anxious to have formed. The Archbishop nominated Dr. Jenner, who wrote out to learn the feelings of the members of the Church, whether they would receive him as their chief pastor. Their representatives were summoned to meet in Dunedin, and passed the strongest resolutions condemning the whole business, and also declaring it premature. This was the prompt and decided answer of the Church out here. These resolutions, however, were never sent officially to Dr. Jenner, having been afterwards vetoed by the Bishop of Christchurch.

We much wish the opinion of our brother Churchmen at home upon the way of doing things out here. The result was that, whether Dr. Jenner received this reply of members of the Church to his question or not, we very shortly afterwards heard that he was consecrated.

The Board met again in February, 1867, and the impression then was that Dr. Jenner was at that time very probably on his way, or would be before communications could reach him; and very naturally resolutions were allowed to pass that he should be welcomed on his arrival. Since then we have heard, but only lately, that he was likely to remain in England for the Lambeth Conference, and steps were immediately taken to make known to him the dissatisfaction felt in the colony, and above all, at his making himself conspicuous among the leaders of the extreme party, which has more and more continually shaken confidence in him. For his own sake, and for the peace of the Church in the future, we would urge upon him the inexpediency of coming out to New Zealand under any circumstances.

By finding room for this dispatch you will oblige a large number of Churchmen, and also

Your obedient servant,

W. F. Oldham
Incumbent of Riverton.

Jenner was to learn about this *Memorial* from a friend in Southland.

There is a movement on foot which, should this find you still in England, may cause you much annoyance, although I trust you will not see in it anything to deter you from entering upon your duties, but rather an incentive to exertion. Let me explain my meaning. I enclose a copy of a memorial, originated, I grieve to say, by my friend Mr. Oldham, to obtain signatures to which the most discreditable means have been resorted to. Garbled extracts from home papers have been industriously circulated, also all sorts of misrepresentations of your words, actions, etc. Every name on the list has thus been obtained by personal canvass. But this is not all. I have positively ascertained that the names of known and professed Non-Conformists have been appended, among the members and office-bearers of the Church. Unless from this class, I do not believe a single person in Invercargill has signed, for the Invercargill vestry very properly prohibited Mr. Oldham from introducing the memorial among the congregation, and passed a resolution requesting him not to interfere in that parish. I cannot express strongly enough my disgust at the discourtesy and uncharitableness of the memorial.

Bishop Jenner, urged by his friends and supporters, wrote a response to the *Guardian* in which he made it clear that his purpose was:

Assuredly not to cause pain or mortification to Mr. Oldham, to whom I cannot for a moment impute complicity with the 'discreditable' measures above described, but only to show my friends in England that the opposition to my appointment, formidable as it seems to be, is by no means universal ...

With Mr. Oldham, and my other opponents, I hope to be associated in many a labour of love, having for its object the glory of God and the building up of his Church. They may be assured that wherever I see real worth, wherever real zeal and earnestness are displayed in the service of our common Lord, thither, whatever differences of opinion there may be, will my warm sympathies extend. For myself, I propose, God helping me, to work as hard as my strength enables me; so that in one thing at least I shall have a bond of union with all true and hearty labourers in the Lord's vineyard.

Is it too much to ask my present enemies, but as I trust future friends, not to judge me, unseen and unheard, on mere vague rumours or unfriendly newspaper reports, or to impute to me views and intentions that I disclaim? I appeal to those who have known me longest, and have had the best opportunities of observing my career as a parish priest, whether, amidst many shortcomings, I have ever been chargeable with disturbing the peace of the Church, or of particular parishes; or of attempting to force or drive people into an acceptance of my opinions. And I repeat here what I declared at York last year, that if anyone expects that on my arrival in New Zealand, I am going to set up advanced ritual, or any ritual beyond what the Colonial Churchmen are prepared for and desire, he will find himself very much mistaken.

But worse was to come, for on 30 October there appeared a letter from a Mr. William Carr Young.

William Carr Young

If there is one person, other than Archbishop Longley, who was most influential in the Dunedin Affair it is Mr. William Carr Young, a Dunedin-based business man and all-round pillar of the local community. He had arrived from England in 1854 and from then on his name appears in the local newspapers as a Shipping Agent, a Stock, Station, and General Commission Agent, Woolbroker and Auctioneer, a member of the Supreme Court Grand Jury, the Secretary of the Royal Marriage Celebration Committee (for the wedding of Edward VII and Alexandra of Denmark), and the Secretary of the local farmers Horse Racing Committee.

As far as the Episcopal church was concerned Young had taken an active part in church matters in Dunedin since he first landed – as churchwarden and lay reader – and had been the treasurer of the Rural Deanery Board in 1862.

Young had also been the treasurer of St Paul's Church in Dunedin – the equivalent to a cathedral in the proposed new diocese. [It was rebuilt and consecrated as the Diocesan Cathedral in 1919.] Indeed the Dunedin Parish Vestry was heavily indebted to Young. In 1864 they paid him the exceedingly large sum of £66.19.0d. as interest; the nature of the loan not being specified, although a report of 1862 mentions that £1,600 remained to be paid for the new St Paul's Church; possibly Young's loan was intended to wipe out this debt.

Young had been a central force in the building and design of St Paul's, which was consecrated in April 1863. This event was reported in the *Otago Witness*:

For a good many years the members of the Episcopal Church have met for worship in what was formerly the Court House. It had been enlarged, but the first great influx of residents, consequent upon the discovery of the gold fields, caused it to be wholly inadequate. Twelve months ago, after a canvass for subscriptions, in which Mr W C Young took a most active part, the foundation stone of the new edifice was laid; and Mr Young has, we believe, throughout held himself responsible for meeting the calls of the contractors as the work has progressed.

There then follows a description of St Paul's, which suggests that its design was actually very similar to the churches being built in England, to the designs of the, er, *Ecclesiological Society,* those evil Ritualists about whom Young was to be so damning in the years to come.

The style of the church approaches the decorated Gothic; the walls are of Caversham blue-stone; the dressings and the whole of the interior wall-spaces, columns, arches, &c. of the easily-worked and well-looking yellowish stone from Look-out Point. The roof is slated. The building comprises a nave 78 feet long and 25 feet wide, divided by very well-proportioned clustered pillars and arches, from an aisle on the northern side 11 ft wide. There is also a chancel 18ft by 25 ft. The tower is 'engaged' at the south-west corner, and a vestry will be added on the northerly side whenever sufficient funds have been raised. The walls rise to a height of 20 ft and the rather plain, open-timbered and varnished roof of the nave completes the height of 38 ft. The windows are all of three lights with decorated and quatrefoil heads. The outlines of the chancel window are filled with stained-glass; and it will be so filled completely, through the liberality of Messrs J H Harris and W C Young.

The internal features are of Oregon pine and the seats are open. There are two small but well-carved lecterns at the intersections of the chancel arch. The communion table is covered with a crimson cloth, and there is a hassock to match, in front of the rails. Near the altar is a credence table. At present there is only a harmonium to accompany the choir, but an organ has been sent for from England.

The seats for the choir are on each side of the nave, closely adjoining the two steps which lead to the chancel.

After having traded in Dunedin for 13 years Young had built up a very good reputation for striking business deals. So it was not surprising that the following article should appear in the *Otago Daily Times* in April 1867.

We announce that Mr William Carr Young proceeds to England as special agent appointed by the Government to negotiate the formation of the

Railway from Dunedin to the Clutha. Mr Young is one of the oldest settlers in the Province, and for many years was a merchant in Dunedin. He stands high in the estimation of the settlers of all classes, and a favourable result to his mission is sanguinely counted on.

Unfortunately, for both the people of Clutha and for Bishop Jenner, Young's negotiations did not fare well. This left him with some spare time on his hands which he used to see the Bishop taking part in a *Feast of Dedication* in Stoke Newington, and then to write home about it.

Bank of Otago, London, 26ᵗʰ June 1867.

The Rev E G Edwards, Chairman of the Standing Committee of the Rural Deanery Board, Dunedin.

Dear Sir,

On my arrival in England I was glad to find that Dr Jenner, the Bishop elect for the Diocese of Otago and Southland, had not sailed for New Zealand, and as he was about to take part in a ceremony to be celebrated at St Matthias's Church, London, I determined to be present, for the purpose of ascertaining whether the reports of Dr Jenner's ritualistic practices were actually true. I regret to say, the reports were no way exaggerated, as the following report of the proceedings which I witnessed at the 'Feast of Dedication' on the 13ᵗʰ ult at St. Matthias's clearly proves:

A procession, composed of clergy, choristers, and the Bishop, all more or less gorgeously arrayed, was formed outside the church, and was met by other officials at the porch. It proceeded down the middle aisle in the following order – boy carrying on high a large gold cross; choir chanting; boy carrying scarlet and white banner, which was afterwards affixed to the pulpit; remainder of choir; boys carrying blue, scarlet and white banners; two boys, each waving censers of burning incense; the clergy, I think eight in number, then the Bishop; lastly a boy, bearing a large purple banner with medallion on gold ground.

All took their appointed places, the candles on the altar were lighted, and the full service of the Church commenced. A sermon was preached by Mr. Bennett, vicar of Frome, of Ritualistic notoriety, when he extolled Ritualism, and almost advocated the doctrine of Transubstantiation, and the Infallibility of the Church. The Bishop pronounced the usual blessing, holding a crozier in his left hand, while describing in the air with his right what appeared to be very like the sign of the cross.

I noticed one young clergyman in the congregation, kneeling down on the pavement in the aisle before the altar, bowing and crossing himself, before he took his seat. Another gentleman in front of me was dressed in gown and cowl, with girdle round his waist, said to be a Brother of the Institution connected with St. Matthias.

Altogether the decorations of the church and on the altar, the genuflexions and the signs of the cross, the lighted candles and incense offerings, were as complete as could be in a Roman Catholic Chapel; and yet all this took place in a professed Protestant Church, in the centre of England.

Moreover, the Bishop-elect, not only took a conspicuous part in the ceremonies, but also afterwards, at the luncheon which I attended, expressed his 'admiration of the services as conducted at St. Matthias'.

Thus Mr. Young begins his letter to the Rural Dean, the Rev. E. G. Edwards, a letter in which there were a great many errors. For example, Bishop Jenner's part was to give the absolution and the blessing. In another letter Mr. Young says *"these are the very things allotted to a Bishop in the Romish mass"*. The Roman Bishop in fact would only so act if he were 'assisting pontifically' in his own diocese, but the Anglican Prayer Book lays down that a Bishop shall say them 'if he be present'. He was attired in his black satin chimere with the hood of his degree, presumably scarlet, pink and violet. Later Mr. Young denied that he had ever said the Bishop was gorgeously attired. The Bishop had proposed the health of the choir, and praised it highly. He didn't say anything about the service itself.

The same month Young wrote to Bishop Jenner:

As a layman in the diocese of Dunedin, where, for the last thirteen years, I have taken great interest in all matters connected with the Church, I beg to direct your attention to the following facts for your consideration, before you decide on sailing for New Zealand. Just before I left Dunedin we had a long and animated discussion at the Rural Deanery Board on the subject of your Lordship's appointment. This was condemned by all as premature; and was totally rejected by some as unauthorised. But there is no doubt that the chief, if not the only serious objection, was purely on personal grounds, for with the news of your appointment, we received public and private reports of your Lordship's High Church views and Ritualistic practices, to which I am happy to say, the Church in New Zealand is most firmly and unanimously opposed. These reports were widely circulated in the public journals, and created so much alarm throughout the Diocese of Otago and Southland that, had it not been for the expectation of your early arrival, there would have been a unanimous protest against your Lordship's appointment, and measures would have been taken to get it rescinded if possible.

For myself, I was disinclined to believe these reports, and I did what I could to diminish the fears of others; but since my arrival in England I have seen enough to convince me that we may well be alarmed for the safety of our Colonial Church, if the doctrines and practices inculcated at St. Matthias's be introduced into New Zealand, especially if introduced under the auspices of a Bishop selected for the Colony by the Primate of England. Finding, however, that your Lordship is not likely to sail for some months, I hope that, under the circumstances, you will delay leaving England, at least until you can satisfy yourself about the views entertained in the Diocese of your appointment. I can assure you that the prospect of obtaining the Bishop's fund, and of providing an appropriate residence, were by no means encouraging when I left Dunedin.

As soon as my report of the proceedings at St. Matthias's reaches the Colony I am satisfied that your Lordship's appointment will be so distasteful to all the Church members there, that to obtain the necessary contributions for the appropriate reception and maintenance of the Bishop will be impossible. I therefore, with every feeling of respect to your high office, would prepare you for the vexations and troubles which await you from the moment of your landing in New Zealand; and I do not hesitate to declare that, as far as I am concerned, I shall do all in my power to prevent the introduction into our Colonial Church of such ceremonies as I witnessed in St. Matthias's; nor can I be mistaken in informing your Lordship that I am expressing the views and feelings of all my fellow- colonists who are members of the Church of England. I think it is right to add that I have written to the Archbishop of Canterbury respecting the facts here referred to, and submitting to His Grace the expediency and propriety of rescinding your appointment as Colonial Bishop.

I remain your attentive and loyal servant,

Wm. Carr

Having received this letter Jenner then wrote to Edwards.

I am determined to remain in England for the Pan-Anglican Synod *. I hope to arrive at Dunedin before Christmas. If a house of some kind can be got ready for us by that time, we shall be grateful. This mail will probably bring you a letter from Mr W. Carr Young, to whom I have been unfortunate enough to give offence. It is right that you should be informed of the circumstances as they appear from my point of view – since an ex parte statement by Mr Young may, if not explained, create a prejudice which it will not be easy to remove.
It is difficult to write on this subject without appearing to cast blame on Mr Young. This I do not wish to do, for I have a sincere respect for him, and desire nothing more than the complete subsidence of the present misunderstanding ...

He then puts down the challenges that Young had made in his letter.

To all this it is only necessary to say that, in the first place, my share in the St. Matthias service was confined to giving the Absolution and Benediction, which I did at the request of the Incumbent, who is a very dear friend of mine. Next, that I do not consider myself in any way bound to avoid taking part in any services that are allowed by the law of the English Church. Thirdly, that nothing can be further from my intentions (and, I may add, from my principles) than to endeavour to force such a ritual as that of St. Matthias's on the clergy and laity of my Diocese. I should undoubtedly discourage the most obvious improvements in Divine worship, unless they were introduced with the most tender and considerate regard to the feelings and even prejudices of the devout laity. Nothing, in my opinion, would be more ridiculous than to attempt to carry out 'high ritual' in New Zealand, particularly in such a settlement as that of Otago.

[Jenner had clearly got some understanding of the place.]

No doubt, as Mr Young tells me, I shall meet with many difficulties from the day of my landing in Dunedin. Be it so. I shall be utterly unfit for the high office to which I have been called, if I were to be disheartened by difficulties. Only let me have fair play, and I have no fear but that, by God's blessing, I shall be able to surmount the obstacles which may be placed in my path.

---

*The *Pan-Anglican Synod* was the first of the Lambeth Conferences, where supposedly all the Anglican bishops got together at Lambeth Palace to discuss the state of the Church of England now that it had set up shop in various overseas colonies.

There had been earlier suggestions that such a gathering might be worthwhile, but momentum increased in the 1860s in the context of the conflict between High Church bishops in South Africa, headed by Robert Gray (the first Anglican Bishop of Cape Town) and John Colenso, Bishop of Natal. Colenso's liberal biblical interpretations and theology led Gray to announce Colenso's removal from office in December 1863. However Colenso, who had refused to attend the tribunal at which his position had been considered, successfully appealed to the Judicial Committee of the Privy Council in London, which ruled that Gray had acted beyond his authority.

This generated concern elsewhere in the Anglican Communion, and in 1865 the Anglican Church in Canada wrote to Archbishop Longley, asking him to convene a meeting of bishops to discuss this and other matters. In February 1867 Longley wrote to 144 bishops from across the world inviting them to convene at Lambeth Palace for four days in September.

There was widespread scepticism about the need for the conference, and only around half of those invited came. Some declined to take part out of support of Colenso. Archibald Tait, Bishop of London, who was to succeed Longley at Canterbury in 1868 and preside over the second Lambeth Conference, is believed to have attended only on condition that the Colenso affair would not be discussed. In the end, it was to dominate the bishops' discussions.

However, there was no resolution or formal declaration in relation to the events in South Africa. Given the level of attendance, the *Pan-Anglican Synod* was widely perceived to have been a failure. But it had demonstrated that staging such an event was not impossible, and important connections had been made.

It is clear that attendance at this Synod would be very important for Jenner, given his own situation with regard to Dunedin, and in the photo of all the bishops lined up in front of Lambeth Palace his distinctive bald head and bushy beard can be seen looking over smaller bishops on the right hand side, in front of a pillar.

In the light of this letter, and the one he received from Young, and the reports in the local press, Edwards decided to hold a special meeting of the Deanery Synod of Dunedin, (the predecessor of the Diocesan Synod) to discuss the matter fully. This they did, starting at 7 pm on the Wednesday evening and not concluding until a quarter past one on the Thursday morning. It was a tedious and legalistic meeting, with arguments based on false assumptions and nit-picking about phrases and sayings, and with opposing resolutions being bounced around the court, with the occasional addition or removal of suggested statements. In Jenner's favour it was moved :

That the Secretary be instructed to write to Mr. William Carr Young, conveying the thanks of this Board for his letter to the Rural Dean; but informing him that, while fully concurring in his opinion that any attempt on the part of the Bishop of Dunedin to introduce, against the will of the members of the Church in this diocese, such practices as those described in Mr Young's letter, or any change of ritual, or obsolete observance distasteful to the laity, would meet with general opposition, and, if persisted in, would lead to most unhappy results, yet, having read the Bishop of Dunedin's letter to his Rural Dean, which, in effect, emphatically disavows any such intention, this Board does not feel justified, in the face of that assurance, in endeavouring to dissuade the Bishop from undertaking the charge of his see.

After a couple of defeated amendments the following was proposed:

That this Board, after considering the correspondence of Mr W. C. Young relative to Dr. Jenner, views with considerable alarm the possibility of Ritualistic practice being introduced into the Church of Otago and Southland, since the introduction of such practices could not but result in the most unhappy divisions ...

and that – as it was the fault of the Bishop of New Zealand and the Archbishop of Canterbury that Jenner had been appointed in the first place – they should be sent copies of Young's correspondence and ...

that they be urged to take such steps as they may think fit to be taken to prevent the deplorable results which this Board thinks likely to ensue from the appointment of a Bishop of such extreme views.

After amendments to this amendment, the legality of the absence of certain members from Southland being challenged, and the occasional re-count, the Board decided, by a very slender majority of two, to ask the Bishops to get Jenner to stay at home.

Young was to write to the *Guardian* again with further thoughts, which included the following:

8 Albion St, Hyde Park, W.1.
October 23rd, 1867

The Editor of the Guardian.
Dear Sir,
I am so convinced of the sympathy of all my fellow colonists on this most important question, that I represented the facts to his Grace the Archbishop of Canterbury, when his Grace expressed his entire disapproval of Bishop Jenner's practices since the appointment was made, and sanctioned the cause which I proposed to adopt with a view to the Bishop's resignation – viz. to obtain a decided expression of opinion from Church-members in the diocese in regard to that appointment.
I accordingly dispatched by the June mail a full report of the proceedings which I witnessed at St. Mathias', together with the result of my interview with his Grace, and have no doubt that the reply, which may be expected shortly, will satisfy Bishop Jenner that the opposition is not only

formidable but universal.

With regard to the Bishop disclaiming in his letter any intentions of 'setting up advanced ritual or any ritual beyond what the colonists are prepared for and desire' we can only judge of the tree by its fruits, and since his lordship has exhibited not only at St. Mathias, but in other so-called Protestant churches, unmistakeable evidences of faith in advanced ritualism, I cannot understand how with his 'real earnestness and zeal', he can do otherwise than both preach and practise it, as opportunities may occur, in the Colonial diocese.

I therefore consider it to be the duty of all true Churchmen in the colony to unite in protecting the Colonial Church against the admission of ritual innovations, which, as police reports too frequently show, are productive of scandal and riot in many sacred edifices, and are assumedly undermining the constitution of the Church generally in the mother country.

I have only to add that I did not fail to acquaint Bishop Jenner with every step in the course which I have pursued in opposition to him, and urged the expediency of delaying his departure from England until he could satisfy himself as to the views entertained in the diocese of his appointment, and the reception he was likely to get in the colony.

The Bishop, no doubt, ranks me among the number of those whom he calls his 'enemies'. I can assure his lordship that, as I entertain every feeling of respect for his high office, so I disclaim any idea of enmity against himself personally, but I am most thoroughly opposed to his extreme views and practices, which I conscientiously believe to be unProtestant, and fatal in the unity of the Church of England.

William Carr Young

The damage in New Zealand was done, not so much by the private opinion of Mr. Young, but by what he boasted to pass on as being the opinions of the Primate of All England. Supporters of Jenner were to say that Mr. Young's verbiage was intended to cover up the lack of his success in his mission on behalf of the Government of New Zealand, but it was difficult for them not to accept what he told them about his visit to the Archbishop of Canterbury at Addington.

Archbishop Longley himself did nothing to contradict in public what he claimed in private were inaccuracies in Mr. Young's report of their interview. He had ample opportunity in his letter to the Rural Dean of Otago dated 1 Nov, 1867 but did not take it:

I certainly think that if Dr. Jenner were to carry out in the Diocese of Dunedin those Ritualistic tendencies which his conduct since his consecration led me to believe influenced him, his presidency over the Diocese would not be beneficial to its interests. But he so solemnly assures me that he has no intention whatever to obtrude them upon his flock, and so resolved is he to give no offence in this direction, that I cannot but believe he may safely be trusted. He has many qualities which will make him a valuable chief pastor, and I hope the clergy and laity of your Rural Deanery may be induced to accept him on the condition he offers, viz. that if two-thirds of the communicants of the Diocese shall, at the end of three years, call for his resignation of the See, he will yield to the call; and in order to carry out this arrangement, he will engage that his resignation shall be placed in the hands of the Metropolitan, should the decision, at the close of that term, be adverse to him.

However, not everyone accepted Young's account of Bishop Jenners' practices at St. Matthias, in particular that church's Vicar, the Revd. Charles Le Geyt, who wrote a lambasting critique of Young's writing in the *Guardian* of November 1867.

He made great capital from Mr. Young's words *"even upon the strength of the vague rumours"*, noting with sarcasm that the Bishop is to be judged before he can act or speak for himself ...

Then he alleges that the Bishop had become a High Churchman only after his appointment (a statement he got from the Archbishop of Canterbury,) but Mr. Young's letter indirectly proves the falsity of that charge, for it sets forth that 'With the news of the appointment' came the public and private reports of the Bishop's High Church views and ritualistic practices. It was perfectly well known both long before and at the time of his appointment that the Bishop was a High Churchman – his membership of the Cambridge Camden Society, his earlier parish placements, and his work on the design of St. Mildred's, Preston, had revealed that. And it was not, only since his appointment, that he had manifested his true views.

He then went on to accuse Young of being a 'spy'. He had come to the service and then had stayed to lunch ...

making himself most agreeable to all present and questioning his neighbour, a young lady, about her spiritual practices and especially about the Confessional. He had then gone back with the Churchwarden, Mr. Porter, and played croquet on the lawn with the Bishop. What a nice kind man they thought him! How they had opened their hearts and loosened their tongues ...

In case Young's thoughts about Ritualism have been lost in the record of letters and meetings it might be helpful to quote from one of his letters, in which he puts them in a nutshell.

... And now a word about 'Ritualism', which involves most serious considerations. Gorgeous ceremonials and vestments are in themselves harmless; and some of us may be inclined to pass them by as unworthy of the attention of rational beings, or even for the sake of peace, to admit them into our churches. But beware in time! Harmless as the gaudy vestment, the soothing incense, and decorated "altar" may appear, bear in mind that these are all valued as symbols by disciples of that school which we believe to be unscriptural and contrary to the teaching of our church. Do not take my word for this, just read and judge for yourselves ...

Fellow Colonists – I am not advocating a "No Popery" cry. The Protestant and Roman Catholic religions are quite distinct and antagonistic. Nevertheless, let all denominations worship according to the dictates of their own consciences. But the Ritualism of the present day is no denomination. It is a poisonous fungus growing upon and sapping the good old tree of the true Protestant faith, causing family alienations, and division of house against house. It has done so in England, and will inevitably produce the same lamentable results in New Zealand, if we once favour its growth in any part of our Colony. Above all things, let it never be said that the hurtful seed was first sown in the Province of Otago!

Meanwhile, back in Preston-next-Wingham, Henry Jenner is receiving this news from New Zealand. It must have been very difficult for him, believing as he did in the spiritual authority of bishops, and in the reality of his own consecration. Of the many letters that he wrote at this time, this one to the Rural Dean of Dunedin, gives a good example of his thoughts.

My dear Mr Edwards,

Mr Young's letter has, no doubt, changed the posture of affairs; but after the communications you have already received from me, you will not be surprised to hear that my determination not to resign my appointment remains unchanged. A delay will unquestionably be caused by the serious nature of the opposition; but I cannot help feeling that my earnest desire to meet the churchmen of the diocese in a cordial spirit of forbearance and charity, and with a tender regard to their feelings and prejudices, must ultimately meet with a response. It may be quite true that my appointment and consecration were premature; but the thing is done, and cannot be undone. 'Factum valet, licet fieri non debuit.' [What was done is worth it, although it should not have been done.] *It was surely a fair offer that I authorised you to make in my last letter – to resign my office as Bishop of Dunedin at the end of three years, in the event of a request to that effect reaching me from two-thirds of the communicants of the diocese. I should do this without hesitation, because I should feel that my chance of usefulness would be small indeed if I failed to conciliate my opponents in three years.*

I see the Otago Witness *prints what purports to be a sermon of mine last May, from a local paper. It is rather hard that one should be exposed to this kind of thing. The report is altogether a 'fancy' one. The* Record, *I am told, in commenting on a speech of mine, attribute to me a deprecation of the Reformation, because I spoke of the corruptions in worship, and in the externals of religion generally, that had crept in since that period. My remarks had nothing to do with the Reformation – any more than with the Conquest; but this is the way in which one is made an 'offender for a word' when it suites the polemical exigencies of controversialists.*

It is a great shame, and says something about the man, that Wm. Carr Young did not think to visit Preston-next-Wingham, and attend a service at St Mildred's, whilst he was in England. It might have soothed his troubled mind a little to see how Jenner led worship in an ordinary parish church that didn't happen to be celebrating a special occasion.

The Expostulating Prelate

In December 1867 the Archbishop of Canterbury, Charles Longley, wrote a letter to Henry Jenner from Addington Park, Croydon. It is a very significant letter in perhaps revealing the kind of thinking that was going on within the hierarchy of the Church of England at that time. The following extract reveals Longley's hostile attitude to the Ritualists, and his mistaken belief that, since his consecration, Jenner had been working to bring about their rise to power.

An Extract of a Letter to the Rt. Rev. Henry Jenner D.D. from the Archbishop of Canterbury,

Addington Park, Croydon. Dec. 19th 1867

… I feel myself to be responsible for your conduct as I had recommended you for a Post in which you were acting in such a manner as to compromise me.

I had on many occasions publicly expostulated my disapproval of the Ritualistic Movement which was bringing the Church of England to the brink of a precipice. If it were really believed that in spite of my protestations to the contrary, I countenanced and encouraged those movements by approving of the course which you had adopted since your consecration, I should have been justly reproached with duplicity. Silence gives consent, and if, when Mr. C. Young called upon me, I had not responded as I did it would have amounted to an avowal of sympathy with your proceedings.

I owed it to myself and to the Church to declare my entire disapproval of them, and I can easily believe that I said I had very seldom in the course of my life been more pained than I had been by the line you had pursued in the matter in question. How could it be otherwise? The whole Bench of Bishops with scarcely any, if any, exceptions had been expostulating, remonstrating against the creep of Ritualism which was imperilling the Church of England, and you, but just consecrated, throw the weight of your influence and example into the scale of these excesses.

Such conduct was felt to be embarrassing and offensive. As to the expressions attributed to me of having recommended Mr. Young and his

friends to adopt such a plan of proceeding as would force you to resign, I
simply disclaim having used such suggestions. I certainly acquiesced in the
course suggested by Mr. Young: viz. that you should be plainly told what
were the feelings of a large number of your future flock on the subject of
the countenance you were giving to the Ritualistic movement, and that if
you attempted to introduce any such system in your future Diocese it would
be fatal to the welfare of the Church there, and that you had better not go
out at all. Happily you have disclaimed all intention of introducing that
system to which you have so prominently been giving your countenance in
England, and it is well that you have done so.
In conclusion I wish it to be understood that I claim no right to control your
actions, but I do claim a right, and I hold it to be my bounden duty to
myself and to the Church, to express my opinion of your actions when I
consider that they are calculated to compromise my character for
consistency of truth, or to affect the interests of the Church.

Believe me
My dear Lordship
very truly yours
C. T. Cantuar.

It should be noted that there were two events at that time that had
perhaps somewhat warped Longley's feelings about Ritualism:
The first was the meeting with William Carr Young.
The second was a complaint thathe had received from a diocesan bishop.

In a letter of 31 August 1867 Archbishop Longley wrote to Jenner:

It is not right to say that I ignore all your former labours in blaming you
for the countenance you have given to those who have adopted the
Vestments. If I had ignored all your former work in the Church, I certainly
should never have selected you as the future Bishop of Dunedin.
I knew all the while perfectly well that you were a great advocate for
Choral Services and surpliced Choirs; but all this did not weigh with me in
prevention of your appointment to that See.
Nor are you correct in arguing as if my views of your subsequent conduct,
which I have called 'a development' was derived solely or principally from
Mr. Young's statement respecting your officiating in Mr. Le Geyt's Church.

That statement confirmed my previously formed opinion but was by no means the foundation of my impressions respecting your recent conduct. I was well aware, before I ever heard of Mr. Young, that you went into different parts of the country, and by your presence and by taking part in the services, gave encouragement to practices which the Bishops of our Church were, I believe without a single exception, most anxious to discontinue.

The Bishop of one Diocese in particular, who was never supposed to belong to what is called the Low Church, but has always been considered to lean the other way, mentioned to me in a tone of complaint what you have been doing in his Diocese. Surely you could not expect me to sanction with my approval such proceedings as these. I volunteered no statement to your disadvantage, but I was compelled to deliver my honest opinion when called upon by Mr. Young. It was then from this ex parte statement of Mr. Young's that I expressed my regret at your proceedings.

On receiving this letter Jenner asked who the complaining bishop might be, but it was not until the 2 December that Longley included in a letter about his meeting with Young:

You once asked me what Bishop had complained to me of your conduct in this respect. I have the leave of the Bishop of Gloucester and Bristol to tell you it was himself.

This led to an exhausting exchange of views between that bishop - Charles John Ellicott – and Henry Lascelles Jenner.

Ellicott's complaint

Although Longley mentions that the Rt. Rev. Charles Ellicott was *considered to lean the other way*, a look at his written work gives a very different impression. On the whole his strengths lay in the field of biblical study and the use of law in church governance, which perhaps made him a little uneasy about any developments in church life that were new – and perhaps incompletely thought through. A good example of his feelings about Catholic revival comes across in his *Some Present Dangers of the Church of England* (1878), a collection of addresses that he gave on archdeaconry visitations.

There are at the present time two dangerously corruptive influences, both of which in different ways are tending to mar the purity and truth of the doctrine of our mother Church. On the one hand there is the distinct tendency to minimise and attenuate the heritage of dogmatic truth which the Church of England has received and maintained through all changes down to this day [i.e. biblical criticism and liberal theology]. *On the other hand, there is the equally patent tendency to stretch our distinctive Church principles until they may be made to include all that was expressly disavowed or tacitly set aside by the fathers of the English Reformation* [i.e. Catholic renewal].

However, it was neither of these 'dangerously corruptive influences' that had made Ellicott complain about Jenner, but rather that he had taken part in worship at a church:

where a debatable usage had been adopted after I had formally stated that I deemed the same undesirable; and I added that I considered such action on the part of a Bishop tended to weaken the authority of the Bishop of the Diocese, and that I regretted it."

In a later letter he wrote:

If you were not aware that any unusual practices, whether in reference to vestments or ceremonial, were adopted at S. Raphael's, I will at once state the same to the Archbishop, and withdraw the complaint.

A bickering sort of conversation continued until February 1868 when Jenner wrote:

As this is the last communication I shall trouble you with, I beg to make the following statements in justification of myself, with slender hopes, however, of convincing you of your injustice towards me:

1. Before my visit to S. Raphael's, I knew absolutely nothing of how the services there were conducted, except that I had heard of the excellence of the Choir.

2. I did not, and do not consider (and have never heard of anyone who did) that a Bishop on going into another Diocese is bound to require the clergy in whose churches he may minister, to produce a clean bill of health from their Diocesan, before he consents to have any dealings with them.

3. At the time I preached at St. Raphael's there was a feeling among Churchmen that you were one of the few English Bishops who would deal fairly, and justly, and generously with those who were pointed at as 'Ritualists'. This consideration above would have prevented me from looking on Mr. Ward as 'taboo', even if I had known of his ritualistic excesses. It would certainly never have entered my head that I was committing any sort of offence against your authority, by advocating the claims of my new diocese in his pulpit.

He then wrote to Mr Ward this delightful letter with its reference to 'embroidered chasubles'.

My dear Mr. Ward,

In November 1866, you were kind enough to allow me to preach for my diocese in your Church on a week-day evening. This, (as it appeared to me) very innocent act on my part, has led to a correspondence with your Diocesan, the purport of which I think it right that you should know. I send therefore a rough précis of the letters. If you can point out any errors in fact, I should be obliged.

Your Bishop evidently disbelieves in my previous ignorance of the details of your services. Yet nothing can be more certain than that, before I saw some embroidered chasubles etc. in your vestry, I did not know that you even wore the vestments. I knew of course that you were a High Churchman, and that you were duly abused as such. But so was the Bishop of Gloucester and Bristol at that time. As to how far you went, and what you did, in or out of Church, I was completely in the dark. It is not agreeable to have one's word doubted, but this Ritualistic Controversy seems to be frightening certain Bishops, not only out of their wits, but what is perhaps worse, out of their sense of justice, and of the requirements of their position as English gentlemen.

Unfortunately Mr. Ward's reply is not to be found among Jenner's papers.

None of which reveals the true nature of St Raphael's. Whether Jenner was here being rather disingenuous, or just incredibly naive, it is difficult to say, given this account of the church by Peter Cobb in his book on the *Oxford Movement in Nineteenth Century Bristol* (1988).

Father Ward was one of the great heroes of the Catholic Revival. He was friendly with many of the leading figures of the Movement, including Neale, Butler, founder of the Wantage Sisters and Machonochie, the controversial vicar of St. Alban's Holborn. He described T. T. Carter, the founder of the Clewer Sisters and virtually life-long president of the Confraternity of the Blessed Sacrament, as 'his spiritual father' ...

He quickly established St. Raphael's as a thorough-going Ritualist church. It had a daily Mass, an early Mass every Sunday and (from 1861) a sung Mass in place of Matins at 11. It was probably the first church in Bristol where Eucharistic vestments were worn and incense used. Some of the ornaments were novel too – banners and a processional cross, crucifixes, Stations of the Cross and a crib at Christmas. With its large choir St. Raphael's became well-known for its music. It had its own hymn book to which William Chatterton Dix, who was a member of the choir contributed various hymns including As with gladness men of old.

The Fundraising Ritual

As has been mentioned earlier, it was necessary for Jenner to raise some of the funds for his Endowment himself, and this he did by asking to preach at services in other churches.

Inevitably many of these were where the incumbent was a friend of his, a member of the Camden Society, or an enthusiast for Catholic Renewal. Also inevitably, these gave rise to newspaper accounts in the English press which, after sailing across the oceans, ended up in the seemingly many Otago local papers, often with a racy 'spin' on them to feed the fantasies of his Dunedin opponents, and thus increase their sales.

In 1867 the *Bruce Herald,* and other Otago and Southland newspapers, included a speech made by the Rev. R. L. Stanford, Vicar of Tokomairiro (now Milton). It was felt to be of such importance that it was published in an eight page pamphlet, at sixpence a copy, available from all good stationers in Tokomairiro, Dunedin, Invercargill, Lawrence and Oamaru.

Gentlemen, I have felt it my duty to call you together for mutual council and advice, in the present very critical state of our beloved Church in the Province ...

followed by a great build up to the crescendo of his introduction ...

I speak concerning one who, unless we bestir ourselves in real earnest, will become Chief Pastor of the Provinces of Otago and Southland. I mean Bishop Jenner ...

then a reappraisal of the concerns about his initial appointment and the problems of the Endowment Fund, leading up to another crescendo ...

I proceed to a more important point – the point which makes the question of the regularity of Bishop Jenner's appointment, and the sufficiency of the endowment, so deeply interesting to every Churchman in the Colony. Has Bishop Jenner identified himself entirely with the Ritualistic party at Home?

I answer confidently that he has done so. Of course, such an assertion may at once be met by the argument, - how do you know this? Have you anything but hearsay to go upon? Would it not be more straight-forward, more English, to wait until you know him? And not to try to poison the minds of the Churchmen here against him behind his back, when he has no opportunity of defending himself.

Such arguments have a show of reasonableness about them, and have misled many of us into a silence which will hereafter perhaps be bitterly regretted. Yet really such arguments are most shallow.

It is a matter of fact that for the last eighteen months there has been hardly any one occasion on which the Ritualists have met together to practise their extraordinary ceremonies at which the Bishop of Dunedin is not mentioned in the press as having been present. We find his name just put among a list of names, with no sign at all of any animus against him, just as a matter of fact. 'Among those present we noticed ...' and so on.

He was present at the Dedication Festival of St, Andrews, Wells Street, and on a similar occasion at St. Michaels and All Saints, Shoreditch. At the octave of services in commemoration of the dedication of St. Mary's, Kilburn he was the first preacher, while he was followed by the notorious Machonochie. On another occasion he preached for that most extraordinary association, the English Church Union and then at St. Michael's Church, East Teignmouth, the clergyman of which church has lately been prosecuted for certain Ecclesiastical enormities.

Again we find him preaching at St. Matthias, Stoke Newington, and attending the funeral of the late Dr Neale. In two of the above churches it is the weekly custom to request the prayers of the congregation for the dead. In two, wafers are used instead of bread in the administering the Lord's supper.

In all, vestments of every hue and colour are displayed, as nearly as possible resembling those used in Roman Catholic Churches. In almost all, incense is freely used as a part of Divine Service. The elevation of the Host, and reservation of the elements for the sick, are the rule, and the rites of extreme unction, auricular confession and penance are advocated. Candles are lit, even when it is not dark.

Now certainly it seems hard that we should be told not to judge Bishop Jenner until we see him, when we have clear evidence of his tendencies before our eyes. As we find his name, mail after mail, among Ritualistic Party associates, and never, absolutely never, amongst those of the opposite school (Evangelical or Low Church Party,) we arrive at a reasonable certainty that he belongs to the party whom he countenances with his presence, and to NO OTHERS.

That this satement was totally untrue was to be repudiated later by Jenner himself.

However, it was inevitably his attendance at Ritualistic churches that grabbed the headlines. A good example being Jenner's sermon in St Matthias, Stoke Newington which turned up in the *Otago Daily Times* having been reported initially in the *Hackney and Kingsland Gazette*:

On Sunday evening last the Bishop of Dunedin preached a sermon in aid of the Missionary cause in the See of which he is the Bishop ... 'I say to you, of this highly favoured and highly blessed congregation, you have an opportunity of meeting in this glorious building, of joining in a glorious service, and witnessing the solemn celebration of the Blessed Eucharist. But there the people of whom I speak have to go hundreds of miles without finding a church, without seeing a priest, and without seeing anything at all except the works of nature to remind them of God and of that Saviour who bought them with his precious blood ... Many go and leave their homes and means of grace behind them to be exposed to the dangers which threaten them. Other dangers seem to sink into insignificance. It is not so much the danger of yielding to any great temptation to sin, it is the danger of gradually and silently losing all remembrance of God, all religion, and the thought of another world ... You are called upon to help a certain particular diocese where you believe the work of God's Church will be carried on in its integrity, and where the blessed Sacraments of the Gospel will be duly administered. Where, in short, the Incarnation of our Adorable Lord and Saviour will be duly set forth.

Again, on 30 August 1867 the *Durham County Advertiser* published this article which appeared in the *Otago Witness* of 13 December:

On Saturday last was re-opened, after having undergone a course of repairs, the neat little church of St. Bartholomew's, Kirkheaton ... The ceremony of dedication and re-opening was performed by the newly appointed Bishop of Dunedin, in New Zealand. The restorations which the church has undergone consist of the entire rebuilding of the chancel, opening a window in the west end, adding a new vestry, and removing the old-fashioned and inconvenient pews, and replacing them with rush-seated chairs*. Mr. Bodley**, of London, is the architect, under whose superintendence the work has been done. The chancel has been fitted up in the most approved style, with richly constructed oak seatings, elegant candelabras, and hangings of a very gorgeous kind. The hangings are revivals from very old designs and *have only been previously seen in the Paris Exhibition of the present year.*

[*In 1844 the Cambridge Camden Society had published *'Twenty-four Reasons for Getting Rid of Church Pews – or Pues'*. **George Frederick Bodley (1827-1907) was one of the most important architects of the Gothic Revival. The Vicar of St. Bartholomew's, Kirkheaton was the Rev. F. Harris, apparently the first northern member of the Oxford Movement.]

The *Otago Witness* then got hold of an account of Jenner's sermon at St Lawrence, Little Waldingfield, Suffolk, two months after it had appeared in the *East Suffolk Gazette*:

A very crowded congregation attended this church on Monday evening, an announcement having been made that the newly-appointed Bishop of Dunedin, New Zealand, would occupy the pulpit ...

The Bishop on entering the pulpit proceeded to give an account of his diocese, and of the work which he proposed to do there. He asked for their alms, their prayers, and their sympathy for him and for his work. The last he particularly needed under the 'trying circumstances' in which he was now placed. As some of them might already know, even before he had left this country for the scene of his future labours, some persons in the Colony had used towards him almost the very language of those in the parable, 'We will not have this man to rule over us.'

The reason for this was that he had done his best to carry out 'the worthy, efficient, dignified, and gorgeous ritual' of the Church. People in this age were not prepared for this; they were content with 'any amount of meanness,' but they were not willing that God should be honoured by the proper celebration of his Holy Sacraments. He, however, having put his hand to the plough, could not look back, and it was his intention to go to his diocese and to win those who had objected to him. A collection was made at the close in aid of the Dunedin mission.

A similar event was copied from the *Church Times* by the *Hampshire Independent* of September 1868, and then appeared in the *Otago Daily Times* in February of the following year:

On Tuesday, the Feast of the Nativity of the Blessed Virgin Mary the parish of Whitwell on the Isle of Wight, was the scene of hearty rejoicings, occasioned by the re-opening of the church after undergoing complete restoration ... A few minutes before 11 o'clock the Lord Bishop of Dunedin, the clergy and choir of Whitwell (assisted by many from Holy Trinity, Ryde and St. Mary, Brooke) processed with processional cross and banners. The processional was Brightly gleams our banner, *and considering that many of the choirs had never previously practised together the result was most satisfactory ...*

Evensong was at 4.30. Again a procession even larger than the morning entered the church at the south door ... At its conclusion a solemn Te Deum was sung before the high altar, which was one blaze of lighted wax tapers and bright flowers, and at this time the effect was most striking – the setting sun shone through the magnificent west window, the work of Messrs Lavers, Barraud and Westlake*, shedding the most brilliant hues through the whole church, and upon the many coloured hoods and cassocks of the priests and choir as they stood facing eastwards. This day will long be remembered at Whitwell, and we must congratulate the vicar upon the success which has attended his exertions in the cause of Catholicism.

[*Lavers, Barraud, and Westlake were part of the Victorian Gothic Revival of stained glass. Lavers, who was a member of the Cambridge Camden Society, started his own studio in 1855 and Barraud joined him in 1858 as the designer. After ten years they were dissatisfied with their designs and on the advice of the architect William Burges hired Nathaniel Westlake as their chief designer. The company also produced designs by freelance designers, including John Clayton, Edward Burne-Jones, Michael Frederick Halliday, and Lewis F Day. Their most accessible work is the *Vision of Beatrice*, a scene from Dante's Divine Comedy on display in *Victoria and Albert Museum*.]

An appearance by Jenner at St Ethelburga's, Bishopgate Street provided some wonderful imagery to be used by Young against Jenner in the *Otago Witness* of March 1868:

At 12 o'clock there appeared at the 'altar' a young man vested in black cassock, and wearing a crucifix and beads round his waist, who proceeded to light two of the tallest of the eighteen candles which stood upon it. Shortly afterwards there emerged from the vestry a procession headed by a lad about sixteen years of age, vested in purple cassock and short alb, bearing a cross some eight feet in length.

Immediately after him walked two boys, clothed in scarlet cassocks and albs, swinging a censer, from which arose an oppressive cloud of incense. Then came the surpliced choir of boys and men bearing aloft two rich banners, one apparently of the Virgin, the other inscribed with a large red cross.

Next walked a youth vested in scarlet cassock and alb, holding on high a bona fide *crucifix, the image and cross being of brass.*

Next came the 'celebrant' the Rev Mr Rodwell, Rector, and two other clergymen, one of whom bore an expression the exact opposite of intellectuality, all wearing the most elaborate vestments ...

The Commandments were recited by the Rector in a very extraordinary and unedifying manner, his chief object apparently being to excel in the art of repeating as many words as possible in one tone without taking a second breath. It is but fair to add that he succeeded in a degree much to the astonishment of many on-lookers.

The Epistle and Gospel were read in a monotone, and without the least intelligence or emphasis ... In the Creed the clergy and congregation generally 'blessed' themselves in the usual Popish style, and many at the article 'and was made man', prostrated their bodies before the 'altar' during a slight pause.

The most observable violation of both rubrics and doctrinal teaching, however, was 'the elevation'. After considerable mystery in arranging the elements, when he came to the words of the consecration of the bread the Rev Rodwell raised the paten high above his head, and the service bell was tolled three times. Then there was silence, the paten was replaced on the 'altar', and the clergy prostrated themselves before it for a considerable time. The cup was then taken, consecrated, and elevated. This elevation was strikingly ostentatious, the cup being held by the bottom rim, and the arms extended above the head to almost their utmost length.

It goes on and on, describing the processions, the singing, the prayers and then the arrival in procession of Bishop Jenner. From what seems to be a very clear account of his sermon Jenner describes the violence and intimidation that the Catholic movement were experiencing at that time.

'Someone has well said that those who oppose God's work by violence are like the bee, which, though its sting causes little pain to others, yet it often costs the insect itself its life. These men of which I speak hate the Catholic principles of the Church. Let us, therefore, help them. Let us support those who have suffered so much and so bravely at Stoke Newington, and by this mission gather many of those misguided souls to whom I have referred into the fold of Christ. Now is the time to show your sympathy with those who have borne so much for Christ, who have been assaulted in the exercise of their lawful duties as God's priests. Look at the great change which has come over that parish in the east of London (St. George's East) where now there is such reverence for the clergy, the Church, and Christ. Go on then in the good work, I entreat you, and especially the young, not to slacken your zeal. While I say be patient, yet don't be slothful, and you are sure to win one day.'' The writer finishes his account with the cry,

Alas! for the Church of our Protestant martyrs, if these, [the Ritualist clergy] *be the successors of the Cranmers, the Hoopers, the Ridleys, and Latimers!*

The Revd. Rodwell gave a brief response in which he pointed out that Young was actually describing two separate services, the first being a ritualistic service at which Jenner was not present, and saying that:

I cannot but regard Mr Young's attempt to connect Bishop Jenner with the observances at the celebration of the Sacrament with violation of rubrics and with glaring idolatry, as about a gross a violation of the truth and of Christian charity, to say nothing of the respect due to a bishop, as it has ever fallen to my lot, in a thirty years experience of a public life, to have met with. Surely it was Mr Young's duty to have ascertained the facts before he gave a world-wide currency to reports which I solemnly declare to be utterly and wholly false.

As the time for Jenner to leave for New Zealand approached, the Rev. W. F. Oldham took pains to pass on the account of the Bishop's participation in a Harvest Festival:

Most opportunely has come out an account of a Harvest Festival at Ardley, Herts, reported in the Church Times, *the organ of the Ritualists, be it remarked; - About three p.m. a procession was formed at the parsonage, consisting of a crucifix, thurifer, choir, acolytes,&c., members of the congregation of Children of St. Joseph, carrying banners; brothers and sisters of the Society in religious habits; two rulers of the choir in copes, the ceremonarius, and the celebrant properly vested in a red cope, biretta, &c. The good Bishop of Dunedin, before whom a priest carried a pastoral staff, came last in the procession. Solemn vespers were then sung. The choir was properly ruled by two cantors, while the presence of a ceremonarius well up to his work, assured that dignity and precision in Ritual details so indispensable in the conduct of high functions.*

Oldham concluded:

On reading accounts such as these, is it easy to exercise patience towards the moral dishonesty of men who remain in a Protestant church, and aid and abet such exhibitions and doctrines as they express?

Still, accounts such as these give the impression that Harvest Festivals were a lot more interesting than the usual tins of beans and turnip displays that we get nowadays.

In 1984 the then Bishop of Durham, the Right Reverend Dr David Jenkins, was lambasted by both the media and fellow ministers for making the widely quoted comment about the resurrection of Christ being *'just a conjuring trick with bones'*. In this, as in other statements that he is reported as making, Jenkins was both misquoted and misunderstood. His views reflected, and tried to interpret for a modern world, the very basics of the Christian faith. One of the problems was that the use of academic and intellectual arguments can easily be picked up and vilified by those for whom the content of beliefs should all be in black and white, or who just don't get the point.

From the reports made about his preaching it can be seen that the Right Reverend Dr Henry Jenner suffered from a similar problem. Like Jenkin's *'conjuring trick'* Jenner is incorrectly reported in several New Zealand papers as preaching that the *'revival now going forward was to* revive the Church from the apathy of the last 300 years. He did not consider that there had been any real worship during these years.

Bishop Jenner was keen to try and put the record straight, and wrote this letter in an English paper of 18 January 1868, which turned up in the *Otago Daily Times* in May of that year:

Sir – Through the kindness of a friend I have just seen your paper of the 18th inst. In which I find that an article from the Weekly Register, *attributed to me the remarkable statement that 'in the Church of England there has not been any true worship of the Almighty for the last 300 years'.*

I am sorry to spoil the argument which your Ultramontane contemporary has built on these words; but I must really ask permission to declare that I never used them or any like them, and that I do not believe them to express the truth …

What I have long felt, what I have sought to express, is this – not that there has been no true worship of God in the Church of England for that space of time, a ridiculous mis-statement that could never be made by one who admires, as I do, the great Jacobean and Caroline luminaries of our Church – but that the 300 years included a period during which the very idea of worship, as well as other signs of life, had well nigh disappeared. This was the period, the corruption of which rendered necessary the efforts of the Wesleys, of the 'Evangelicals', and later of the 'Tractarians' and their followers.

No Churchman, surely, High or Low, can recall without shame the state of the Church – say 100 years ago. For during the eighteenth century the Church had gradually sunk into a condition, not indeed of death, but of suspended animation. Loving hands, from time to time, endeavoured to induce reaction, but no real lasting good was effected until a treatment had been adopted which can hardly fail to succeed, and which has succeeded wherever it has been fairly tried – viz., the full and faithful and practical yet loving and considerate, exhibition of the Church's system of doctrine and worship.

The impression given by the press of both England and New Zealand was that Jenner only preached at or attended Ritualistic churches. However, as he himself made clear, it wasn't only in such churches where he had graced the pulpit. In a letter published in the *Otago Witness* of May 1868, in which he answers the criticisms made of him in a resolution from the Invercargill vestry, Jenner wrote:

I quite admit that my sympathies are with the High Church party, as they have been for a quarter of a century at least; yet, a reference to my diary shows me that my ministrations during the last year and a half have been exercised far more frequently in Churches where a moderate Ritual prevails, than in those which are extreme. The fact is, I have preached and performed other ministerial functions in almost every Church to which I have been invited, without troubling myself about the views of the incumbent.

In a similar letter defending his position, this time in the *Otago Daily Times* of April 1869, Jenner again admits his support for 'Ritualists' and goes on to say:

I will confess, moreover, that on many occasions, before and after my consecration, I have officiated in churches where the plainest rules of the Church are habitually ignored; where no announcement is ever made of holy days and festive days to be observed; where no services are ever held except on Sundays; where the bread and wine for holy communion are never placed on the holy table by the priest at the time specified by the Rubric; where the offertory sentences and the prayer for the whole state of Christ's Church Militant are never read, unless there is communion; where holy baptism is never administered at the time appointed; and where a vestment unknown to Church law is always worn by the preacher.

An interesting letter from a John Grahame Morton in the *Otago Daily Times* speaks very well of the balanced approach that Jenner took in his attendance at other churches:

Having had the pleasure of hearing Dr. Jenner officiate several times since his consecration I most strongly object to one point that is being put forward against him, that of his identifying himself with the Ritualistic Party, so called. The churches in which I heard Dr. Jenner officiate were churches that had certainly obtained notoriety for their ceremonial and services; but what sensible or thinking Churchmen would consider this an objection to his being made their Bishop?

By all parties in the Church (sad it is to have to use that phase) Dr. Jenner is greatly respected and revered, not only for his attainments as a Theologian and Scholar, and his talent as an eloquent and powerful preacher, but also for his active and useful life in the service of the Church, shown by his striving to make her services partake more of the 'beauty of holiness', to make them more frequent, hearty and devout, and to place them within reach of the poorest of her members by having Churches free and unappropriated.

Surely a priest who devotes himself to work like this is deserving of the warm support and confidence of every Churchman, and as Dr. Jenner has been to, and taken part in, services of the most gorgeous description, so he has been to and taken part in services of the plainest and simplest kind. As the Archbishop of Canterbury observes, 'he is an earnest minded, but judicious man, holding his own opinions without giving offence'.

Jenner's participation in the worship of noted Anglo-Catholic parishes wasn't only because of his membership of the Cambridge Camden Society, or his preference for that sort of thing. Diocesan Bishops also used his affiliations with Ritualism to avoid having to be involved with such churches themselves. For example, the Bishop of London asked Bishop Jenner to take the confirmation service at Mackonochie's church of St Alban's, Holborn, an interesting account of which appears in the *Guardian*:

The church was densely thronged, many women with children in their arms being present, and a large number of bonâ fide working men and gamins [street urchins] from the streets, several of whom knelt and appeared to enter heartily into the service ...

His lordship confirmed each candidate severally, and less than half an hour was occupied in administering the rite singly to about 100 candidates. His lordship then, in an earnest, affectionate address, urged the candidates to perseverance in good works, and especially in the reception of Holy Communion, to which they were now admitted.

His lordship, who has held several confirmations for the Primate, will confirm again for the Bishop of London at St. Matthias's, Stoke Newington, shortly.

In November 1867 the *Otago Daily Times* included this revealing account:

In the Christian World *of Sept. 1867, an account was given of the series of services in St. Lawrence Jewry Church, Gresham Street, in connection with the Pan-Anglican Synod. These services commenced on Saturday, 14th September, when the Bishop of London was to have delivered the inaugural sermon; but he did not attend, and the Bishop of Louisiana preached instead.*

On the following Sunday the Bishop Designate of Derry and Raphoe was to preach in the morning, but he too stayed away and the Bishop of Antigua occupied the pulpit.

In the evening the Bishop of Dunedin preached a ritualistic sermon, in tune with the service which had preceded it.

And it was not just in preaching or confirming that Bishop Jenner was asked to fill in. *The Bath Chronicle and Weekly Gazette* for 29 August 1895 announced that:

The bells of the parish church of Clutton, which have been disused for nearly seven years, have been rehung, and the peal was yesterday week re-dedicated by Bishop Jenner, late of Dunedin, in the absence of the Lord Bishop of the Diocese. It is proposed to add a sixth bell shortly.

Which they presumably hoped would be dedicated by the Diocesan Bishop.

In his *Bishop Jenner and the Diocese of Dunedin* John Evans makes a very helpful analysis of Jenners churchmanship:

It is important to understand that ecclsiastical labels such as 'High Church', 'Low Church' and 'ritualistic' are generally imprecise and frequently misleading, and therefore require thorough scrutiny and careful definition.

Was Jenner a ritualist?

He was asked this question at the Dunedin meeting, and said that he declined to be called 'by any name whatever'. Those who asked the question, he said, must tell him what they meant by the term.

He was, of course, perfectly right in his refusal to accept a label, for an Anglican bishop cannot afford to be known as a party man in a Church that comprehends so many shades of doctrine, and he was fully justified in demanding a definition.

However, in the same speech he made two statements.

He did not think that any service could be too carefully, beautifully, and he might say, gorgeously rendered for the worship of Almighty God; and the services in his church were more conspicuous for their frequency, their beauty, and the efficiency of the choir, than for anything else. Also for a large congregation joining in divine worship.

If this was ritualism, then Jenner was a ritualist.

What is particularly galling about this affair was that, around the same period (1858 to 1866) Edmund Hobhouse, the Bishop of Nelson – at the other end of New Zealand's South Island – was a noted Anglo-Catholic whose churchmanship displeased the strong evangelical element in Nelson. Although he rejected the Tractarian label, he firmly believed that his church was 'Catholic' as well as reformed, and openly said the daily offices.

Interestingly, an Ango-Catholic English priest, who was to become Vicar of St Peter's, Dunedin, arrived in the diocese shortly after the Dunedin Affair, but managed to either hide his churchmanship, or for it to swiftly became acceptable after Bishop Jenner had gone.

Bryan Meyrick King was the son of the Rev. Bryan King, who was notorious for his efforts to introduce Anglo-Catholicism into the London church of St Georges-in-the-East such that crowds of people regularly disrupted the services by bringing in their dogs, heckling, jeering and singing songs to drown out the hymns. Things were so bad that, after services, King needed a police escort between the church and the Rectory. The rioting went on from May 1859 to July 1860.

For some reason Bryan the younger decided to sail for Western Australia, where he was ordained by the Bishop of Perth in 1879, finally arriving in New Zealand in 1885. He became vicar of St Peter's in 1892, and was appointed Canon in 1897. It is recorded that Canon King was in possession of his father's full set of eucharistic vestments and a chalice encrusted with magnificent jewels. This latter is kept in the bank by the Dunedin Cathedral and only used on special occasions. The chalice was said to be a gift from Dr. Edward Bouverie Pusey, a prominent leader in the Oxford Movement, and the chasuble previously the property of Rev. John Purchas, a priest prosecuted for his Ritualistic ceremonies. Canon King continued at St Peter's until 1911.

The *Alaska* is a vessel of
5000 tons, paddlewheel,
and very ugly. Built on the
same principal as the
huge saloon ferry boats of
the American rivers.
9 Dec

THE ISLAND OF OPARA, SOUTH PACIFIC OCEAN

The South Pacific Island of Opara
Visited 16 June
(An engraving from *The Graphic* of 1878)

The Ruahine
Panama to Wellington

Stafford Street, Dunedin 1862 (Burton Brothers, Dunedin)

The Dunedin Athenaeum and Mechanics' Institute
Where Jenner went to read the papers.
(It is here being demolished, having been replaced by a much larger and architecturally
grander building in 1870)

Port Chalmers 1868

St. Paul's Church, Dunedin, behind Cargill's Monument in 1864 - then in the middle of the Octagon. Interestingly the monument itself has been described as a Gothic Revival masterpiece.

St. Paul's and the Octagon, taken from the top of the Presbyterian First Church spire in 1874.

*The Town Belt,
Dunedin
(1890 engraving)*

In our walk yesterday we passed through the "town belt" i.e. a part of the bush still surrounding Dunedin. It gave me some idea of what bush scenery is like. The ferns were lovely. There were at least 20 different species, growing on the ground, on rocks, on trunks and even branches of trees. I saw several tree ferns, not very tall, however. There were but few plants in flower but the foliage of the trees and shrubs were exquisite.
11 Feb

*The view of Dunedin
from the 'town belt'
(1890). (Photos by
Burton Bros.)*

*New Zealand bush scene
watercolour by George French
Angas (1844)*

N. Z. Cabbage Palms

Clyde

Queenstown

Just above the junction with the Kaiwarra, a wooden bridge crosses the Molyneux at a great elevation. *24 Feb*

Means of transport in Otago during Bishop Jenner's visit.

I saw several Chinese today. They are industrious and successful gold diggers, making a livelihood, very often, out of "claims" deserted by the English. *24 Feb*

I walked out to look at some gold seekers hard by on the bank of the river. I found two men "prospecting". They very kindly showed me how the gold was washed out of the dirt in which it is found. There is a great deal of iron sand here. This, from its weight, sinks lower than the earthy matter, but the gold, of course, lower still. So in the "prospecting dish" (which is something like a tin milk pan), when the water is poured off, and the dirt allowed to settle, one sees nothing at first but a mass of this black iron sand. But on inclining the dish, a little piece of sparkling gold dust appears on the edge of the sand; this is carefully removed and in this way my two friends told me they could earn about £8 a week per man. *28 Feb*

Preparing for departure

Given the somewhat unfriendly noises coming from New Zealand, a sane man would have been having second thoughts about travelling half-way around the world to do a demanding job amongst people who wished that he hadn't come.

However, it could be said – at the risk of being uncomfortably hagiographic – that Jenner perhaps did suffer a little of the 'insanity of the saints'. His beliefs about the church and its clergy, rooted in the beliefs of Catholic renewal, and his understanding of the will of God, meant that he took his vocation as a priest – and more importantly his call by Archbishop Longley to be the Bishop of Dunedin – immensely seriously, to be pursued and honoured to the limits of his endurance.

This is revealed in some very powerful extracts from his letters as he prepared to leave England:

There is one aspect of the case which, I think, has not been considered, either by my supporters, or my opponents – viz., that although I am supposed to be bent on maintaining my position as Bishop of Dunedin, in the face of a hostile diocese, I am not thereby promoting to any great extent my own temporal interest.
On the contrary, if comfort and position and the like were my objects, I could secure them much more easily by remaining at Home, in my snug vicarage, and in the midst of most affectionate parishioners and friendly neighbours, than by proceeding to a distant Colony, where all such advantages must, at any rate, be waited for, if they are ever attained. Add to this that my friends are never weary of urging upon me that I should be more useful in England, where I am known, than in New Zealand, where I am misunderstood. That there is ample excuse now for drawing back, and so forth.
To all of which I have only one answer – that I believe from my heart that God has called me to do a work for Him in New Zealand, and that I must obey, coûte qu'il coûte [no matter what].

By late 1868, based on the news that he was receiving from Dunedin, Jenner thought that it was now worth placing himself personally in the hands of his accepters and accusers.

It was perhaps a mistake that I did not go out to New Zealand some months ago. But it must be born in mind that, had I gone, it would have been in the face of assurances that there was no chance, in the then financially depressed state of the Colony, of raising anything like an adequate endowment, a consideration which I could not afford to disregard.

Then came the Pan-Anglican Synod and, about the same time, repeated entreaties (including two telegrams,) that I should not leave England until I had heard the results of the efforts that were to be made at the Rural Deanery Board to keep me at Home. So I was not without inducements to remain. I am happy to say that all obstacles are now rapidly disappearing. The endowment is all but complete; the general opposition to myself, though by no means at an end, is deprived of much of its strength by the resolution of the Rural Deanery Board.

Some weeks before he travelled up to Liverpool and boarded the first of the many ships in which he was to travel, Jenner wrote the following letter outlining his views. It gives an interesting glimpse into his manner, and his thinking. The recipient's name is not known.

There is one thing which, since my consecration, has prevented me from rejecting invitations from 'ritualistic' clergymen as a matter of course, lest I should compromise 'the dignity of the Episcopate', and that is, that I have not yet been able to acquire the art of turning my back on my old friends, or my old principles. What these principles are, and have been for years past, may be gathered from the following extract from a letter written by me in 1851, in reply to inquiries by one near and dear to me respecting my views on various points of Church ceremonial: -
On the whole, then, my theory is this – I consider none of these things [certain details of ritual] essential in themselves, but the principle of obedience, and of doing one's best, that the English ritual should lose none of its Catholic character, I do consider essential. But whereas my own taste lies to a great extent in the aesthetics of divine worship, I think I am bound

to be very watchful, lest, by indulging this taste to the disregard of the prejudices of others, I should fatally offend those among whom I might be appointed to minister. On this principle I should feel it my duty to abstain from many things which I would otherwise consider desirable to introduce, so that no vital doctrine were involved.

These words show what my principles were seventeen years ago. I have not changed them since – I do not see any reason for changing now. They have kept me, on the one hand, from 'dissembling my views,' to quote the accusation of some of my Dunedin friends; and, on the other, from forcing them upon people. And they have, moreover, made it impossible for me to withhold sympathy, still more stand aloof from those who, in spite of occasional excesses, are doing the true work of the Church as few have ever done it, at least in modern times. There is a danger, surely, against which we shall all do well to guard, lest, in opposing the efforts of those who are giving up all for Christ and His poor, we be found in the ranks of the 'fighters against God.'

In June 1868 Bishop Harper wrote what seemed a reassuring letter to Jenner which included the following:

I do not see how it is possible that any such Ritualistic charges can be entertained by either General or Diocesan Synod, though it is possible that they may influence the votes of some of the members on such questions as the division of my diocese, or the confirmation of your nomination.

The statement which I suggested, you have in part given in the first portion of your letter. It recounts the acts of others through which you were consecrated a Bishop in New Zealand. And, as you say, it is a matter of simple justice that you should not suffer through any haste or undue exercise of authority of others.

What I should like to have, is this statement in a separate form, somewhat enlarged upon, and supported by extracts from such letters and documents as may be within your reach, with exact dates. Such a statement I could put into the hands of the more sober-minded members either of the Diocesan or General Synod.

If it can be shown, as I think it easily can, that the New Zealand Church is bound in justice and duty to accept you as one of its Bishops, an interest may be created in your favour, which may not only neutralise the prejudice against you, which some have allowed themselves to entertain, but call out an amount of energy and activity in collecting what is yet needed for the completion of the endowment.

Jenner was immensly relieved to receive this letter, and replied to Harper:

It is a great satisfaction to me to find that your opinion coincides with mine as to what is the real question at issue. It appears then, that no charge against me of 'Ritualism' can be entertained by the Synods, and that the question will resolve itself into one of bona or mala fides towards me. If this issue be fairly submitted to the Synods I have not the least fear of the result - only I do wish that I had not been kept all these months on a false scent.

I will draw up a statement to be presented to your Synod. It will be one, however, in which I shall plainly, though, I hope temperately, assert my RIGHTS and it will be understood that I send it simply in order that I may help the New Zealand Church out of the dilemma in which it has been placed, and not in order to obtain any favour at its hands.

Whilst Jenner was preparing to leave for New Zealand, the Bishop whose letter had led to his rather premature consecration was sailing in the opposite direction. Bishop Selwyn had been offered the Bishopric of Lichfield and, after much umming and aaaahing, had decided to accept it.

For a while he was both Archbishop of one of Britain's newest and largest far flung colonies, and also Bishop of Lichfield, one of the oldest and most shrinking dioceses in England – it would be carved up into new dioceses with the growth of industrial cities like Coventry and Birmingham.

In October 1868 Selwyn, when he was about midway between the two and a passenger on the steamship *Hero*, wrote to the Rural Dean of Otago and Southland.

My dear Mr Edwards,

The question of Bishop Jenner has received our most careful attention; but as I have not been instructed to communicate to you officially the decision of the Synod, I shall confine myself to a statement of my own opinion. The following facts appear to be admitted by all:-

1. That Dr Jenner was nominated by the Archbishop of Canterbury, at my request.

2. That he signed the Declaration of Obedience to the laws of General Synod – 'in consideration of being appointed Bishop of Dunedin'.

3. That the Declaration thus signed by him was read by the Standing Commission of the General Synod and recorded upon their minutes.

4. That the £1,200 or £1,300 was collected by me in the Province of Dunedin, in the name, and for the use of Dr Jenner as Bishop of Dunedin.

5. That all these various preliminaries were carried out, without any remonstrance, or objection, on personal grounds, in England, in Dunedin, or before the Standing Commission.

6. That during the course of these proceedings there was an interval of time amply sufficient to allow objectors, if they had wished, to petition the Archbishop of Canterbury to postpone the consecration.

7. That Dr Jenner was consecrated some months after the above transactions, on the 24th August, 1866, with the consent of the Secretary of the State for Colonies, by Royal Mandate, in lieu of Letters Patent.

It appears by the minutes of the Select Committee appointed by the general Synod, that it was accepted as a principle to guide their proceedings - 'That the burden of proof should rest upon the opponents of Bishop Jenner.'

The Committee seems, therefore, to have recognised him as in possession, de facto, at least, of the office of the Bishop of Dunedin; and to have called upon his opponents to show cause why he should not enter upon the duties of his office. Three objections might have been raised by the opponents of Bishop Jenner.

1. The want of due formality in the appointment, according to the law of the General Synod.

2. Charges against Dr Jenner, on the ground of doctrine or ritual.

3. The insufficiency of the Endowment Fund, and other difficulties of a pecuniary kind.

On the first point, nothing is said in the report of the Committee; and, when I attended as a witness I was not asked any question on this subject.

On the second point, again, no question was asked of me, nor was any mention made of it in the report of the Committee, except to say that they had not thought it necessary to inquire into the charges of ritualistic excess brought against Bishop Jenner; and, further, that charges of that nature would be likely to prejudice the collection of the Endowment Fund.

On the third point, viz, the insufficiency of the income of the Bishopric, and other pecuniary difficulties, questions were asked; but certainly the answers which I gave were not intended to lead the Committee to the conclusion to which they seem to have arrived – that these difficulties are such as cannot be overcome.

I feel, therefore, that nothing has been proved by any opponent of Bishop Jenner, which ought to debar him from entering upon the duties of his office, whenever a sufficient income, clear of all encumbrances, can be supplied.

In the absence of any definite charge or insuperable difficulty, such as ought to exclude Dr Jenner from the Bishopric of Dunedin, we all concurred in the request that, for the sake of the peace of the Church, he should resign his claim. But this argument of peace has a double aspect. Bishop Jenner may claim of his opponents with greater justice that, for the sake of the peace of the Church, they should withdraw their opposition. If he has done anything unlawful according to the law of the Church in England let it be proved. That he will do nothing against the laws of the Church in New Zealand, we have his own solemn promises, which we are bound to believe. For his sake then, and for the sake of the Synod, and for the sake of the peace of the Church, I do most earnestly entreat my dear friends and brethren in the Rural Deanery of Otago and Southland to withdraw their opposition, and to accept Dr Jenner as their Bishop. This way of peace is more complete than the other, because it will bring to an end all controversial discussions, and will obviate the necessity of electing another Bishop; and above all, because it will show that we have confidence in the power of our Synodical system to restrain those eccentricities of private zeal which have disturbed the peace of the Church at Home.

The content of this letter was communicated to Jenner, and so, with such seemingly affirmitive letters from New Zealand, he decided it was time to face the foe.

THE JOURNAL

In his Introduction to *Seeking a See* John Pearce wrote:

Bishop Jenner, it would seem, kept Journals for most of his life. Their present whereabouts, alas, is not known. It has been felt, nonetheless, that the Dunedin Journal *stands on its own as a journal, and gives opportunity for putting into print a brief memoir of a man universally neglected in biographical studies and books of reference; a man overshadowed, in the public esteem, in his early life by his father, and in his later life by his son.*

I am deeply grateful to Lady Rawlings for allowing me to transcribe the Bishop's Journal, for lending me original letters and printed matter relating to the Dunedin Controversy, *and for graciously giving her consent for the publication of the book.*

Rev John Pearce MBE
Lanner Court,
Helston,
Cornwall

The Rev. John Pearce (1913-1985) was ordained deacon in 1968 and priest in 1969 in the Diocese of Truro. As well as his parish work he was greatly involved in issues of social concern, was secretary of the Cornwall Council of Social Services, and wrote many publications about the history of Cornwall. His interest in Bishop Jenner arose from his passion for the life and work of the Bishop's son, also Henry, who could be said to be the father of the Cornish Movement.

Whilst the introduction to *Seeking a See* is a well researched and carefully argued account of the lead up to, and development of, the Dunedin Affair, its main ingredient is Jenner's *Journal*. It is the record of his day-to-day experiences on the voyages by sail and steam to Dunedin, of travelling around Otago and Southland by horse and on stagecoach, of his meetings with priests and people of that region, and of his painful return, with dashed hopes, to Preston-next-Wingham, Kent.

It begins with the Bishop leaving Preston on 16 November 1868, and ends with his return on 16 July 1869 – a period of just eight months.

As can be imagined, a daily account of such a journey is both very long and, at times, a little boring and repetitive. For example:

The wind changed in the night and, being now right ahead, causes the ship to pitch fearfully. I awoke at 6 and turned out at 8. Went into the saloon for breakfast, but having no appetite I returned to my cabin, and read in a recumbent attitude till 1 p.m.

There is a lot like that.

However, there is also a great deal that is both interesting and educational. For example his descriptions of being at sea on an early steamer, of seeing an exhilarating beauty in other lands, of riding on horse across the gold producing and sheep farming province of Otago, and of meeting a variety of different people along the way. All of this is woven through with his emotions at leaving Preston, and his concerns for his future in Dunedin.

To make the *Journal* accessible – and this book not too bulky – it has been pared down to include only the more relevant or interesting sections. The notes in brackets were included by Pearce.

On the 16 November Jenner caught the London train from Grove Ferry and made the railway journey to Liverpool. Here he stayed with the Rev. Cecil Wray, the perpetual curate of St Martin's church, and a pioneer of the Anglo-Catholic cause. Wray's daughter had recently married Canon Allen Page Moor, known to Jenner as sub-warden of St Augustine's College, Canterbury.

On the 18 November he boarded the *City of Boston* which took him to Queenstown Harbour (now Coba) in Ireland, the major departure point for emigrants to America. Whilst there Jenner travelled to nearby Cork in order to see the partially built *Saint Fin Barre's Cathedral*, designed by his friend William Burges.

When the *City of Boston* left the harbour he wrote -

After dinner I walked about the deck till 7. I saw much of the Irish coast. We passed the Old Head of Kinsale about 7.30. I could not take any tea; and, it is no use disguising the fatal truth, premonitory symptoms are certainly manifesting themselves. Before I left the deck, all sails had been set, and we were going rapidly along with a fair breeze. Turned in (nobody goes to bed at sea) at 8.

During dinner, the ship gave several awful shakes. This is caused by the screw propeller rising out of the water, when, meeting with no resistance, it revolves with uncontrolled rapidity. It is extremely difficult to walk in the saloon, or indeed, in any part of the ship. I turned in at 9. The wind had risen to a strong gale. No chance of sleep I fear. The screw keeps on shaking fearfully, and really seems to be as much out of water as in.

Our eighth day out. A most lovely morning, hardly any wind and a nearly smooth sea: but I suspect there must always be some swell on this mighty ocean. I breakfasted with good appetite in the saloon – only I could not quite stand fried tripe and onions, which was on the table. After breakfast I went on deck, and quite enjoyed myself for a couple of hours talking to the officers.

An immense number of gulls and divers (and diverse other birds), were swimming and flying about the ship; and, to my great satisfaction, the chief officer drew my attention to a whale spouting, about a mile off. He had hardly spoken before the monster showed the whole of his enormous tail above water, and immediately disappeared. They said it was a very unusual sight, so much of him being exposed at once.
I have made the acquaintance of a New York man, who tells me that his brother is a Lincolnshire clergyman, and he himself a former chorister in Lichfield Cathedral. He knows the Bishop and most of the clergy of N. York.

Advent Sunday. It is strange indeed to be at sea today. I calculated that the Celebration at Preston would be going on from 7.30 to 8.20 a.m. during which time I said the office for Spiritual Communion in the

Manual of the *Confraternity of the Blessed Sacrament* with infinite comfort.

I had a walk on deck before breakfast. This morning the weather was most beautiful. The ocean quite calm, the sun shining. Fore top sail and top gallant sail set with main and fore topsail. I made a good breakfast and then arranged with the Captain to have a service in the saloon at 10.30 and another in the steerage in the evening...

The saloon was crowded and very hot. It was a queer sort of service. I wore my cassock, surplice, stole and hood. Said Matins and Litany – read the Epistle and Gospel and preached for 17 minutes on the Two comings. During the service nobody thought of standing or kneeling. They seemed to consider that it was all done by deputy, i.e. me. The responses were said by a few. They were all very attentive to the sermon, which I found I might have prolonged, as we did not take quite an hour over the whole function, but I was afraid of wearying them.

At 6, I had the service in the steerage. Before beginning evensong, I suggested to the congregation that they should stand at the Psalms and at the prayers, if they could not kneel. I impressed upon them that standing not sitting was the next best attitude to kneeling. They fell into my wishes very well and the result was satisfactory. After evensong I preached for 25 mins. as plainly and earnestly as I knew how. They were extremely attentive, and many of the women were visibly affected.

Nov. 30. S. Andrew. I turned out early. A most glorious morning. Full moon, Venus and a few stars visible. Fire Island Light on our starboard quarter. Long Island just appearing. The sun rose at 7.10 (thirty-five mins. sooner than at London) the most magnificent sight - not a cloud to be seen - the sun coming clear out of the ocean.

Till breakfast time, I walked about the deck with the Captain, who was very pleasant. After breakfast, on deck again to see the American coast - Long Island - Staten Island and the entrance of the harbour, a most striking scene to me. Hundreds of Yankee Gulls were flying about the ship. They seemed to me, but it might be only fancy, to be of a more impudent and swaggering kind than ours.

The Brooklyn Fire Brigade, in red shirts, and with band playing, was parading as we passed up the harbour. We anchored in quarantine for half an hour, during which time the government medical officer came on board and examined the emigrants. Then we proceeded up to our berth, anchored again, and after an hour's delay were landed in a tender. The luggage was examined at the Custom House and passed very leniently. My boxes of books were not opened.

I got a letter from the Bishop of N. York inviting me most cordially to his house. [Jenner had met the Bishop of New York at the First Lambeth Conference, the previous year.] At the Custom House, I met Mr. Withers who was extremely useful to me. What I should have done without him, I cannot imagine. He got my things carried to a cab and paid everybody for me. The New York cabmen are the greatest ruffians possible. There being no law of fares, each driver tries to get as much as possible out of his passenger.

The drive to the Bishop's in 22nd Street is through Broadway and Fifth Avenue. The pavement is very bad, but there are splendid shops, and crowds of people. The Bishop was most kind and hospitable and so was Mrs. Potter. After lunch Mr. Withers took me out for a walk. He showed me a good deal of the City, and took me into St. Alban's Church, a mean building with, however, a well arranged Choir and Altar - the only one I fancy in N. York.

We dined at 5.30. There are two Miss Potters. The other guests were a couple of clerical cousins and a Mr. Charrington, cousin to my Chislehurst friend. The dinner was peculiar but very good. Soup, fish (cod), roast turkey, Venison steaks (Red deer). The second course and dessert were mixed up together and comprised excellent scolloped oysters, apple pie and an enormous ice cream, with which preserved ginger was handed round.
I had a very pleasant evening. One of the Rev. Potters is a professor at some college in Massachussets. The other is Rector of Grace Church, N. York City. The Bishop takes me tomorrow to a diocesan Convention

at Albany 150 miles up the Hudson. He telegraphed to the clergy that I was coming.

I can hardly believe that I am in America. It seems so like a dream. I am perfectly well in health, and there is something very invigorating in the New York air. Looking back at the voyage from Liverpool, I see cause for the deepest thankfulness, for its general prosperity and comfort: and I was not a little pleased to get a few minutes of quiet recollection in S. Albans this afternoon. I heard today that the steamer *William Penn*, which comes hither from London, via Havre, was very nearly wrecked in mid-ocean. She was 17 days coming from Havre, and got in on the 22nd, so we must just have escaped the storm which she encountered.

Dec 1. I had an excellent night's rest in a very comfortable room. Outside there was a hard frost, but the whole house is warmed, and I felt nothing of the cold.

We, (i.e., the Bishop of N.Y. and I,) started at 12, on our journey north to Albany. We went by train. All the railway arrangements were (to me) new and curious. The "cars" all of one class - with a passage up the middle - the vendors of newspapers and periodicals, of fruit, cakes and sweets, perpetually passing through; the store at one end of the car, and the vessel of iced water at the other. The general "free and easiness", combined with perfect orderliness of everybody and everything were some of the more striking details. The line runs along the east bank of the Hudson river, and takes us through some lovely scenery.

The Indian summer is over, and the trees have suffered as to their foliage by one or two sharp frosts. Yet, in sheltered places, the leaves still remain on many of the trees. A few miles after leaving N. York, we got a fine view of the "Palisades" - lofty granite cliffs on the west bank of the river - which spreads out into a noble reach as you approach them. In another half-hour we came in sight of the beautiful Catskill Mountains. They were just dusted over with snow, and the sun shining brilliantly on their southern slopes produced a most exquisite effect. We were very lucky in having such a fine day.

The winter seems to have begun a week ago with a very sharp frost. The Hudson will soon be frozen, and the navigation stopped. As it is, there is a fringe of ice, twenty feet wide, along the banks. This must be a terrible cold catching country. The railway cars, and all the churches and houses, are heated - the two latter overheated, and the contrast when you go out into the frosty air is far too great.

About 3 p.m. we passed West Point, the great Military College, where Grant, Lee, etc., were educated. It was dark before we reached Albany, so we missed some of the finest scenery.

We went straight from the station to the house of a Mr. Meads, a lawyer here. He is most agreeable and intelligent, and takes a warm interest in Church matters. [Orlando Meads was one of the most prominent of the upstate laymen, who had played a part in the extended negotiations which led to the founding of the Diocese of Albany, was a member of the first standing committee, at the Convention attended by Jenner, and became an incorporator of the temporary cathedral on 27 May, 1873.] He gave us an excellent dinner, and I had a most comfortable room to sleep in.

Dec 2. At 10 this morning the Diocesan Convention was opened. We had Matins and Celebration at St. Peter's Church. (Completed in 1860 from the design of Richard Upjohn 'the Elder' (1802-1878), a leading architect of the Gothic Revival in the United States of America.) The Bp. of N.Y. preached, and I celebrated.

The American Liturgy is superior to ours in one respect – the oblation immediately following the consecration. In other respects it is inferior where it differs. And the variations in the ordinary offices struck me as needless, and in more cases absurd. After service quite a crowd of clergy came round me in the vestry, to thank me for giving them '*so Catholic a service*'. I hinted that it would hardly be so described in England. At St. Peter's, the Basilican arrangement is used. (Celebrant facing east). I did not like it. One awkward feature of it is that the Celebrant, when standing at the Altar, has one or more clergy facing him.

The Bishop and I went to a wedding to which we had been invited at the house of Governor Fish. The bride was Miss Fish, the bridegroom a Capt. Benjamin. It was a very grand affair, and all the best society of New York were present. We were magnificently entertained. The breakfast surpassed anything I had ever seen – the principal element, as at all New York feasts, was the oysters. Of these there were bushels, dressed and undressed. Mountains of ice cream in every possible shape, stewed terrapins (a sort of small turtle) and wines of every known kind. There was a good band playing in the hall almost all the time.

The religious ceremony took place in the drawing room. A clergyman in surplice and stole officiated. The American office is very short. Few of the company could see what was going on and as the talking never ceased for an instant, it was not easy to hear the words of the service.

The rooms were as full as they could be packed. The costumes of ladies and gentlemen were rather "loud", the conversation and manners the same. General Grant was there. I was introduced to him. He shook hands with much cordiality, but did not say much. The *New York Times*, in reporting the wedding, says '*Most noticeable among the guests were General Grant and Bishop Dunkeddey! of New Zealand; the latter in full canonicals,*' by which I presume the reporter meant my 'apron', and, perhaps, gaiters. [General Grant had been nominated as presidential candidate by the Republicans that year, and became President of the United States in March 1869.]

Dec 9. At 7.30 I was roused by a voice at my door, announcing that 'your brother has come'. I was up in a moment, dressed hastily and imperfectly, and found Arthur in the drawing room. It was a delight indeed to see him again, after 12 years. He was looking well, though thin. His spirits seemed very good, and his manner and appearance very much as of old, except his long light red beard.

Arthur accompanied me to the *Alaska*, which was alongside the wharf, and I got my luggage into my stateroom with no difficulty. Mr. Withers joined us before the ship sailed and brought my Crozier * which he had obtained from the Customs Office. It was grievous to have to part so soon from Arthur but there was no help for it.

[* The crozier given to Jenner by the Ecclesiological Society. See page 268]

At 1 p.m. we cast off, and steamed down the harbour. It was very cold – a stiff breeze blowing, with snow. The *Alaska* is a vessel of 5000 tons – paddlewheel – and very ugly – built on the same principle as the huge saloon ferry boats of the American rivers.

Before going to bed I had a look at the stars. Sirius had just risen, and with Orion looked beautiful. Jupiter also was very bright. It was odd to see Ursa Major so near the horizon and right astern of us, our course being due South. I have been taking Petroleum for sea sickness, but it was hardly required.

Dec 10. We are due at Colon this day week, and tomorrow we shall find the weather quite warm. So at least says the Captain. It is pleasant enough today, and by no means cold, whereas when we left N. York it was bitter.

Our course lies past the Bahamas, through 'Crooked Island Passage', and near the island of that name. We shall sight, also, several of the smaller of the Bahamas group. We pass between Cuba and S. Domingo and may possibly catch a glimpse of Jamaica.

The Captain had ordered the steward to keep me a place at his right hand, the post of honour, where I am sure of being well attended to. One thing struck me as curious, and different from what I had heard of the habits of Americans. No one drank anything but water at dinner. I felt quite ashamed of my modest bottle of Vin ordinaire. But I discovered afterwards that there is an institution on board called a 'bar' where the passengers 'liquor up', and the Yankees have a habit of soaking in the solitude of their own cabins!

It is amusing to see the thorough organisation of the regiment of waiters. When the passengers are seated at the dinner table, a bell strikes, and immediately all the stewards form in a line near a side table, on which the dishes have been previously placed. A second bell, and they seize each man his dish, and stand motionless as before. A third bell, and they march off to place the dishes on the dinner tables. Bell again, and all the covers are simultaneously whisked off, and the serious business of eating begins. This is all repeated at the second course.

Before turning in tonight, I looked over the stern of the ship and saw the most brilliant phosphorescence in the wake. It was like liquid fire pouring from the paddle wheels.

Dec. 11. I slept very well till 6, when I was awakened by sounds of the wind freshening. On turning out, I found that it was blowing rather hard from the N.E., a change having occurred in the night. It has been raining hard too. The *Alaska* cannot hoist much canvas, but what she has is set. The north-easter, I suppose, prevents the air from getting warmer.

I felt very comfortable all the morning, but about noon it began to blow heavily, and by 3 p.m., there was a strong gale with a tremendous sea. We got some severe shaking about, and shipped a good many seas. I sat all the afternoon in the Captain's Cabin, feeling anything but at my ease. The steward encouraged me by hinting that there was a possibility of the cabin and wheelhouse being swept into the Ocean!

Dec. 17. At 8 p.m. today, we arrived at Colon (Aspinwall).
The approach is very grand, the mountains on the South American coast particularly so. Unfortunately it was rather hazy. The heat is great, but by no means insupportable. It was quite dark when we came alongside the wharf. A crowd of Negroes on the shore made the night horrible with their noise.
Soon after we arrived a benevolent fellow passenger brought me a delicious banana. I did not intend to go ashore before morning but I was persuaded to alter my intention. I was only absent from the ship for half an hour. The place seemed excessively dirty. One saw scarcely any living creatures but Negroes. There was an absurd dance going on outside a grog shop. The "music" was a drum and two pieces of wood

knocked together. I noticed two cocoa nut palms, splendid fellows, close to the landing place. The air was full of fireflies. I hope the mosquitoes will not find me out in the night.

Dec. 18. The train left Colon at 1 o'clock. There was a great crowd to see us off, of niggers, male and female – the latter gorgeously attired. The pace was pretty good till we got within 15 miles of Panama where a stoppage occurred, through the breaking down of the return train from Panama.

There being but one line of rails. We had to wait no less than three hours, the result being that we did not get in till 6.20. Thus we missed the scenery of the latter part of the route, which is said to be the finest. But it can hardly be superior to that which we did see, which is beyond description beautiful. It far surpassed my utmost expectations.

Such prodigality of vegetable beauty I never believed could exist. It was as if the Palm House in Kew Gardens were indefinitely repeated over the loveliest imaginable hills and valleys. But there were palms and other trees that would not stand in the Kew building, if it were raised to ten times its height. The flowering trees were specially magnificent. Such masses of blossom; gold, white, scarlet, crimson and blue, everywhere dispersed. And the wonderful butterflies of every possible hue, and the humming birds (behaving precisely as our hummingbird moth does,) and to crown all, the noble *Chagres* river, with its steep and lofty and profusely timbered, banks, appearing again and again, as we went on. It was almost too glorious. One longed to linger at each fresh bit of landscape, in spite of the malaria. The marshy places produced the finest and most showy displays of floral beauty. The rich orange of the *Arnica Indica* was here especially noticeable. I saw no monkeys, except one old fellow (who might however have been a bear), sitting in a fork of a tree. Neither did any alligators show themselves. There are plenty of wild beasts in the forests, jaguars, pumas and bears, besides snakes of various kinds. All along the line we passed villages of huts at intervals, with the funniest little naked Negroes running about!

It was curious to see the sensitive plant (*mimosa pudica*) growing between the sleepers of the railway. A woman brought a tame anteater which she tried to persuade some of the passengers to buy. Others had bananas and oranges, the latter quite green, but deliciously sweet and juicy.

Dec. 19. Panama. I had a little adventure today. In the morning one of the waiters of the Hotel, a Jamaica mulatto, came and asked me if I was a clergyman, and being satisfied on that point, told me that a friend of his wanted her child baptized in the 'Protestant faith'. I told him I did not know what that might be but promised to go and do what I supposed was required. There is no clergyman of our communion at Panama.

In the evening, as Mr. Henderson and I were sitting at tea, in walked my friend the waiter, unannounced, and with a low bow informed me that 'they were all ready'. I said 'Who are ready?' 'The sponsors' replied he. 'Why,' I said, 'I never undertook to go this evening'. 'Oh no' said he, 'I am perfectly aware of that and I don't blame you in the least'. 'Don't you?' said I, 'I shouldn't *much* care if you did.' However, I went with my cool friend, and he took me through a number of lanes and alleys, and up several flights of stone stairs and along a balcony, through a window in which we entered a good sized room, well furnished, where I found a poor girl not more than 16 with a child 6 months old. After I had baptized the child, I turned the sponsors out and had a talk with the mother. I think I made some impression, for she promised to come to my Evensong next day, and kept her word. But alas! Marriage is a rare thing here, comparatively. Just as I was leaving the house, the waiter made his appearance with a tray of large glasses of Champagne, each with a lump of ice floating in it, and insisted on my taking one. It was one of the most delicious draughts I ever had, the night being extremely sultry.

I heard today that the *Ruahine*, in which I hoped to go to Wellington, has been seized for debt, and would not be allowed to leave Panama.

The general opinion, however, seems to be that the Royal Mail Co. will pay the demand, and that the *Ruahine* will get off as usual.

Dec. 22. I had been asked to consecrate a cemetery for British residents, and at 4.30 p.m. Mr. Carvine, the very obliging agent of the Pacific Mail Co., drove me to the cemetery. There were a good many people, black and white, large and small, assembled. The service went off very well, I thought. I wore my robes and carried my Crozier. It was very hot work, and the mosquitoes were troublesome, and threatening, though they did not actually attack me.

At 6, Mr. Carvine had provided a four-oared gig to take me to the *Ruahine*, which was lying about 3 miles off. I steered the gig with my usual discretion – but it was rather ticklish navigation to a stranger – and the boatmen and I not understanding each other's language, made it still more awkward. There were plenty of sharks to receive us, if the boat *had* been upset on one of the numerous reefs. However we got safely on board.

I had some supper, and was presented to Captain Beale. I cannot say I liked him. I sat talking with him on the quarter deck till 9 p.m. He amused himself and tried to amuse me by abusing everybody and everything mentioned, *except Capt. Beale.* He is a Sandwich man, and knows most of the residents in the neighbourhood.

The live stock on board consists of a fine Newfoundland dog (Rover) who swims about the ship regardless of the sharks, a monkey who is very amusing, a cow, two Panama bullocks, and a number of fowls, ducks and turkeys. The cocks begin crowing at a most unreasonable hour every morning.

The *Ruahine* seems a comfortable ship, though she is much smaller than the *City of Boston* or the *Alaska*. I hope I shall retain possession of my cabin. There are only 25 passengers to embark and 16 of them are children.

Christmas Day. 9 p.m. I woke early and have been following the Preston services all day. I had matins on the quarter deck, a very fair attendance of sailors. I preached after service for about 20 minutes. The Captain returned to dinner with the encouraging news that the mails have been seized as a security for the non-departure of the *Ruahine*, and the passengers are not allowed to embark.

So we are here for another day at all events. What an intolerable nuisance. I was forced to do without evensong. According to the Captain, sailors don't seem to have any souls to speak of. Hence the minutest proportion of religious services is enough for them. The crew were shouting and singing uproariously, far into the night – the result, I presume of extra grog.

Dec. 27. Sunday, S. John. Evang. We had a large party at breakfast this morning. To my great delight I was allowed to retain undivided possession of my cabin. My immediate neighbour at breakfast was a Mrs. Morant, a widow with several girls, the youngest of whom, aged 5, is called Dora. Opposite, sat Dr. and Mrs. Turner, friends of Mrs. Morant, who have boys and girls on board. These are all bound for Nelson. For some time past they lived at Hayling Island and know the Hardy's. Dr. Turner is a Glamorganshire man, and knows all about us, and everybody in the county.

But the strangest thing is there being a cousin of mine on board – Arthur Lascelles. He is the son of Frank L., my first cousin – Rowley's brother. We fraternized warmly after breakfast. I liked what I saw of him very much. He is going to Auckland. His wife and 8 children are on their way out by sailing ship. He is a barrister, and has spent most of his life in India.

Jan. 1. 1869 Circumcision. A happy New Year to all my precious ones. The year began well. The morning was magnificent. A good run today – 252 miles. Lat.5°9 ' S Long. 92 W. I got one of my boxes up from the hold today, and extracted my desk together with the photos of Preston Vicarage, over which I gloated in my cabin. The wind has been fair all day, and every stitch of canvas is set. Flying fish have been very abundant.

Meanwhile, back in England, the *Sun* (London) of 2 January, ran the following item:

A REJECTED BISHOP

Some time ago Dr. Jenner, Bishop of Dunedin, finding that his active and prominent participation in English ritualist services had rendered him very unpopular in his diocese, deferred his departure, and after a long delay he agreed to submit the differences that had arisen to a diocesan synod, and to accept any decision to which that body might come.

The Synod has now decided that it will be for the benefit of the Church that Bishop Jenner should not take charge of the diocese, and he is therefore requested to resign the bishopric.

He will be the more able to do this because, although he has been consecrated three years, he has not resigned his living, but has placed in charge of it the Rev. A. Cherol, formerly curate of St. Raphaels', Bristol, an 'advanced' ritualist Church.

It was stated a short while ago that Bishop Jenner had set out for his diocese, but the Church News *of this week states that he was last month taking part in services at a clerical gathering in Albany, New York.*

Jan. 4. Run 286 miles. A shorter run than we ought to have made, but the Chief officer tells me the engines have been "priming" i.e. water getting in where steam should be – a result of the swell. The Captain is rather more amiable than he was. He is never tired of talking about Sandwich and the neighbourhood, and he romances not a little in relating his youthful exploits. This afternoon he pointed out to me what he called a *young waterspout*, hanging like a jelly bag to the clouds.

Jan. 5. I had a sad disaster this morning. I was sitting reading in my cabin with the port open, when in came a sea and flooded the whole cabin. I was wetted to the skin and had to change everything. My desk was half filled with water , so was the Crozier box, and even the tin robecase did not wholly escape. The cabin floor was 6 inches deep in water.

Jan. 6. Epiphany. The recollection of this day as it used to be, compared with what it is, did not tend to raise my spirits. After breakfast, I sat at the piano, and sang, by myself, all the dear old Epiphany hymns. The vane of Preston Church, as we used to see it on our way to Matins on this day, shining in the sunlight, and reminding us of *the* Star – came constantly into my thoughts.
The *Magellanic Nebulae* I saw for the first time, tonight. They are like splashes of the Milky Way.

Jan. 15. At 11.30, the officers made out a tall rock, far away to the South, which proved to be one of a group called the Four Crowns (also called Bass Island).

At 3.30 Opara – about two thirds of the way from Panama to Wellington – was sighted and rapidly became very plain.
By 5, we could make out the coast outlines – which are very bold and irregular.
An attempt was made to get into the harbour before nightfall, but it would not do. The channel is very narrow and intricate, with coral rcefs on each side, on which account it can only be entered by daylight. We were abreast of the island by sunset and shall have to stand on and off till 5 a.m. and then go in.
We shall begin coaling directly and it is hoped that we shall get off again tomorrow evening. I believe we are to have a French Naval Officer on board to dinner tomorrow. He is governor of this wonderful island (which has also a king). Opara (or Rapa) was not originally one of the regular coaling stations of this company: but a reserve of coal

was kept, in case any of the ships should exceed their ordinary consumption, and be in danger of running short before reaching Wellington.

Jan. 16. We got alongside the coaling hulk at 7 a.m. The passage from the open sea is short, but extremely intricate and dangerous from the coral shoals.

Most lovely is the landlocked harbour. Such magnificent green hills, with deep indentations, and ravines. Rocks project everywhere, and, at the head of the harbour, a conglomeration of round topped eminences, gives the impression that a general boiling up of the earth had taken place, followed by a rapid cooling, before any subsidence could occur. Indeed the whole island is volcanic, and the harbour itself has the appearance of having once been a crater. Large flocks of wild goats were feeding on the hillsides.

We began coaling at 9, before which time many boats and 'catamarans' came alongside. First, a soldier in full uniform, being the French army of occupation. Then, numbers of natives with bananas, cabbages, flowers, calabashes, and magnificent pieces of coral like enormous mushrooms, for sale. They all came on deck, and it was amusing to hear the officers and men talking to them. They, of course, understood not a word of what was said, but they grinned good humouredly, and showed their teeth. Many of them are tall and good looking, colour dark brown.

Before these ships began to call here, i.e. about two years ago, the natives knew nothing of money, and attached no value to it. But now they are the keenest of traders, and will sell nothing under a shilling. About 8 a.m. the sharks began to gather round the ship. Some passengers got out a salmon line (!) on a reel, and baited some gimp hooks with beef. A shark laid hold of one, and snapped the line in a moment. Major Stafford shot at another without effect. A young shark without experience cruised round the gangway in an impudent manner, and a cunning quartermaster, watching his opportunity, slipped down the ladder and laid hold of the fast young gentleman's tail. He was very soon flapping about on the deck in great disgust.

At 10, a boat was sent ashore with a large party of passengers, myself among the number.

The chief plants that we met with were a verbena-like weed, which grows everywhere, a lovely *Ipomoea*, large, blue and sweet scented. A yellow *Oxalis* and ferns without end, all new to me. The most striking was a magnificent one like Hart's tongue, but an asplenum not a *Scotopendrum*: with fronds three feet long, and three inches wide, bright green, with a nearly black rachis. There were of course a good many other plants, but very few in flower.

The trees are low and insignificant. There is a plantain, and a nut bearing tree called *candle nut*; also a few oranges, whose fruit is not worth much; and a tree bearing splendid yellowish white flowers, resembling *Stephanotis*, and with as delicious a fragrance. These are used by the natives, men and women, as ornaments. They wear them round their necks, or stuck through their ears in which large holes are pierced.

Before returning to the ship, I called at what we chose to designate the 'Palace', a low, one roomed house, thatched with plantain leaves. The King was in the garden, digging without his coat. He shook hands with us with much affability. The Queen had a baby a few days old. We were introduced to her, and to the young 'princes' and 'princesses'. They are all dark, but by no means black.

This 'nation' is rapidly dwindling away. The total population, including the last royal baby, is 129. The only religious teaching they have had appears to have been from the London Missionary Society.

[In 1826, there had been almost 2000 inhabitants. The first European to visit Rapa was George Vancouver on 22 December 1791, who named the island Oparo. Contact with Europeans brought alcohol and disease, and between 1824 and 1830 over three quarters of the natives died. Peruvian slavers raided the island as well, and when a handful of their victims were returned to the island, they brought with them smallpox, which caused an epidemic.]

Jan. 27. I came on deck at 7.20 when the N. Zealand coast, just north of Cape Palliser, was plainly visible. Most interesting to me was the sight. The coast is very grand; full of wonderful "effects" of light and shade. We soon came near enough to make out the vegetation – great masses of fern and scrub, a few huts here and there, and several bush fires, but not a human or other being to be seen till we got into Wellington Harbour.

We dropped anchor at about 4 p.m. and then went to dinner. The first news we heard was that there had been terrible doings at Poverty Bay and elsewhere, on the part of the Maories. At 5, Mr. Prendergast, Attorney General of N.Z., came on board, and brought me a packet of papers from Mr. Edwards, which I took down to my cabin and read. I am requested, it seems by the Gen. Synod, to resign my claim to the See of Dunedin, for the sake of the 'peace of the Church'. Most unfair this, to lay such a responsibility on me! I certainly never anticipated such action as *this* on the part of the Synod. Probably I should have acquiesced, if I had not left England before it reached me, but now – well I can only hope and trust that I shall be guided to a right course. Bp. Selwyn has written a letter entreating the Dunedin Churchmen to receive me as their Bishop, and this justifies me in postponing my decision till I have visited the diocese.

Wellington is a straggling place. All the houses are of wood, on account of the prevalence of earthquakes. The harbour is very beautiful, the surrounding hills lofty and bold. The wind here is terrific. The *Phoebe* to Port Chalmers sails tomorrow, at 3 p.m., weather permitting. The Bp. of Christchurch asks me by telegraph to stop *there* on my way south. I replied, begging him to meet me at Lyttelton.

Jan. 28. I hardly slept at all on account of the worry. My brain was in a state of utter confusion all night.

Jan. 30. No change in the weather all night, and as it still blows a gale, we are not to sail today. I went ashore after breakfast, and walked about with A. Lascelles. We spent the evening at Mr. Prendergast's. While I was there a telegram reached me from Edwards. 'Come to Dunedin as soon as possible'.

We are to sail tomorrow (Sunday) morning – so my hopes of a Sunday ashore will come to nought. The wind has gone down. I have dropped the title of Bishop of Dunedin, and have become plain 'Bishop Jenner'.

In the *Otago Daily Times* for 30 January a member of the Dunedin Deanery, James Smith, wrote to the editor:

Sir,

I observe in your recent issue an advertisement with the names of Mr Wm. Carr Young and other gentlemen appended, inviting those members of the Church of England who are opposed to Ritualism, and the election of Dr Jenner to the Bishopric of Dunedin, to meet this evening to consider the best means of opposing the claims asserted by Dr Jenner, and to secure ultimately the nomination of a Bishop acceptable to the Church in this Diocese.

This proceeding is thoroughly in keeping with the singularly unfair spirit which has hitherto characterised the opposition to Bishop Jenner, which some few persons, taking ungenerous advantage of the Bishop's absence, have persistently carried on. They have industriously laboured to persuade the members of the Church to condemn Dr Jenner unheard, upon the exceedingly vague and pointless charge of "Ritualism," unsupported by any evidence except loose (and probably one-sided) newspaper reports of doubtful authenticity, which were entitled no weight in competition with the solemn and convincing testimony borne by the late Archbishop of Canterbury to Dr Jenner's ability, zeal, and usefulness during many years spent by him as a parish minister, under the eye of the Archbishop of Canterbury.

But the now rapidly approaching event of Dr Jenner's presence here, and of his being, for the first time, in a position to meet his accusers face to face, and to answer fully for himself, might, one would think, have recalled even his most inveterate opponents to a sense of the forbearance due to a still absent man, and have prompted them to abstain from any further proceedings until all those members of the Church who are willing to hear before they condemn, had had an opportunity of learning from Dr Jenner himself whether there is any truth in the insinuations which his opponents have circulated, to the effect that he is heretical in doctrine, and desirous of introducing ceremonial observances destructive of the true worship of God.

In a later edition there was a letter from someone called 'Z':

Sir,

I was present at the meeting tonight called by Messrs Young, Martin, and others, and was much surprised and pained to hear Mr Young, in opening the meeting, saying that it was simply one for the opponents of Dr Jenner, and that any one holding contrary opinions would not be allowed to vote, even if allowed to speak. Now, I consider this most one-sided, and I trust that it will be properly represented to the Bishop of Dunedin, that this meeting, held so shortly before his arrival, was not one of the members of the Church of England in Dunedin, but simply of a select few who were opposed to him.

One thing that came out of this meeting was a further advertisement, criticised in this letter in the *North Otago Times:*

Sir,

In common, no doubt, with many members of the Church of England in this diocese, I read lately with the greatest indignation an advertisement in the Dunedin papers to the following effect -

'To the members of the Church of England in the Diocese of Dunedin – the Representatives you are about to elect as members of the Diocesan Synod will be called upon to decide whether we shall accept Dr Jenner as Bishop of Dunedin or not. Therefore do not promise your votes before the 10th March, when the candidates are to be nominated. A candidate opposed to Dr Jenner (Ritualism) will be nominated for every seat in the Synod'.

The *Tuapeka Times* for 30 January had this more positive item:

We are glad to observe in the list of passengers per. s.s. Ruahine the name of his Lordship the Bishop of Dunedin. The arrival of his Lordship among us will do much to heal all dissensions; and all, we have little doubt, will aid him in carrying out his work in this diocese. With what may have occurred in England we have nothing to do; by his Lordship's conduct in New Zealand he must stand or fall, and we have no fear of the result. It would only be an act of Christian courtesy to set about preparing congratulatory addresses on his safe arrival among his flock.

Jan. 31. Sexagestma Sunday. The *Phoebe* sailed at 9.30. There was a fresh breeze, and a heavy swell outside the harbour. At 7 I went on deck for half an hour. We were just passing the Kaikoura range. They looked most majestic. The summits were covered with snow, and stood up well above the clouds like the mountains on the Lake of Lucerne. An extremely impressive scene! They are far higher than I had imagined, yet Mt. Cook in Canterbury is nearly twice as high as the Kaikouras, which are even surpassed by the Otago ranges. So at least says 'the Hon. I. Hall', member of the Legislative Council, who is a passenger. He lives at Christchurch. and seems to be a good Churchman. We are to arrive at Lyttelton at about 6 a.m. I wonder what the Dunedinites would say, if they knew how dreadfully I am tempted to take the General Synod at its word and start off home at once.

Feb. 1. At 7 I came on deck, the ship was stopped twice during the night on account of the dense fog, which continued until 9, when it lifted and showed Bank's Peninsula close to us. We steamed into Lyttelton Harbour and anchored about 10. I went ashore in the Customs boat with Mr. Hall. The Bp. of Christchurch never came to Lyttelton.

[When Mr. Young later addressed the first Dunedin Diocesan Synod he made great play of this incident:
At Wellington he received his Lordship the Bishop of Christchurch's letter, and in that letter his Lordship expressed a desire to see him. He

did not even reply to his Lordship but went to Lyttelton. Why did he not telegraph from there? Did he expect his Lordship to meet him at Lyttelton. and was not his act of omission one of disrespect?
A member of Synod responded that Jenner did indeed telegraph, but that the telegram miscarried. It was given to a Captain Kenson by mistake.]

There was no time to go to Christchurch and back before the *Phoebe* left, so I walked about with Girand and a Dr. Donald, one of the original settlers, who showed me the Church and the Town Hall. Lyttelton is very pretty. Beautiful green heights on each side of the harbour with bold projecting rocks everywhere, but very little timber.

The *Phoebe* left her anchorage at 1. A heavy fog was driving up from the sea. We went very slowly, stopping to take up Capt. White of the *Blue Jacket*, a sailing ship, which is to start for England about the middle of the month. She furnishes her cabins and provides linen, etc, and charges only £50 – not more than other ships which give no such advantages. I feel *very* much inclined to go back in her. After dinner (at 3.30), the fog increasing, we dropped anchor, as the Captain did not know where he was. Shall I ever get to Dunedin, I wonder? It takes 18 hours in clear weather to go from Lyttelton to Dunedin. We remained at anchor till 9, when, the fog clearing, we weighed and went ahead.

Feb. 2. Purification. There have been many sharks round the ship today. The Captain shot at several without effect. At about 6 p.m. we passed through acres of "whale feed" - minute crustaceans like young lobsters, on which the whale lives. They give a reddish colour to the sea.

At 8.30, we anchored outside the 'Heads' , and are to move up to Pt. Chalmers at 4.30 a.m. I do not expect any kind of "reception" at Dunedin, so, as they can scarcely mob me, I shall not be disappointed whatever happens. Mr. Edwards in his letter, promised to meet me at Port Chalmers, but, the *Phoebe* having been so long coming, I doubt whether he will. Probably I shall have to walk *solus* from the jetty to the town.

Feb. 3. The *Phoebe* weighed at 6, and anchored at Pt. Chalmers in half an hour. A most exquisitely beautiful place, this, surpassing anything I have seen, in N. Zealand or elsewhere. To my great relief four Dunedin gentlemen came on board to see me. viz. Rev. E. Granger, Messrs. Quick, Howorth and Panthin, all warm sympathizers. There seems to be huge excitement at Dunedin.

I could summarise the features of the situation, after the fashion of American newspapers:

GREAT EXCITEMENT AT BP. JENNER'S ARRIVAL!
Commonly supposed that he will insist on preaching.

MEETING LAST FRIDAY CONVENED BY YOUNG & CO.
Measures adopted against Bp. Jenner's reception.

BISHOP HARPER "TELEGRAPHS TO YOUNG THAT HE SHALL NOT ALLOW HIM TO OFFICIATE"!!!
Vestries and congregations of St. Paul's and All Saints indignant at his exclusion fr

TELEGRAM SENT TO BP. HARPER, WHO REFUSES TO WITHDRAW INHIBITION.

My friends took me ashore, and gave me a good breakfast at the Hotel. At 8.30, we left in a small steamer for Dunedin. The morning was fine; the scenery as we passed up the harbour unspeakably lovely. The shores, steep and bold are covered with bush, and, where cleared, with the greenest grass. Here and there appears a settler's homestead, with blue smoke curling up through the trees. Then there are several small but lofty islands, among which our course winds. These are clothed with verdure from the water to the highest elevation, except where the rich brown rock peeps out.

In about an hour, the City of Dunedin came in sight. It is far more imposing and larger than I had expected. At 9.30, I landed, not without deep feelings of thankfulness to God, for His most merciful protection throughout my long voyage. There were crowds of people on the jetty to see me, much respect was exhibited. Edwards, Dasent and others took me to the Parsonage in somebody's carriage.

Mr. Edwards, I liked much. He is most kind in every way. Almost all day, I was receiving visitors. Heartiest welcome from everybody. The excitement at my inhibition is by no means abated. S. Paul's vestry met again and adjourned till tomorrow, after sending another telegram to Bp. of Ch. Ch.

In the afternoon, I walked out with Edwards, and called on Mrs. Bell. Dunedin is a surprising place, S. Paul's Church is better than I had expected. Poor Edwards has just received the news of his mother's death, and is in great 'affliction'. A memorable day this, my islands reception has far surpassed my expectations.

A colourful description of the impact of Jenner's arrival is contained in Henry Jacobs *Colonial Histories: New Zealand*, published by the SPCK in 1887.

Travelling via Panama, Bishop Jenner arrived in Lyttelton at the end of January, 1869, did not come over to Christchurch - a distance of seven or eight miles by railway - to confer with Bishop Harper, but hastened on by the same steamer to Dunedin.

There his sudden arrival electrified; not church-people only, but the whole community, and provoked intensely painful dissension and bitter controversy. The newspapers teemed with remonstrances, rejoinders, attacks, and recriminations. Many took up the bishop's cause warmly, and loudly complained of the harshness and injustice of the treatment to which, in their view, he had been subjected.

An attractive presence and the bearing of a gentleman - not to speak of his renown as a church musician and composer - won for him many supporters. On the other hand, newspaper reports of services and ceremonies of an advanced Ritualistic type, in which he had recently taken part in England, accompanied by a letter of disapproval written by Archbishop Longley, were scattered broadcast throughout the two provinces, and, while they excited much ignorant prejudice, perplexed and irritated even the moderate and soberminded, and awakened doubts and misgivings in the minds of some even of the warmest advocates of the bishop's cause.

In a word, the new diocese was split in two from end to end. As had been the case in the Synod, so it was now; some clamoured for justice to Dr. Jenner; others pitied the diocese more, and, according to their temperament, either mildly deprecated, or vehemently protested against, the appointment as a menace of perpetual discord. Some believed in, and appealed to, his promises of moderation and caution for the future; others scouted them, as utterly untrustworthy. 'Can the leopard,' said they, 'change his spots?'

Feb. 4. I found a letter from the Primate [the Bishop of Christchurch] – very hard and unsympathetic. He desires me 'not to attempt to officiate either as a Bishop, or as a Minister of our Church in Otago or Southland'. Assuming that this was my intention, he lectures me on my duty to the N.Z. Church. An uncalled for proceeding this. It would be well if the N. Zealand Church would remember its duty towards me.

In S. Paul's vestry there seems to be increased excitement. They appointed a committee with orders to keep on telegraphing to the Primate until evening, or until they got a direct answer to the question, whether he forbids me to accept the invitation of the Vestry to preach next Sunday at S. Paul's, but the Primate declines further correspondence except by letter. The Vestry were unanimous in wishing me to preach.

I answered the Primate's letter in the afternoon, but I was perpetually being interrupted by sympathising visitors of whom there seems no end. The milder of the adversaries are beginning to come, e.g. Mr. Whittingham and Mr. Oliver. The former an opponent in S. Paul's vestry, the latter, a member of Mr W. C. Young's committee. Mr. W. was pleased to express himself to Mr. Edwards much gratified by his interview with me, though he was angry with himself for it and said 'that's the worst of having to deal with a gentleman'! Mr. Young at his meeting, warned the audience against me on this ground!!

Feb. 7. Quinquagesima Sunday. Being under inhibition, I went to Church as a worshipper only. There was a large congregation, and a good many communicated. The singing was not bad – Anglican Chants to Canticles – Hymns A & M. It was strange my being compelled to be silent. The congregation at Evensong was very large. It appears that an idea prevailed that I should preach after all.

Feb. 10. Ash Wednesday. At S. Paul's there was Litany Commination, and the 'Communion Service' (no Celebration) at 11. About 25 persons were present. Capt. Hamilton called this morning. A very good man, but almost, if not quite, a 'Plymouth Brother'.

In the prevailing torpor of the Church, it is no wonder that earnest minded, but ill instructed, men, should go off to other bodies of religionists. Such is the case, unhappily, here.

Feb. 11. In our walk yesterday we passed through the 'town belt' i.e. a part of the bush still surrounding Dunedin. It gave me some idea of what bush scenery is like. The ferns were lovely. There were at least 20 different species, growing on the ground, on rocks, on trunks and even branches of trees. I saw several tree ferns, not very tall, however.

There were but few plants in flower but the foliage of the trees and shrubs were exquisite.

Every now and then we came to a little gully with a long perspective of ferns of all kinds, and trees arching overhead. In one charming little spot, about 6 yards square, the ferns were *arranged* (so to speak) against a rocky bank just like – but infinitely more lovely than – a fernery in an English garden. Only one bird was singing – the *Tui*, or parson bird. The note is very sweet but melancholy and undecided. *Feb. 12*. I spent most of the day indoors, preparing for the meeting this evening, which is convened for the purpose of hearing an address from me. It was held at S. Georges Hall at 8. With one exception all was most satisfactory. I was received with great applause.

The Chairman was Dr. Buchanan, who said he came prejudiced against me, but declared himself perfectly satisfied. The vote of thanks was unanimous and enthusiastic.

Mr. W. C. Young's name was received with hisses, and a letter explaining his absence, with still more emphatic marks of disapproval. The one drawback to the success of the meeting, was the absence of the 'opposition' leaders, who were specially invited to attend, but thought it prudent to stay away.

Feb. 13. Started at 8 in the coach for Waikouaiti. Mr. Graham, an up country station holder, was with me inside, with four others, two being diggers. The morning was wretched – heavy rain, which found its way into the coach to our great discomfort.

In spite of the weather the scenery was charming. Every turn of the road – and, on account of engineering difficulties, the road winds a great deal – reveals fresh beauties. Huge masses of uncleared bush, with the richest foliage conceivable, clothe the lofty hillsides. I was much struck with the enormous *fuchsia* trees. Tree ferns abound. I saw some more than 8 ft. high. Here and there a cabbage tree (or Ti palm) rears a naked trunk crowned by a palm like head. Flax *(Phormium tenax)* abounds everywhere, and in the valleys, grows to a large size. The cleared land is carpeted with the small white clover, which introduced a few years ago from England, is becoming naturalized in the most astonishing way.

After an uncomfortable journey of 3 hours, we arrived at Waikouaiti, where Mr. Dasent met me, and drove me to his house. This is a scattered township, occupying a considerable space of ground.

Feb. 14. 1ˢᵗ Sunday in Lent. Matins and Evensong in the little wooden church. A small congregation. Service dull. I was a worshipper only. After dinner, I walked out on the beach, a very fine piece of land, with Miss Dasent, aged 14. Picked up some shells, and saw the vertebra of several whales imbedded in the sand, also enormous masses of a sea weed, for all the world like confused heaps of *saddles*!

Feb. 15. At 8 a.m. Mr. Dasent and I left Waikouaiti in a four wheeled 'buggy' for Palmerston, a small township on the north road. The scenery is very pretty in places, though of a different character from any I had as yet passed through. On the left hand, after leaving Waikouaiti, there was a considerable bush, with the prettiest little houses and gardens belonging to squatters, at intervals on the very edge. Far away to the westward, extend an interminable range of grassy hills, with rocky peaks interspersed.

At 9, we came to Capt. Fallerton's station. Here we had a capital breakfast, served in admirable style. Such cream, butter and hot cakes! with most superlative coffee. After breakfast Capt. Fallerton drove us the 25 miles to Hampden.

The road was 'metalled' for the first 6 miles, after which it was rather rough, except in sandy places where the travelling was very pleasant. After passing the Shag valley we had to cross the Horse Range, and very steep it was – 800 feet above the sea level. From the summit, there is a magnificent view over the country we had passed – endless plains and hills to the West, and Port Chalmers and Otago Heads to the South.

The descent on the Northern side of the range took us through 'Trotter's Gorge' - a most glorious piece of rock scenery. On the right, a lofty cliff, formed of enormous piles of conglomerate massed together in the wildest confusion: on the left, a lovely green gully bounded by precipitous heights, and strewed here and there with rocky fragments that had fallen down from time to time. The contrast of the grey rocks against the brilliant verdure of the grass and ferns was most striking.

The road hence to Hampden is less interesting. The land is highly cultivated, and the crops of wheat and oats looked very well. At Hampden we found a party from Oamaru to meet us, viz. Messrs. Miller (an Eton and Trinity man, was at Eton with Robert and Alfred and knew several friends of mine), W. Black and Allen, besides Mr. Gifford.

After dinner at the Hotel, I attended a meeting in the schoolroom. (N.B. the schools of Otago are numerous and, as far as regards secular instruction, excellent, but they are under government management, and the clergy have nothing to do with them). About 30 were present, I addressed them for 20 minutes. Everybody was most friendly.

I acknowledged the thanks, which were carried by acclamation, and wound up by saying that, having been doubtful as to what character I ought to be regarded as bearing in Otago – whether Fenian, Hau Hau, [After 1865 armed Māori were almost invariably termed Hau Hau,] or other lawless intruder – I had come to the conclusion that I was only 'a new chum out prospecting'. This piece of digger's slang tickled them amazingly.

At 5, we got into Mr. Miller's 'buggy' and started on our 26 miles drive to Oamaru. We crossed several rivers, the largest being the Otepopo. We saw a great deal of land under tillage today. One field, or paddock, as they call it, belonging to a company lately started, contained 1500 acres of wheat. We arrived at Oamaru Parsonage, a stone house of some pretensions, at 8.15.

Feb. 16. At Oamaru all day. In the forenoon Mr. Ashcroft, a very pleasant man called. We had a long conversation and he lent me his horse, on which I rode for a couple of hours with Gifford. The day was magnificent.

The town and bay looked extremely pretty from a headland which forms the southern extremity of the bay. 'First Rocky Point' it is called in the maps. There is a tremendous surf here sometimes. We went into the Church, which I suppose must be called good for New Zealand, this of the white Oamaru stone, an excellent material.

Feb. 17. The meeting was at 7, in the 'Drill Shed'. Mr. Miller the Chairman was not very brilliant. I spoke for half of an hour. There was much silly talk, especially from one Clendinner, who seemed to me to have been having a strongish 'nobbler'. The feeling of the meeting was highly Protestant.

Gifford spoke well but said one or two things, *ad captandum vulgus* [to capture the crowd] that I thought unworthy of him. The meeting on the whole was depressing. I found afterwards that there were many Presbyterians present and that certain rude Protestant demonstrations came from *them*. The attendance was large, upwards of 300. I got a kind letter from Mr. Vincent Pyke, the Gold Warden of Clyde, this evening, pressing hospitality upon me.

Feb. 18. At 2.30, I started with Mr. Graham, for his station, Ben Lomond. The road was very rough, and the scenery not particularly interesting. Mr. G. is a reckless driver and very nearly upset us several times. The heights on either side of the plain along which our route lay, are striking at first but soon become monotonous. They are covered with tussocks of grass which was quite brown, and never seems to be green at any time of the year. No bush or tree to be seen except now and then a solitary Ti palm (or cabbage tree). The plain is under cultivation and the fields of wheat, barley, oats and potatoes, were looking very promising.

About 5, we came to the Waitaki and skirted its banks for some miles. The opposite heights are in Canterbury province. Ben Lomond is not so high as its Scottish namesake, but the fog prevented its summit from being seen. We arrived at Mr. Graham's station at 6. There is a Mrs. G. and several children. After dinner I baptized their baby.

A copy of the Baptism Certificate for Graham's child (issued with 'Seeking a See'.)

Feb. 19. I wrote to tell the Primate that I had baptized Graham's child, in spite of the inhibition.

Started at 10 with G. for Otekaike. The horses were slow, and the road exceedingly rough, often taking us through rivers and over shingle beds. We started in the afternoon for 'Rugged Ridges Station' owned by Messrs. Julius. Their father, G. Julius M.D., and his two brothers, I knew very well at Richmond and at Cambridge. Off again in half an hour for Ptimatala, where we were received by Mr. and Mrs. Gardner, a nice old couple from the lowlands of Scotland. Presbyterian I fancy. Our drive today was 34 miles long. We kept close along the Waitaki. No distant mountains were to be seen for the mist, but the Canterbury hills and Ben More, 6,000 feet high, showed out very beautifully as the sun went down. We passed some fine bits of rock. On the smooth face of one sandstone cliff some quaint Maori devices were executed in a red pigment. My companion was at a loss to understand how and where they got the paint. Everybody we met talks of nothing but sheep and wool and washing and shearing.

Feb. 20. After breakfast Mr. Gardner showed me over his homestead. Everything seems to thrive marvellously in these Otago gardens. All here looked most healthy, especially the standard apple and peach trees.

At 9.30 I took leave of my kind friend, Mr. Graham, and the Gardners, and set off on a tall horse (16.2 high) for Omarama. After riding 5 miles through a hilly country without a single tree, but interesting for its bold and rugged character, I came suddenly in sight of a noble snowy range, which greatly delighted me. The sun was shining brilliantly on the summit which seemed enormously high. There was snow in patches on other mountains nearer at hand. Inconceivably barren was the country through which I passed. Between the huge tussocks of grass, the ground was absolutely bare, except that here and there appear a small yellow flowered and red leaved *Oxalis*, and a *Cineraria* or *Senecio* with yellow flowers and woolly leaves. I also passed a patch of a strong scented *labiate*, probably *marrubium*. At 2, I arrived at Omarama. My horse belonged to Mr. Ostler of Ben More, who is to be my host tonight. He (the horse) carried me well, but wanted spurs ...

At 2 Mr. Ostler appeared. He gave me his horse to ride, and mounted my 16 hands steed himself. Then we started on our ten miles ride to Ben More, in the 'McKenzie' country. This district derives its name from a man, who, in the pro-Canterbury days, stole a 'mob' of sheep, and for more than a year kept them on these plains. At that time unknown to the rest of the world. He was caught at last and made to disgorge his booty.

Our ride was very hot and dusty (the more, as Mr. Ostler had to reclaim some horses on the way and drive them home, and the dust they raised between them was prodigious,) along a vast plain, bounded by low rugged hills on our right and left and by the snowy ranges far away in front.

Mr. O. showed me an iron fence, which, he said, enclosed a 'paddock' of 90,000 acres, and enabled him to keep a flock of 40,000 sheep without a shepherd. I imagine the Waitaki river forms one boundary of this nice little meadow. The plain is 1200 feet above the sea, and is very cold in winter, when the snow lies deep and the rivers freeze.

We rode through a great many streams, most of which are admirably fitted for trout and even salmon, but, except eels, none of them at present contain fish bigger than white bait. We got to Ben More station at 5. My horse was a pleasant one, and I was much less fatigued by my first ride of 25 miles than I expected.

Mr. Ostler has been married only six months. His wife is a rather good looking Victorian. The house is beautifully situated, with a glorious view up the plain, terminated by the snowy mountains. What we see, by the way, are glaciers, which are perpetually melting and feeding the rivers below. This is part of the Mount Cook range. Mt. Cook proper is further to the north, and is twice as lofty as the heights we see.

There is a lake to the Westward of this house, whose high and precipitous banks appear quite close. I was proposing a walk thither tomorrow afternoon, when Mr. Ostler told me it was at least ten miles off. One is constantly being deceived, in judging distances, by the extreme clearness of the atmosphere.

Mr. O. called me in after dinner, to see a sick man, one of his hands, suffering from a bilious attack. Mrs. O has a *case* and Dr. Hering. I gave him *nuxv*. [Jenner was an ardent believer in homeopathy, of which Dr. Hering was an early american pioneer, and *nuxv (Nux Vomica)* a classical medicine.] My patient is a 'lag', colonial for a man who has worn the irons on his ankles.

There is a nice *Broadwood* piano in the living room here. Mr. O. is only manager. The station belongs to Messrs. Campbell & Low.

Feb. 21. 2ⁿᵈ S. in Lent. I slept well, and was only a little stiff, and not at all *galled* by my ride. My patient is much better this morning. The day was extremely hot. No wind at all. A little haze on the distant hills did not prevent them from being plainly visible.

At 10.30, *interdict* notwithstanding, I had a service in the woolshed. I said part of Matins and expounded the first lesson. There were about 27 present. All were very attentive. It was an odd scene. The men sat in tiers on the wool, high above my head. In the afternoon, we had a similar service, viz. a selection from Evensong, and an exposition of S. John X. Mr. & Mrs. O. expressed unbounded delight at certain 'local allusions' in my addresses about sheep and shepherds.

Feb. 22. Still fearfully hot. The sun has prodigious power in this country. Mr. Ostler drove me after breakfast to Omarama, and thence to Mr. Hill's station 'Longslip' where we lunched.

Then Mr. Hill lent me a horse (piebald) on which I rode to Mr. McLeans, Morven Hill's station; 20 miles along a rough country, but more fertile than that which I had just left. There was some very fine rock scenery, the Lindis Pass. I fell in with several plants I had not seen before. A tall and rather handsome *Primulaceoe* with white flowers and a long tap root. *Verbascum Blattaria* fine and abundant, but introduced: and a pretty little *Campanulaceoe* (or *Campanula* or *Wanlerbergia gracilis*) with light blue sometimes white flowers. There were no animals except lizards, a hawk or two, and the ever recurring 'pipit'. Not even flies to tease the horse.

Mr. McLean is a delightful old person. A Presbyterian, but a warm and indignant supporter of my cause. He is 'the Honourable', i.e. a member of the upper house of the New Zealand Legislative. It was quite refreshing to hear him talk of the tactics of W. C. Young & Co. Most of the men of the station - there are 60 of them - are away 'mustering' sheep. Mr. McLean has the largest run in Otago - 400,000 acres. A Mr. Haines is his manager. Son of a former prime minister of Victoria, and nephew of 'Haines of Caius' whom I knew well at Cambridge.

Feb. 23. At 9.48 Mr. McLean and I started in a nice 'buggy' drawn by two greys (Donald and Hector) for the Wanaka Lake, or, rather, a station near it, belonging to Mr. H. Campbell. The road for the most part was a mere track, over a very undulating country, indeed a succession of "terraces". We crossed the River Lindis several times, and for some miles kept along its banks, through a very lovely rock gorge. Here we saw several families of the Blue Mountain Duck, a remarkably pretty bird, colour slate, with some white about the head. They seem very tame. It was pretty to see them rise out of the water, fly some yards and then light on a rock in the middle of the stream.

The approach to the Molyneux, which runs close by Mr. Campbell's station, is very fine. Magnificent mountains seem to rise out of the Lake, covered with immense glaciers. The Otago glaciers are said to be more extensive than all the Swiss ones put together. The Molyneux is a notable river, though unnavigable on account of its extreme rapidity.

We left the buggy and horses on the other side of the river and crossed in a very frail boat, and leaky, which I thought must be swept down the stream. There are a number of houses here, and an 'hotel'. Mr. Campbell's house is a very rough affair. We had tea and the inevitable mutton at 6.

Feb. 24. St. Matthias. Left at 9, in a buggy driven by a 'cadet' on the station, called Monro, a very unskilful charioteer. I took the reins after a couple of hours. 16 miles from the Wanaka we fed the horse. I walked on about 4 miles over an uninteresting country, a vast undulating plain, without seeing a living creature except 'pipits' and an occasional 'mob' of merinos. A little further on we met several wool drays, drawn by bullocks, sometimes by horses, on their way to the coast, Oamaru being their port of shipment.

From hence to Cromwell, the road is monotonous. The Molyneux appears at intervals on the left of the road. At Cromwell, a small digging township, with a single street of corrugated iron houses, the Kaiwarra joins the Molyneux. For some distance the muddy waters of the former run side by side with the clear stream of the Molyneux; but before long the whole becomes turbid and the combined streams rush southwards between their steep and rocky banks.

Just above the junction with the Kaiwarra, a wooden bridge crosses the Molyneux at a great elevation. The scenery here is very fine. Great quantities of gold have been, and are being, found in the neighbourhood. The banks of the river are 'sluiced' by the diggers for many miles.

At Clyde, Mr. Vincent Pyke received me most courteously. I dined at his house, and slept in lodgings provided by the 'Church Committee'. The house was an iron one, but very comfortable. It was arranged that I should go to Queenstown tomorrow returning on Saturday.

Clyde is another diggings township, larger than Cromwell. The houses are of wood and iron. There is no clergyman here. None in fact, nearer than Queenstown, which is 50 miles off. Mr. Pyke, who is 'Gold Warden' officiates as lay reader in a 'church' which belongs to *us*, but is lent for one service every Sunday to the Presbyterians! A grievous state of things, this, but being without a head the whole diocese is naturally in a state of confusion and decay.

The Clyde people are anxious to have a clergyman, and would support him and build him a house. He would itinerate between Clyde and Cromwell, and his duty would be to work among the diggers through the district.

I saw some numbers of the Dunedin newspapers today. There are many letters about me, all *contra*. I got a note and a telegram from Edwards, also a polite invitation from Stanford, which I determined to accept. Several members of the 'Church of England Committee' waited on me in the evening. There seems to be an excellent feeling here. I am to hold a meeting on Saturday evening, after my return from Queenstown, and on Sunday I shall have to worship in the 'Church' here, under Mr. V. Pyke's auspices.

I saw several Chinese today. They are industrious and successful gold diggers, making a livelihood, very often, out of 'claims' deserted by the English. Halfway between Clyde and Cromwell, there is a very thriving and well cultivated market garden. The owner saluted me most respectfully. I should have liked to make his acquaintance. I was told that he was gradually extending his cultivation, and was making a good thing of it.

Feb. 25. After sending a telegram to Dunedin, I started in a buggy and pair for my 56 mile drive to Queenstown on Lake Wakatipu. My charioteer was a Dane – Mr. Beck – a pleasant and civil man. The first ten miles of road was that which I came along last evening. After passing through Cromwell, the country was new to me.

The road skirts the banks of Kaiwarra, the grandeur of which is beyond description. Such rocks I never beheld. Twice we crossed the river, in wonderful self-acting ferry boats. These swing across by the force of the current, which is tremendous. There is not a tree or shrub to be seen for many miles. The banks of the river are extremely lofty and precipitous. The stream is of course unnavigable, on account of the rapid current.

There is quite a large digging population scattered along the banks, dwelling in huts of all kinds of materials; iron, wood, turf, canvas or even calico. 'Hotels' appear frequently. Mere shanties bearing appropriate signs, e.g. 'The Diggers Rest', 'The Sluicer's Arms' and, close to a waterfall called 'The Gentle Annie' is an 'accommodation house' of superior pretension bearing the same name.

Another mountain torrent of noisy and obtrusive character, but very beautiful, is called 'Roaring Meg'. The rocks are a micaceous schist, and glitter brilliantly in the sun. The miners must often have reason to remember the proverb 'all that glitters is not gold'. Indeed the mica is commonly spoken of as 'New Chum's Gold'.

About halfway to Queenstown, we stopped to bait the horse, at an accommodation house, connected with a ferry over the Nevis, (a tributary of the Kaiwarra) and kept by a man named Edwards and his wife. He is a Truro man, and she from Swansea. Both were greatly interested at my knowledge of the two localities. Mrs. E. got into an excited state when she heard that my wife was born at Swansea, and that I had been there so recently. Her children had all been baptized by either Bishop Selwyn or Harper, except the baby, 2 months old, which I promised to baptize on my return from Queenstown.

There are diggings close to the house. Mr. Edwards told me the river is full of gold, if it could only be got at, and even in the road near his house, little grains could be seen after a shower. He showed me a small heap of gold dust, weighing 1 oz. and worth about £5.0. And he gave me a little nugget (worth 10/-) which I thought very kind. The latter part of the road was not quite so rich in scenery until we approached the lakes, when some glorious mountain ranges, the 'Remarkables' (an idiotic name) showed themselves. One snow covered peak was 10,000 feet high and there were many of rather less elevation.

Six miles from Queenstown, we crossed the *Shotover*, not without some risk, the ford being swollen by rains and the track uncertain. We stopped at a public house just before we reached the river, and asked the woman who kept it, how we were to find the way. She said 'O, you had better drive down to the ford and *coo-ey*; the boy is sure to hear you, and he'll show you over'. We followed this advice, and a boy on a white horse, responding to our 'coo-eying', came and piloted us across. The water came into the buggy, in spite of the height of the wheels, but we got across without serious difficulty.

And now we entered upon a tract of land, which, highly, and to all appearance successfully, cultivated, was more like home than any I had lately seen. Such prodigious fields of wheat and oats, just cut, and standing in stooks, or else being reaped by machine. The crops seemed very good, but the difficulty of getting them in must be immense, on account of the scarcity of labour.

Lake Hayes is a charming little sheet of water, about 2 miles from L. Wakatipu. The land is cultivated to its very banks; and there are little white dwellings dotted about, some close to the water, others higher up the green slopes; a scene of exceeding loveliness.

We reached Lake Wakatipu just as the sun was setting, and the nearly full moon rising. Very sweet and peaceful it looked. There was hardly a ripple on the water. One does not get a view of the whole lake from this part of its banks, (there is a 'town' here consisting of half a dozen houses, called Frankton,) but as far as can be judged, it appears quite equal to the Swiss lakes. In shape it is not unlike the Lake of the Four Cantons.

Queenstown lies in a hollow, on the edge of a little cove. You come upon it quite unexpectedly. It is a fair sized place; the houses are all of wood. This is a 'diggings' town, but superior to Clyde or Cromwell. Mr. Beetham, President of the 'Church Committee', came to meet me, and took me to his house, where I was to sleep. He entertained me hospitably, and was pleasant but Puritanical to a degree. Not that he knows much, or indeed anything, of theology. There had been a meeting about me a day or two back, when some silly resolutions were passed, which will make my work tomorrow night very simple. But we shall see.

The congregation at Queenstown had already been forward enough to send a resolution to the Archbishop of Canterbury in December 1867, which stated that:

The members of the Church of England in this district view with the greatest apprehension the appointment of Dr. Jenner to the Bishopric of Dunedin, as they consider the Ritualistic practices and performances with which he has so fully identified himself are pernicious and dangerous in the highest degree, having for their sole object the subversion and corruption of the firm faith and doctrines of the Church of England, converting its beautiful and impressive Liturgy into an absurdity.

Feb. 26. Unfortunately a windy day, which prevented my going out on the Lake, where squalls are dangerous. After breakfast Mr. Beetham, who is Gold Warden and Magistrate of the district, went to his office or court, and I sat down to write letters and diary, hoping to have a quiet morning.

Vain expectation! I had hardly begun before two young ladies walked in with infinite composure, and proceeded to make themselves at home, with the room, and with me. They pulled everything about within reach, and catechised me on my occupation and antecedents. They steadily refused to take hints to go away; but at last one of them proposed that we should take a walk, which gave me an opportunity, of which I was not slow to avail myself. I agreed at once, and off we set, hand in hand. Where should we go? 'Oh', said one, 'to the Peninsula'. So to the Peninsula we bent our steps.

This is a very lovely spot, with a grand view of the Lake. There is a cemetery on one part of it. My young friends, one of whom was 5, and the other 3 years old, terrified me by picking up some berries and eating them. They turned out to be 'snowberries', and are quite harmless and rather nice. We all sat down in a shady place, and I told the young people all about my darlings at home and showed them the photos. Then I related 'Alice' to them, after which I proposed that we should return home, i.e. Mr. Beetham's, to which they graciously consented, and after some difficulty, I succeeded in getting rid of them. I found they were the daughters of a Mr. Worthington, who lives close by.

The meeting at 8 o'clock was a full one. There was a scene, as I expected. I had said not a word of my intentions to anyone, but when I was called upon to address the audience, I rose and observed that it would depend entirely on themselves whether I should address them or not. Then I proceeded to refer to the 'resolutions' which had been passed and handed to me. I said it was preposterous to prejudge the whole matter, as they had done, when they knew I was on my way to see them and defend myself. It was like hanging a man first and trying him afterwards. Then I continued:

You call upon me to do certain things, to make statements which you dictate to me, and you tell me, that if I refuse to do your bidding, any further explanation will be useless. Now, I positively and distinctly refuse to do anything of the sort. It is, therefore, for you to say, whether I am to proceed with my address or not.
If this meeting holds itself bound by the ridiculous resolutions of last Tuesday, not a word more can I say, since you tell me beforehand that it

will be useless. If, on the other hand, you like to declare that you do not accept those resolutions, and, as far as you are concerned, are prepared to rescind them, I will gladly proceed with the address that I came to Queenstown to deliver.

Then there was a good deal of wild talking. A Mr. Coffey and Mr. Worthington fell out. W. said that the resolutions would have been differently worded, had they known I was coming when they were passed. C. said, 'No, they would not'. The latter appealed to me to say a few words to the assembly, but I steadily refused; except on the conditions already mentioned, which they would not accept, and so the meeting ended.

Feb. 27. We started at 7.15 for Clyde, and waited at the Nevis Ferry again. I walked out to look at some gold seekers hard by on the bank of the river. I found two men 'prospecting'. They were extremely civil, one was English, the other Scottish. The former had been gardener at the Rev. Hunt's, Sunninghill, father of the late Chancellor of the Exchequer. He lamented the paucity of religious privileges, and, indeed, nothing can well be more distressing. What seems to be required is a priest (two even would not be too many,) whose duty it should be to itinerate perpetually among the digging population.

My two diggers very kindly showed me how the gold was washed out of the dirt in which it is found. There is a great deal of iron sand here. This, from its weight, sinks lower than the earthy matter, but the gold, of course, lower still. So in the 'prospecting dish' (which is something like a tin milk pan,) when the water is poured off, and the dirt allowed to settle, one sees nothing at first but a mass of this black iron sand. But on inclining the dish, a little piece of sparkling gold dust appears on the edge of the sand. This is carefully removed, and in this way my two friends told me they could earn about £8 a week per man. I was afterwards told that this was probably an understatement.

We got to Clyde at 5.30. I dined at Mr. Pyke's and went to the 'meeting' at 8. There was a good attendance and everybody was amiable. The vote of thanks was most hearty and unanimous. A great contrast, this, to what took place at Queenstown.

There is no clergyman here, alas! They are anxious as I before observed to have one, and would guarantee him £350 a year and a house. I said when Mr. Pyke told me this, 'I think I shall offer myself'. 'Oh', said he 'if *you* will come, we will make it £500.' There is little doubt that a thoroughly competent man would get even more, for the diggers are extremely generous, when their hearts are won.

The *Dunstan Times* of 5 March contained this account of the meeting at Clyde:

BISHOP JENNER AT CLYDE

A meeting of the members of the Church of England and Ireland within the Dunstan District was held in the Church at Clyde on Saturday evening last, to meet Bishop Jenner, and hear from him an exposition of his views. About one hundred persons were present, including a few ladies. Bishop Jenner said that he was not before them for the purpose of canvassing for their their votes. He occupied his position in order to refute some of the charges laid at his door. He did not intend detaining them with other than a few explanations in self-defence.

The charges against him were numerous, and, in some instances, idiotic. For instance, he was charged with being a gentleman, and with being too great a favourite with the ladies. But the most grievous charge was that he was unfaithful to the Church. He had been called upon to resign all pretentions to the Diocese of Dunedin, to which he had been nominated. He refused, as for the past two years he had considered himself Bishop of Dunedin.

With respect to the latter charge, he could only say that it was a calumny, which appeared to have originated from his attending at churches where certain rites were performed which are repugnant to the people of this colony. He would say that, had he known that the feelings of the people of the Diocese had been so keen, so sensitive on the matter, he would not have attended those services ...

A Mr George Fache put a question to his lordship.

'Will you state whether, as Bishop, you would be in favour of introducing or permitting the introduction into the Church of practices and ceremonies known by the designation of Ritualistic.'
His lordship in reply said that he would not.

Feb. 28. 3ʳᵈ Sunday in Lent. At 11 I went to 'Church' when Mr. Pyke read prayers and a sermon given (by Dr. Guthrie), giving the Benediction (!!) at the end. The 'Church' is a wretched affair, used once a day (i.e. Sunday) by the Presbyterians.

I lunched with Mr. Pyke and in the afternoon was driven, by Mr. Beck, to Galloway Station in Mr. Low's. The road to Galloway Station took us past Alexandra, a diggings town of some importance. We did not go through the town but left it on the right, following a somewhat intricate path across an open country, and through a wide and rapid river, the Manukerikia, which falls into the Molyneux close to Alexandra. 'Blacks,' another gold miners' settlement, we saw on our left hand. All these places and many more in the neighbourhood have a scattered population of some thousands, at present altogether destitute of the Church's ministrations.

Mr. & Mrs. Low at Galloway are very charming people. She is a daughter of Dr. Buchanan. I baptized their baby, *Ethel Stanley* and said Evensong in the dining room. We went through part of the 'Messiah' in the evening. Mrs. Low sings rather well. My spirits rose under the influence of the cordial sympathy displayed by my host and hostess, and I enjoyed my visit to the Galloway station not a little.

March 1. I meant to have taken the coach to Hamilton's. It passes on its way from Clyde, close to Mr. Low's house. But my kind host offered to lend me a horse, on which to ride as far as Dunedin, if I liked it. A plan which I greatly preferred. So at 10 I set off.

A very rough trotter was my steed, and as he refused to canter, I had rather a hard time of it. When I had ridden five miles, my eyeglass fell off. I spent half an hour looking for it, but without success. It had got among the 'tussocks' and, perhaps, had been carried off by a woodhen, a bird which is naturally a kleptomaniac.

The sun was extremely hot, especially towards noon; soon after which I arrived at Mr. Bell's station. Here I found quite a little village, peopled by the station *employees*. This was my first unannounced visit to a strange station and I was a little nervous at first. It seemed such a very cool proceeding, to ride up to a man's house, and claim food and shelter, for it comes to that, however meekly you may deport yourself. But the genial and sympathetic manager, Mr. Stronock, soon put me at my ease.

He came out to greet me, sent my horse to the stable, and led me into the house, where he entertained me at his family dinner table. Nothing to eat, of course, but mutton, in various forms.
After dinner Mr. Stronock most kindly accompanied me quite ten miles on my way, and, more than that, he insisted on my riding his chestnut mare, a most delightful goer, after my bone dislocating animal.

On our way Mr. S. spoke a good deal about my prospects. He was energetically on my side. I think I won his heart by being able to talk intelligently about cricket, a game in which he takes a deep interest. The road was more or less uphill for nearly the whole ten miles to the top of 'Rough Ridge', a mountain 3,000 feet above the sea.
About three miles from the highest point, the ordinary 'tussocks' began to disappear, their place being occupied by huge clumps of 'snow grass', a most elegant, and useful plant, affording nourishment to the sheep when there is nothing else to be got or seen, for the snow. The leaves are very long, and the plant resembles the Pampas grass, but is much less rigid and serrated. Mr. Stronock left me just after we had passed over the ridge of the mountains.

About 3 miles off, at the foot of the mountain, the descent of which is extremely rapid on this the southeast side, is the station of Mr. Jas. Murison, where I was to stop for an hour. The track down the mountain side was very hard to find, and when found was quite precipitous. I had to get off and lead my horse, using my stick as an 'Alpen stock'.

The last mile of road is through a fine gorge, carpeted with 'English grass' which grows luxuriantly here. But before I got so far as this, I stopped to rest on the hill side, under the shadow of a great rock, whence I could enjoy the prospect before me, without being scorched by the intensely hot sun.
It was a scene never to be forgotten.
The view of the valley, or rather plain, of the Taieri, was quite uninterrupted. From the foot of the Rough Ridge to the other side of the valley the distance is about 10 miles. It looks much less: for except the river winding through the middle, the eye finds nothing to dwell upon, until it reaches the foot of the opposite range of hills. The plain is perfectly level and the hills on either side rise with great abruptness to a considerable height.

From where I sat I could just distinguish the settlement, partly mining, partly pastoral called 'Hamiltons', nestling under the mountains over against me. Mount Ida, a rather important 'digging' settlement, lies more to the northward. I could not make it out, there being a haze in that direction. And now, having thoroughly examined the prospect, I had leisure to remark the (to me) extraordinary stillness that prevailed.

The day was perfectly calm. Not a breath of air stirring; and the consequence was that a silence, overpowering in its intensity, reigned on the mountain; and broken only by the champing of my horse's bit, as he made the most of his time in cropping the scanty herbage of the rugged hillside. The absence of all sign of animal life is almost awful. One would give anything for the caw of a rook, or the chirp of a sparrow, or even a sheep bell. There are no flies, or other insects, to be seen or heard. A little brown lizard or two came out of the clefts of the rocks, and played about in the sun. What can they find to live upon?

Well, I must get on, or I shall be benighted.

So down the hill again till I reach the gorge near the foot. Here I meet with evident signs of a habitation close at hand; and in a few minutes I arrive at Mr. Murison's station, called 'Rough Ridge', after the mountain I had just descended. Nothing can be more snug than its situation.

Mr. M. I find is sub-manager, and is shortly leaving. He has made a very nice place here. The house is well arranged and furnished and the garden charming. The gum trees have grown wonderfully, as have the apples and other fruit trees. Vegetables and flowers alike look healthy, as is almost invariably the case in this colony.

Mr. Murison gave me the choice of two routes: No. 1, easy to find, but longer than No. 2, which though nearly straight, involves a hunt for the ford across the river, which it is possible I may fail to find.

As the sun is fast approaching the horizon, I elect the shorter road, Mr. M. exhorting me not to leave the dray track, as long as I can see it.

For the first four miles all seems easy enough, but then alas! I come to a spot where there are *two dray tracks* divergent. Which to take is the question.

Probably I made a wrong selection. At any rate, I shortly got into a part of the plain where no track could be discerned. A mob of sheep crossed my path on their way to the river, no doubt. I determined to follow them in the hope of hitting on a fordable place.

Stay! What noise is that? A faint bleat, it sounds like, and close at hand. I look about me, and soon discover two unhappy sheep, standing up to their necks in a hole, full of water, with a muddy bottom. Well, they must be got out, no doubt about that. So I dismount, and with my arm through the bridle, proceed to haul the creatures on to dry land. First one, which proves to be an old ewe who ought to have known better than to get into such mischief. Then the other, clearly her lamb. What to do with them is the next question.

They cannot stand, having probably been in the water some days. The only thing I can think of that is at all likely to benefit them, is bloodletting. So I took out my pen knife and made an incision in the ear of each. Whether it was this operation or what, a decided improvement speedily took place. They both stood up and got with a stumbling kind of walk. So, turning their faces away from the water into which they both seemed inclined to stumble again, I left them.

[I was blamed afterwards for taking so much trouble about two sheep, *as if their lives were of any appreciable value to their owners, who probably possessed many thousands'*.]

I was also jocularly informed, that, so far from having done any good, I had created confusion by my surgical operation; which of course altered the ear marks, by which the ownership is determined.

The episode of the sheep delayed me more than half an hour. Meanwhile the sun had reached the summits of the western heights, and it was growing dusk. The only thing to be done was to make for the river with all speed.

In a few minutes I reached the bank, not without difficulty, on account of the density of the tussocks, over which my horse who was getting weary, stumbled constantly. Here is a fordable place, I *think*. I try, but find the opposite bank too steep, and the bottom too soft to be practicable. So I ride along the bank for a mile, slowly and cautiously, for the darkness deepens, rapidly. Quack-Quack! I hear, a few yards off and, turning my head sharply round, I see a large family of 'Paradise ducks', amusing themselves on a bank of mud in the middle of the stream. They are beautiful birds (though geese, not ducks at all) and so tame.

Soon I came to a shallower part of the river, which seems to invite me to attempt the passage. And this time I am successful, though the water at one place reaches to my saddle flaps and I only just succeed in keeping my feet dry. As soon as the Southern Cross was visible I took the bearings of the hills which I was endeavouring to reach. More than once I rode through a large mob of merinos, to their no small terror.

The further side of the valley was reached about 9 o'clock. Here I found a good road; but it was hard to decide except by guesswork whether to turn to the right or left. It is so dark that I cannot see a yard in front of my horse's head. Mr. Murison had told me that Hamilton's station, whither I was bound, was considerably to the left of the digging settlement of the same name. The latter I fancy must be where I see some lights, which I determine to leave behind me, judging that the station cannot be very far off.

I stopped for a few minutes and practised *cooeying*. Such a stillness everywhere! More oppressive even than in the daytime. No one responding to my *cooeying*. I resolved as a *dernier resource* to let the horse try to find the way. I see lights ahead, but the track I am pursuing appears to be taking me past them. Yet the horse seems to have no doubt.

I make a reconnaissance in the direction of the lights, and soon find there is a considerable creek between me and them, so back again to my track, which leads me down a very steep bank, over some dangerous ground that has been sluiced by gold seekers, and is full of holes; through another small creek, after crossing which I am startled to find myself close to a house, apparently garrisoned by an army of dogs, who bark furiously on my approach.

My *cooeying* is not responded to, possibly not heard, amid the din of canine indignation. So I go on for a mile, and, coming to another dwelling, stop and *cooey* again. A man comes out and, to my great joy and relief, tells me that I am at Hamilton's station, and within a stone's throw of Mr. & Mrs. Rowley and Hamilton's house. In ten minutes more my horse is in the stable, and myself sitting in an easy chair in Mrs. Rowley's drawing room, while my supper is preparing in an adjoining apartment.
It is nearly 11 o'clock. I have ridden between 50 and 60 miles since 10 a.m. and am thoroughly and completely knocked up.

March 2. After breakfast, I started for another long ride, about 45 miles, to Mr. Wayne's, 'Shag Valley'. Mr. Rowley and his brother-in-law accompanied me the first 6 miles. For the next ten, I had a companion in the shape of a well bred bay filly, of whom I could not get rid. No one I met seemed to know to whom she belonged. Eventually I stopped at an accommodation house, and got the landlord to put her into a stable.

The road by which I am travelling is the regular coach road from the Lakes and Clyde, over the 'Rock & Pillar' mountain, by Palmerston and Waikouaiti, to Dunedin. Some parts of it would make an English stage coachman, if there is such a being, stare.
I ascended today some of the steepest and worst hills that ever horse, to say nothing of wheels, attempted. On the highest I encountered a long train of drays, laden with stores for the up country districts, each drawn by I forget how many horses, and progressing at the rate of about 2 miles an hour. From this point there was a very extensive, but not particularly fine, view. This I fancy is part of the Kakanui range.

At 1 o'clock, finding myself in a pleasant valley, through which a creek of the clearest water was flowing, I determined to halt and eat my luncheon, viz. a huge sandwich, provided by Mrs. Rowley, and carefully packed in my 'swag'. My horse meanwhile regaled himself with some delicious 'English grass'. We had an hour's rest, and I amused myself with a little 'prospecting'. That is to say, I tried to wash some of the sand taken from the bed of the creek, in an old sardine tin which I picked up on the road side. It is curious, by the way, to notice the number of articles of this kind, that one meets with everywhere along the road. My gold washing was far from successful. Not a grain was to be found.

Mr. Wayne's house is very superior to any of my former resting places. It is close to the *Shag* river, or *Waihemo*, a wide, but shallow, stream, here. Gum trees, which have thriven amazingly, are planted on each side of the house, and give it quite a long established look. Just before I reached it, I crossed a regular village green, where some men and boys were just leaving off playing at cricket. Very home-like was this. I found only Mrs. Wayne at home, with Mr. & Mrs. Dasent staying in the house.

I was not expected, yet some letters were waiting for me. I was dreadfully tired.

March 3. I left my horse at Mr. Wayne's, to enjoy the rest he had so well earned, and to find his way back to his owner, when an opportunity presented itself (according to the free and easy custom of the station,) and rode on a very nice mare of Mr. Wayne's, to Palmerston; Mr. & Mrs. Dasent accompanying me. The day was very hot.

At Palmerston I found some newspapers, with English news. Among other items, it reported the judgement of Jud. Com. in Mackonochie's case.

[In 1867, a prosecution was brought against the Rev. Alexander Mackonochie by John Martin, supported by the Church Association, under the Church Discipline Act of 1840. The charges brought were; elevating the host above his head, using a mixed chalice and altar lights, censing things and persons, and kneeling during the prayer of consecration. The first decision of the Court of Arches was against Mackonochie on two counts and in his favour on the other three, with no decision as to the payment of costs. Despite Mackonochie agreeing to comply, the anti-ritualists appealed to the Privy Council, which found against Mackonochie in the remaining three charges; and he was ordered to pay all costs.]

It will be hard to bear at home. I hope people will be temperate, but I fear great discontent, and not a few rows.

The coach left Palmerston about 1 and it was 6 before we got to Dunedin. The road, especially from Blueskin Bay was most lovely. The Bush scenery looked wonderfully rich. I found Edwards waiting for me at the Octagon, and letters from home at the Parsonage. All well, thank God! Edwards was in poor spirits about my prospects.

Whilst on the coach to Dunedin Jenner wrote a reply to a letter of criticism from James Smith concerning distorted reports of a 'ritualistic' service that he had been part of in England:

My dear Mr. Smith,
I cannot be surprised that you should write as you have done. If it were true
that I had acted, or rather spoken, as has been suggested, I should indeed be
unworthy of your support and confidence, or of the support and confidence
of any faithful English churchman ... The banners and candles would, no
doubt, be thought 'excesses' in this colony, but in England they are so
commonly seen that few people are offended at them. I believe that the
Black Days are observed in the English church, that they were deliberately
replaced in the Reformed Kalander after having been once omitted. Several
of them are religiously observed at several of the Colleges in Oxford and
Cambridge. Indeed, nothing is more common throughout England than to
hold the annual commemoration of the building or restoration of a Church
on the festival, whether black or red, of the saint whose name the Church
bears ... The account given of my sermon is false and calumnious ... My
language was misrepresented most outrageously. I am made to advocate a
doctrine or practise which I reprobate. I care little for this, but I do care for
the prospect of alienating such friends as you. The truth is, my dear Mr.
Smith, I am nearly wearied out with this business. The isolation, the
humiliation of my position – which culminated last Sunday in my having
to 'sit under' a lay reader – have well nigh broken me down. I feel inclined
to let matters take their chance, and give myself no further trouble, and ask
my friends to leave me to my fate. I shall see you no doubt in a day or two.
Pray forgive me for leaving off abruptly. I am writing under difficulties in
the coach on my way to Dunedin. I only got your letter last night, and I am
anxious to lose no time in coming in.
I am etc. H. L. Jenner.

March 6. I went with all the Edwardses' by the two o'clock steamer to Port Chalmers. Unspeakably beautiful was the sail down the bay. The islands and wooded banks looked heavenly, revealing fresh beauty at every turn of the circuitous channel.

We landed at Port Chalmers, and walked about the place. I had no sooner set foot on the jetty, when an oldish waterman (apparently) placed himself in the way, holding out a basket of peaches. 'Take a peach', said he, in a tipsy voice. 'No thank you,' said I, and tried to escape. It was useless. 'Ah, but you must', said my friend, 'you are our Bishop, you know', the word 'Bishop" being pronounced with explosive emphasis. Once more I resisted, but I was defeated, and to get rid of the man, I took a peach which I put in my coat pocket, and on which I presently *sat*, to the detriment of the coat.

I fear people who are addicted to 'nobblers', are very commonly my supporters; for I had no sooner gained the deck of the *Rangitoto* which was to take me to the Bluff, than a fishy-eyed man, of vast stature, accosted me with much fervid sympathy, and I had no small difficulty in getting him to leave me alone.

At 6 p.m. the *Rangitoto* got under way, and steamed out through the Heads. There was a large number of passengers on board (*too* large, in fact, for, as I heard afterwards, the captain was heavily fined at Melbourne, for carrying more than his lawful number).

March 7. At 9 we arrived at the Bluff. We passed several islands, e.g. Ruapuke and the Dog Island, and we got an excellent view of Stewart's Island, which appears to be very beautiful. The Harbour is excellent, when the entrance, which is rather intricate, is once passed. It is the port of the province of Southland, and ought to be a more important place than it is.
The settlement, consisting of a few small houses, is called Campbell Town. There is a railway hence to Invercargill, a distance of 17 miles.

At 10.30 the train came in from Invercargill, bringing Mr. Butts, the postmaster to meet me. We returned together at 11, reaching Invercargill at 12. A most forlorn place, this, the most Southern town in the world. It is built on a vast plain. The area of the 'town' is immense, the streets being as wide as Regent Street: but the early promise of the place has never been fulfilled, and the dwellings are far between, and moreover, are rapidly decaying. All are of wood. The *trottoirs* [pavements] of the streets are also of wood, a sort of grating formed by laying pieces 4 inches square, across, about 2 inches apart. An unspeakably dreary appearance is caused by the dead trees of a half cleared bush remaining close to the town, and sometimes even amongst the houses, on the outskirts.

March 8. Tanner took me to the 'Club', and introduced me to several of the Southland 'Squattocracy': and to Mr. Kingsland, the Choir master, who is an Ashford man, and knows all Kent.

March 11. Indoors most of the day. Mr. Oldham called. I was with him for half an hour conversing most amicably. In the evening there was a grand 'tea fight' at the Club, which went off very successfully. Mr. Tanner introduced me to everybody. I made two speeches, which were very well received, and (I was told) converted many opponents. Mr. McCullock (who is the resident magistrate) proposed a vote of thanks and a welcome to me, which was carried by acclamation. A great number of people were present. Mr. Oldham did not appear. There was some singing, in part of which I joined. It was rather poor.

The 'tea fight' was reported in the Southland Times a few day later:

CHURCH OF ENGLAND TEA MEETING TO WELCOME BISHOP JENNER

Last Thursday evening a large number of members of the Church of England assembled at the Southland Club to welcome Bishop Jenner on his arrival in this part of the diocese. The proceedings took the pleasant form off a social tea meeting which was most numerously and influentially attended, over 150 being present, including members of the other religious bodies.

A liberal supply of refreshments was displayed on a table across one end of the room, the remaining being left clear for promenade. The room presented a very cheerful and animated appearance. There was no stiffness or constraint, all conversed socially together, and with the distinguished guest, who seemed to win golden opinions on all sides, especially from the ladies.

In his address Bishop Jenner said that he had arrived among them as a stranger under the most peculiar circumstances, and it was most gratifying to be received with such courtesy and social feeling. He confessed he had received a good many hard knocks since his arrival, but there might be no harm in that for, if they were honestly and sincerely given, he believed they would be like blows which, falling on the head of a stake, drove it more firmly into the ground, (applause) and they would make him fit more closely to the position he hoped to hold, (applause).

He went on, that a social meeting was not a fitting time for controversy, but he would say this, that he hoped as they had so kindly received him they would make allowances for differences of education, and peculiarities of modes of thought, and say:
'We dare say you mean well, but we don't quite understand you yet,' and that they would endeavour to understand him, that they would try what good, and not what harm they could extract from him, and they might find him not so dark as he had been painted. Some people delighted in dark colours, he preferred bright ones (applause). Let them try a new plan, and paint in lighter colours.

March 12. At 2.30 I left for Riverton, on a chestnut horse. Mr. Tanner riding with me part of the way. The road passes through a very pretty bush, the 'town belt', I think, of Invercargill. It was full of Bell birds and Tuis, which sing delightfully. Many of the trees were on fire, a further clearing being in progress. A sad pity it seemed.
A little further on, a well built wooden bridge spans the estuary of the *Orete*, or *New River*. There is a turnpike gate at one end. I suggested that clergymen ought to pass through without paying, but the toll-taker civilly enough, informed me that it was private property on which no exemptions were ever allowed.

Two miles more brought me to an extensive sandy plain peopled by innumerable rabbits, which are becoming a serious nuisance, I heard. All this time I was approaching the ocean, and after a five mile ride from Invercargill, I emerged upon a beach stretching for 14 miles, until Riverton is reached. It was nearly low water, and the riding was very good, or would have been if my steed had been better behaved. He was a terrible slug, and shied violently at all the common and uncommon objects on the sea shore.

Very bleak and bare was the country indeed. Seawards, through the haze, beyond the mighty rollers that eternally break on the flat sandy beach, rise the grand heights of Stewart's Island. Behind, the Bluff appears, looking like an island, as Bishop Selwyn notices in his journal. Now and then you catch a glimpse of snow-capped mountains, to the north. These are part of the Moonlight Range. As you advance along the sands, the bay curves suddenly round, and a beautiful wooded headland seems to bar all progress in that direction. This is some distance beyond Riverton.

There was no lack of objects of interest on the beach. Immense quantities of sea-fowl accompanied me, of several kinds and sizes. I was struck with a black and white bird, with a red bill, about the size of a curlew. It was singularly tame and inquisitive, and would run almost under the horse's feet as I rode along. There were sea weeds and shells and sponges without end. Innumerable vertebra and other bones of whales lay about everywhere, some of a monstrous size. And in a space of 7 miles, I passed three vessels that had been wrecked at various times, more or less imbedded in the sand.

One must have been lost many many years ago, for the timbers alone remain, and of these only the tops are visible. A terrible and hopeless lee shore, this, I should imagine. These ships must have been caught in a 'southerly burster', and gone ashore in running for the Bluff.

About 5 miles from Riverton, a river, the *Waimatook*(?) has to be crossed. I had some little difficulty in finding a practicable ford.

It was about 6 when I got to Riverton. The way into the town from the beach took me through a Maori cemetery (there being a village close at hand, though very few of the huts are left,) and past their little wooden chapel, the gates of which were decorated with crosses. Then came a quarter of a mile of half clear bush where 'English grass', growing in profusion, makes a pleasant surface for the horse's feet. I asked my way to Mr. Oldham's, which is at the further end of the town.

He had expected me earlier. I received great kindness and attention from Mr. & Mrs. O. In the evening the churchwardens and others came in.

March 13. An excellent night's rest. I was up by 8, and after breakfast set to work finishing up letters for the horse mail. At 12, Mr. Nurse arrived, with another gentleman, and at 2 we all set out, Mr. Oldham accompanying us part of the way, for Mr. Nurse's residence Blackwater Station, about 8 miles from Riverton.

For the first three miles there was a fair road, then we struck off across a rough moorland country, through tracts of fern and flax. The fern is the common 'brake' of New Zealand, *Pteris aquiliua var esculenta.* It has quite the same effect as our brake. The flax, i.e. *Phormium-tenax* is very fine here, often above my head as I rode through it. My horse goes better in company with others, but we were very nearly coming to grief in crossing a boggy place in a steep gully where the horse sunk nearly to his shoulders in a very tenacious clay. Mr. Nurse's house is charmingly placed on the northern (the sunnyside here) edge of a most lovely birch bush. The birch, is a splendid tree with a white bark, the branches and trunks of the older specimens clothed with the most luxuriant growth of mosses, lichens and ferns. A prostrate trunk is a perfect cryptogamic garden. In a birch bush, there is hardly any undergrowth or 'scrub'; in which it differs from all other N.Z. forests.

March 15. I was awakened at 6.30 by the combined songs of Bell birds, Tuis and woodhens. The latter makes a great and not melodious noise, but the other two birds are charming.
I sent my letters and journal up to this date, to the post at Wallacetown, 3 miles off.

I greatly admired the exceeding beauty and snugness of their little homestead. There is a large paddock of excellent grass in front, with the stockyard (for Mr. Marten feeds bullocks, not sheep) in the middle.

Their garden is fenced on the north by the finest sweetbriar hedge I ever saw, to which Cabbage trees standing at regular intervals, give a singularly picturesque character.

The bush, after running in a straight line on each side of the house for about half a mile, makes a turn at right angles on the western side, and then begins a sort of fringe of Manuka trees, which, seen from a little distance: are marvellously beautiful. The habit of the foliage is light and feathery. These specimens are 40 feet high and are set off by a background of lofty black and white pine, and other forest trees, of which there seems an endless variety.

In the evening Mr. C. R. M. and I sang some duets, and he accompanied himself and me in various songs. He has a remarkably good tenor voice (with a chest B flat) and sings extremely well. The heat has been great all day. No wind at all.

March 16. The morning was chilly 'till about 9 a.m. when the sun began to have great power. Mr. Marten took me into the bush after breakfast. It was difficult to find the path, which indeed hardly deserved the name, being swampy and much overgrown. But the trouble of penetrating into the bush was well repaid by the sight of several exquisite ferns. *Hymeniphyllum Tunbridgeuze* is quite common here, and another and larger species of the same genus, *H. Colensoi*, is found in good sized clumps.

As we were returning, I became aware of a most overpowering stench which I could not at all account for. It was nearly an hour before my nostrils got rid of it. I discovered that it arose from my having accidentally come in contact with the most offensive tree, I should think in the world, the odour of which is exactly described and by no means exaggerated, by its generic and specific names, viz. *Coprosma foetidiss* (stinkwood).

In the afternoon the heat of the day being intense, I sat reading indoors till 5, when I went out for a walk by myself. I entered the bush in another direction, where the walking was pretty good, as many of the trees had been felled. I saw an amazing number of ferns, again.

The commonest is a *Polystichum*, which grows everywhere. There are no *fern trees* about, but a *tree fern* in its earlier stage, occurs here and there. This is *Cyathea dealbata*. I sat down with a book for half an hour, on the trunk of a prostrate tree, and watched the birds, which, it seems, are always busy and excited just before sundown. I noticed some good sized pigeons, a great number of Tuis, N.Z. 'Tom tits' and robins and *ought* to have seen some ka-kas, a large grey parrot, which abound here, and is very destructive in the gardens, but none appeared. The native robin is exactly like ours in habits and manner, but he is dressed in a dark grey, almost black coat with a dirty white waistcoat.

March 19. I meant to have left for the North this morning, but the Martens persuaded me to remain till Monday. And indeed I shall not be sorry to have my Palm Sunday in a civilized place.

Today there was a ceremony in the stock yard, which I was glad to have seen once, but should not care to see again. The branding of some of the stock. This, it seems, is required by law. The animals had been mustered and driven into the paddock, the day before, by the younger Martens, armed with tremendous stock whips. This morning they were driven into the stock yard, which only just held them, and where they did nothing but hustle and tumble over each other, and get their horns and legs entangled. When a bullock was wanted, a rope was thrown over his horns, and another round one of this hind legs: both ropes were then hauled in, and made fast to the stockyard fence. The struggles of some of the creatures were prodigious. One young bull gave very great trouble. He bellowed and fought most energetically, and was only subdued by the united efforts of the whole establishment, ladies excepted, including myself. The brand, a red hot iron, is applied to the hip, and it is not pleasant to hear it hissing into the flesh. Mr. Marten's brand is OX. Every stock owner has a distinctive one, which must be registered. The ropes used today were new ones, made of *Phormium*, and marvellously well they stood the severe strain to which they were subjected.

In the evening, the young ladies having borrowed 'Alice' from a neighbour, I read it aloud, to the gratification of the company. Southland surely cannot be in so hopeless a state as people make out if it possesses a copy of 'Alice'.

March 20. The greater part of the day was fine, but there was rain in the evening. I spent all the forenoon in my retreat in the garden, reading. After dinner Mr. Tanner came and stayed an hour. I had a conversation with him on the state of affairs. I observe a desire springing up, that I should get the members of the Church out of the mess they are in, by resigning before the Diocesan Synod comes to vote on the question of my claims. But I have positively made up my mind not to resign. The Synod will have to decide (although it is a case not for the Diocesan but the General Synod, and ought to have been decided last October,) whether the engagement made with me by the New Zealand Church, in virtue of which I received the episcopal character, is to be fulfilled or not.

The non-fulfilment by the Church here of its side of the contract would inflict on me an injury such as few have ever suffered, and for which there *must* be a remedy. The bitter hostility of my opponents and traducers. The hard, unsympathizing bearing of Bishop Harper. The degradation to which that unheard of step, the inhibiting, has exposed me. And the unscrupulous electioneering tactics resorted to by, or on behalf of the 'opposition' candidates for seats in the Synod, justify me, I do think, in reminding churchmen, that, although I have kept my *claims* in the background hitherto, preferring to be chosen by the voluntary action of the church, the main question to be decided is whether anything has been done to vitiate the engagement under which I was consecrated. I must put all into the form of a letter, and publish it before the 7 April.

March 21. Palm Sunday. A most violent storm of hail and rain at 9 a.m. I said Matins and read the Epistle and Gospel, with a short piece on the Passion, which I had translated from L de G. on board the *Ruahine*. C. R. M. played Venite, Benedicite and Benedictus on the piano, and we sang them to (1) Farrant in F (2) 8th Tune 1st Ending (3) 1st Tune 1st

Ending. It was a treat to join in the dear old tunes again. It rained and blew hard the whole day. A "Southerly Burster" this, and very cold and raw it was. At 6.30 I said Evensong, and we chanted again. Magn. to 1st and Nunc D. to 3rd tune. We sang "Gloria laus et honor" after service.

My thoughts were much at Preston today, and dwelling on the services there this week. The scantiness of Church privileges here is quite awful. At Invercargill there are no services in Holy Week, except on Good Friday.

March 22. Monday in H. W. A most tremendous gale, still from S.W. with torrents of rain nearly all day. At 1 I left my kind friends, and rode to Invercargill. C. R. M. accompanied me most part of the way. The rain came on so furiously that we had to take shelter for an hour in the stable of an accommodation house. The landlord came out, and was most obliging. He insisted on lending me a white mackintosh, in which I must have looked a pretty figure, but which kept me quite dry. The wind today was more violent than I ever remember to have felt it. I got to Invercargill at 3.

March 23. Tuesday in H. W. The gale still continues (and seems even to increase in violence) with heavy rain. It makes it extremely awkward for me, since it is impossible to leave in such weather. The roads, not to mention the rivers, being utterly impassable, and the sea frightful. I had arranged to spend Good Friday at Tokomairiro, and Easter at Green Island (Dunedin) but this is out of the question now. The good people of Tuapeka have been passing some idiotic resolutions about me, nearly identical with those adopted at Queenstown, only sillier and ruder. So I read today in a Southland paper.

March 26. Good Friday. Incessant rain all day. On the whole a better Good Friday than I had hoped for. The services were tolerable, and there were opportunities of retirement. Matins at 11. About 35 present. The singing was not bad, but *Te Deum* sounded very odd today. Hymn 100 (A & M 1861)[O come and mourn with me a while] quite *did* for me. I could hardly sing a line of it. I got on better in 101 [When I survey the wondrous cross,] which is not a Preston Hymn. We had Evensong at 7. Only 12 people present. The singing was very poor. There was no sermon. I wonder whether they had all the usual Good Friday services at Preston. The dear old parish was much in my thoughts today.

March 27. Easter Eve. I took a walk with Mr. and Mrs. Tanner, in the forenoon. There is a hitch it seems about Easter Day. The Paschal full moon happens *here* on Sunday (tomorrow) so, according to the letter of the rule, Easter Day ought to be tomorrow week, and in the government almanacks it is actually so marked. I believe there is likely to be some difficulty and confusion in the matter. In the evening I drilled the S. John's Choir. We had a very satisfactory practice.

March 28. Easter Day. A very fine day. Not much like former Easters, however. The services were fairly attended, and the singing was much improved. Most of the faults that I had pointed out being corrected. Not more than 20 communicants. I sat in the choir, and sang alto. I was following the Preston services all day in my mind.

March 29. Easter Monday. Mr. C. R. Marten, who came into town on Saturday for the Easter services, went out with Mr. Tanner to get people to vote for the *right* candidates for seats in the Deanery Synod. They were very successful and will probably turn the scale. Not that it matters much.

March 30. Easter Tuesday. At 2 I took leave of the Tanners with much regret. They have been *most* kind and attentive. I went by rail to the Bluff, hoping to set off this evening, by the *Gothenburg*, to Dunedin. She ought to have arrived from Melbourne, but did not. I slept at Mr. Longuet's.

Mr. O'Toole his son-in-law was at the house all the evening. He takes a very right view of the present controversy. He and Mr. Longuet seem firm believers in the future prosperity of Southland. *Ainsi soit il.* (So be it). There is no doubt that gold exists everywhere in the province, as well as in Stewart's Island. Mr. Longuet told me also that Platinum is found in considerable quantities in the sand of the beach to the westward of the Bluff. And he showed me a small tin box full of rubies, some of a respectable size, which he had picked out of the same sand. He says there is 'any amount' of them.

March 31. After breakfast Mr. Longuet took me out on the beach. It was low water, and he had a large landing net with which he proposed to catch some shrimps. It was wonderful what success he had. The shrimps abounded in the pools left by the receding tide, whence Mr. Longuet scooped them out with his net by hundreds. They were remarkably fine and large. There are prawns, it seems, to be caught on the rocks further out; and oysters are found all along the coast. Fish of various kinds may be caught, but few people trouble themselves to catch them. That is one evil of the scanty population. There is not enough men for all the branches of industry that offer themselves, so the resources of the Colony remain undeveloped.

At 12 Capt. Underwood of the *Gothenburg* came up to call on my host; and with him some of the passengers from Melbourne, two gentlemen and four young ladies. Mr. Tanner and his sister with Miss Bree came by the 3 o'clock train to the Bluff. They, the two ladies, were going northward, and had taken their passage by the *Lord Ashley*. This made me regret that I was committed to the *Gothenburg,* but I was very comfortable in her.

Both vessels left together, and kept together the greater part of the trip to Otago Heads. The sea was perfectly smooth. This is a charming way of travelling. At 7.30 we had tea, a very good meal. I produced the shrimps, which Mrs. Longuet had boiled and put up for me. They were highly appreciated, but they did not come up to the Pegwell Bay *Crustaceans.* They were pink, not brown, when boiled.

April 1. I had an excellent night's rest, and when I awoke we were stopping just outside the Otago Heads. This was about 5 a.m. I had another nap, and turned out at 6.30. Breakfast was served at 8, after we had anchored off Port Chalmers. The morning was most glorious.

After breakfast the *Golden Age* came alongside, and took me and others up to Dunedin. It was very warm. The view, or rather views, of the Port and Bay were indescribably lovely. It is singular, that N.Z. scenery always looks best in the morning. This autumn scene will always remain one of the choicest of my gallery of mental pictures.

April 4. Low Sunday. I drove Mr. Jone's buggy and pair into Dunedin, for a service at S. Paul's. The horses were rather fiery, and wanted to gallop *down* all the hills, and as the hills were very steep and had awkward turns, a good deal of driving was required. The roads were in a dreadful state, showers of mud were perpetually flying about, and (unlike the mud thrown by Messrs. Young, Watt & Co) sticking wherever it fell. So we were pretty figures when we arrived at the Parsonage.

There was a small congregation, and 21 communicants. Edwards preached a remarkably good sermon on Job XIX.25. Wonderfully apropos of the Synod next Wednesday, was the 2nd Lesson, Acts 1. The mail brought no letters from Preston, a heavy disappointment. The alteration of the mail day, consequent upon the discontinuance of the Panama line, must have put them out at home.

April 5. At 3.30 I drove the 'Express' and pair to Dunedin. The horses went much more soberly today. I remained at the Parsonage. Messrs. Smith and Granger came in the evening, and we talked over the state of affairs. Mr. S. has a resolution to propose at the Synod which will raise the whole question of my appointment.

I sent a letter to the Bishop of Christchurch, protesting against the treatment I had received from him, and calling on him, as Primate of the N.Z. Church, to see that justice is done to me.

At supper we had a dish of what the newspapers here call 'luscious bivalves' i.e. oysters, from Stewart's Island. Most excellent they were. Edwards and Granger wanted me to stay at Dunedin to meet Bishop Harper, but I did not think it advisable, for his sake, or my own. So I leave tomorrow for Blueskin Bay.

Jenner's letter to the Bishop of Christchurch and Primate of the New Zealand Church

My Lord,

I beg leave to address your Lordship in your two-fold capacity, as Metropolitan of the New Zealand Church, and Bishop, for the present, of the Diocese of Dunedin. I trust that your Lordship will communicate the few words that follow to the Standing Commission of the General Synod, and to the Diocesan Synod of Dunedin.

1. Referring first to the resolution passed by the General Synod last October, in which I am requested, for the sake of the peace of the Church, to resign my claim to the position of Bishop of Dunedin, I beg to state that, having, by careful enquiry, and by experience gained during a tour through the Diocese, satisfied myself that the peace of the Church will in no wise be secured by such resignation, I respectfully decline to comply with the request.

2. In the second place, to approach a most painful subject, I am reluctantly constrained to advert to the disgraceful and humiliating position which, by an arbitrary exercise, not to call it stretch, of your Lordship's authority, I have been forced to occupy during the last two months. My Lord, I beg to record, in the face of the Church, my most solemn protest against the insult offered to me, and to the office which we bear in common.

It is not only to the private letter wherein your Lordship urged me to 'abstain from all attempts to officiate, or in any way to exercise my office as a Bishop or as a Minister of our Church in Otago and

Southland,' *that I allude. For, having myself resolved before I heard from your Lordship not to officiate in New Zealand until my status should be more clearly defined, I should have had no reason to complain had you contented yourself with a private intimation of your wishes. But I refer also to the telegram,* ('Bishop Jenner has come out without authority from me; nor do I propose giving him authority to officiate in Otago or Southland. H.J.C., Christchurch',) *sent by your Lordship to a gentleman at Dunedin applying to you in the avowed character of spokesman of my opponents, and requesting an answer for the satisfaction of those with whom he was acting; and to your letter to your commissary, the Rev. E. G. Edwards, requiring him to communicate to the clergy of the diocese your refusal to allow me to officiate. And I say that these three utterances taken together, can bear but one interpretation, namely, that it was your Lordship's intention, deliberately and publicly, to inhibit me from ministering even as an ordinary clergyman in that diocese, for the oversight of which I received consecration.*

The natural effect of this degrading inhibition has been not only to place me under a very serious disadvantage in my character of aspirant to the See of Dunedin; but also to give great encouragement to those who are banded together in opposition to my aims. For it is to be borne in mind, that the measures adopted by your Lordship were those suggested, not to say dictated, by the opponents themselves. Once more, my Lord, I protest against the attitude thus assumed by you.

3. In conclusion, I beg leave to remind your Lordship, and through you the Church in New Zealand, of a circumstance which I cannot but think has been unjustifiably kept out of sight, the existence, namely, of an engagement of the strongest moral, if not legal, obligation between this branch of the Church and myself, in virtue of which alone I am in possession of the Episcopal character.

Thus, my Lord, I present myself, not for the first time, before the New Zealand Church, as a party to this solemn contract, the fulfilment of which I claim as due to me on the commonest principles of justice, honour, and morality. And unless it can be shown that the contract has been nullified by any act of mine, I respectfully call upon your Lordship, as head of the New Zealand Church, to take such measures as the law of the Church, prescribes for its fulfilment, that is to say, for placing me in actual and formal possession of the See, for the occupation of which, and for no other purpose, I was consecrated a Bishop.

I have the honour to be, &c.,
HENRY LASCELLES JENNER, D.D.,

April 6. At 8 a.m. I started by coach for Dr. Buchanan's station on the Port Chalmers' road. The coachman by mistake took me some distance past the house, and I had to carry my bag a mile back.

The Buchanans have a very nice place. They gave me some breakfast, and then took me in their 'express' to the Waitati [local market]. The last time I travelled this road, the weather was wretched, and prevented me from enjoying the scenery. Today it was very different. The beauty of the prospect defies all description. For the first four miles after leaving Dr. Buchanan's house the road gets more exquisitely lovely every step. The greater part is through the bush, which is being rapidly cleared, especially where Manuka timber is growing. This is the firewood of New Zealand. It burns to perfection, and I imagine Dunedin is supplied from the forests we passed. It is cut up and sent down the steep hillside on which it grows, by means of wooden trough like 'ways'. But the timber is not all Manuka. On the level ground on the top of the hill overlooking Port Chalmers there is a profuse conglomeration of all kinds of trees, black and white pines, cabbage trees, wild fig (as it is called, though only on account of the resemblance in leaf and branch to our fig) supplejack, and numberless other creepers, twisted and matted among the branches, and the brilliant leaved tutu, spreading luxuriantly over the road side banks. Tree ferns of course here and there.

The view, from this point of the bay near Pt. Chalmers, with its islands and promontories, the bush just mentioned in the foreground, and the deep blue of the limitless Pacific in the distance, I do not believe can be surpassed, if equalled, anywhere on this earth.

The road is said to be clumsily engineered. Certainly it appears to wind about, to a needless extent, but this is an advantage as far as the scenery is concerned. At one turn, at least four miles from our starting place, we stopped, and, looking back, the city of Dunedin appeared quite close to us, on account of the zigzag course we had steered. The approach to the Waitati, a very long incline, very steep in some places, is almost as fine as the ascent from Dunedin.

At the Waitati Hotel, Mr. Pitt was waiting for me and drove me across the sands of Blueskin Bay, to his house, which bears the name of Warrington. The situation is magnificent, almost on the edge of the low cliff, which here forms a rampart against the Pacific. There is a noble view over the ocean. The Otago Heads on the South extremity of the bay are close enough to allow all vessels going in or out to be very plainly observed. Mr. Pitt feeds a few hundred sheep, and keeps turkeys (magnificent black ones), poultry, pigs, and several horses. There is a good extent of cleared land, with English grass appearing everywhere, a cabbage tree here and there, serves for a land mark.

April 7. The weather which last night was threatening, has cleared up. The morning is calm and bright, and the bay and ocean beyond are looking magnificent. Turn in what direction you will, the view, especially in the early morning, is exquisite. Autumn is rapidly advancing, yet the Bush is as green, and the foliage as massive as ever.

We went to the Waitati at 9.30. There was a cattle show. The exhibition was not very wonderful, except that here again the roots were marvellously fine. A mangelwurzel weighing 38 lbs, grown without manure, is, I am told, nothing uncommon. There was a magnificent display of butter, the best I ever saw. Most of the roughs of Otago were congregated at the show. At least it is to be hoped that the province does not contain many more. We had a very pleasant picnic lunch, just inside the bush which skirts the road here.

There was an absurd paragraph in the *Otago Times*, today, copied from a Scottish paper, to the effect that a Ritualistic Free Church is to be formed, of which I am the Patriarch! What idiots people are. No doubt I shall be held responsible for this scheme. The Synod meets today.

April 9. Mr. Pitt went to Waikouaiti for the election and was away all day. In the afternoon walked down to the Ocean beach with Mrs. Pitt. A quantity of greenstone implements and weapons had been found there, and I was not without hope of picking up a few specimens, but all I could find were a few chips, showing that there had been a workshop in the neighbourhood.

Mr. Pitt returned at 8. I saw a newspaper today, and Mr. Pitt brought the astounding intelligence that the Synod went on sitting until 6 this morning, and had not adjourned when the information left. What this means, I have not an idea.

The Bishop's attempts to make out that there had been no inhibition, though he admitted that he had publicly refused to give me permission to officiate, were pitiful enough. In his opening address he distinctly implies that justice to me is quite a secondary consideration! Mr. Smith's speeches yesterday were very strong. I only hope he will not overdo the thing.

April 10. The luxury of a soft water bath is attained by a bucket full brought every morning to my door, which opens into the garden. I walked out on the rocks before breakfast. The clear bright pools of water left by the tide, and lined with seaweed of all colours are of surpassing loveliness. The Ocean was quite calm; a steamer was just entering the Heads, and a brig becalmed, was trying to get clear of the land, not far off. The sun, even at 8.30, had great power.

After breakfast (the principal feature of the breakfasts here is the most exquisite honey I ever tasted,) I continue my letters home. At 2 the papers came. The proceedings of the Synod caused me much pain and perplexity. Mr. Smith spoke for more than six hours on my side. He rose to *reply* at 5.15 a.m. after in vain urging an adjournment, which it was surely disgraceful to refuse. At 6 the division was taken, and the lay opposition, elected by the votes of not even nominal churchmen, carried my rejection. Bishop Harper displayed a strong bias against me throughout. Of course, I utterly refuse to accept this as any real expression of the mind of the Church.

The Oamaru papers covered the Synod in full, which, given the length of the meeting – over two days – took up many columns of fine print. Local papers covering other parts of New Zealand gave their readers a more edited and readable summary of the events. A fairly accurate précis was published in the *Wellington Independent*:

The first Synod of the Diocese of Dunedin met on April 7ᵗʰ and was presided over by the Primate, Bishop Henry Harper. Present – 8 clergy and 26 laity. The Primate stated in his opening address that the Synod had been called for the purpose of nominating a Bishop for the new diocese – for which nomination the assent of the majority of the clergy, and of a majority of the lay-synodsmen was necessary. The Bishop so nominated would then have to be approved by the General Synod or its Standing Committee. The Synod had peculiar duties to perform, inasmuch as a Bishop (Dr Jenner) had been avowedly consecrated by the late Archbishop Longley for the see of Dunedin, yet the last General Synod had requested him to withdraw his claims to the bishopric, for 'the peace of the Church'. Still he felt that, should the Diocesan Synod express its wish to accept Dr Jenner, the General Synod might fairly be asked to reconsider its determination – since no discussion had been raised in the Synod either upon the alleged irregularity of Dr Jenner's appointment, or upon charges of ritualism, but merely whether the church members in Otago would accept him and raise the necessary funds for the endowment of the See. And this not seemingly probable to the General Synod, owing to the general mistrust of Dr Jenner's views, it was decided to ask him to withdraw any claims he might be supposed to have for the sake of 'the peace of the Church'. This being the case, he, the Primate was only carrying out the wishes of the General Synod in declining to permit Bishop Jenner to perform any duties of his episcopal office in the diocese until his claims or position had been finally settled.

[The expression 'any duties of his episcopal office' would not have covered his duties as a priest, so it is hard to see why these were included in the inhibition.]

The Primate laid upon the table a letter of Bishop Jenner's addressed to himself – 1. Declining to resign his claim to 'the position of Bishop of Dunedin'. 2. Protesting against the inhibition to officiate in the diocese. And 3. Calling upon the Primate 'as head of the New Zealand Church, to take such measures as the law of the Church prescribes, for placing him in actual and formal possession of the see, for the occupation of which, and for no other purpose, he was consecrated a bishop.'

On the 8th Mr James Smith, a barrister, in a long and able speech moved the following motion;
That having considered the origin of, and the circumstances connected with, the appointment of Bishop Jenner to the see of Dunedin, and in particular the resolution of the late Rural Deanery Board of Otago and Southland, passed on the 21st February 1867, whereby the duty of receiving Bishop Jenner as the Bishop of Dunedin was solemnly affirmed by that body, duly representing as it then did, the church in this diocese, this Synod hereby declares and resolves that the good faith of the Church of England in this diocese has been distinctly pledged to the acceptance of Bishop Jenner as bishop of this diocese, and that therefore his said appointment to the see of Dunedin should, in justice to him, and for the honour of the church, be duly confirmed – unless it can, and, within a reasonable time, actually be proved before the proper tribunal of the church for the trial of ecclesiastical offences, that Bishop has been in point of either doctrine or discipline, unfaithful to his ordination vows as a minister of the Church of England – and that therefore this Synod hereby requests the General Synod Standing Committee to give effect to Bishop Jenner's said appointment by formally sanctioning the same, provided that no such charge as above mentioned shall be brought and duly established within three months from this date.

Mr Smith said that the question before the Synod was:

Were they or were they not bound in honour to consider Bishop Jenner as to all intents and purposes, actually Bishop of the diocese, and only awaiting the legal confirmation of his appointment at the hands of the duly constituted authorities?' 'It was not,' *he contended,* 'the functions of the Synod to judge Bishop Jenner on matters of doctrine or of discipline – if the opponents of the Bishop considered that he had been unfaithful to his ordination vows they should proceed against him in the proper courts. Bishop Selwyn, acting for the Church of New Zealand, had procured Bishop Jenner's appointment in exactly the same way as that in which he had procured the appointment of the Bishop of Christchurch, and the church-members in Otago were as much bound to accept Bishop Jenner as church-members in Christchurch were bound to accept Bishop Harper – unless they could substantiate some charge against him. And more than this, the Rural Deanery Board at its various meetings had again and again acknowledged Bishop Jenner as the Bishop of the diocese, and so set aside any question as to the irregularity of the appointment.

The Synod was not competent to decide upon matters of doctrine, and therefore unless Bishop Jenner was proved to be unfit for his office by some competent tribunal, the Synod was morally bound to acknowledge his claim. This view had been urged by Bishop Selwyn in his letter of 22nd October 1868 to the Rural Deanery Board, in which the Bishop says:-

'The Rev. H. Jenner having been nominated by the Archbishop of Canterbury, and consecrated under Royal Mandate, Bishop of the See of Dunedin, this Board recognises the duty of making preparations for his reception by providing a suitable residence, and completing the requisite endowment.'

The Rev. Mr. Gifford observed that the General Synod has requested Bishop Jenner to resign his claims not because it had judged him guilty of any unsoundness of doctrine or breach of discipline, which had not been considered, but simply because the endowment fund for the proposed diocese was insufficient for the support of a bishop, and that owing to the objection felt against Bishop Jenner there was little prospect of this fund being completed. He reminded the Synod of the words of the Bishop of Wellington at the General Synod, speaking against the resolution asking Bishop Jenner to resign:

'If this resolution went home in its present bare form, it would be the greatest blow that could possibly be given to the synodical system, as it would be undermining all confidence in its fairness. Thus the system by which they trusted to regenerate the whole church would be brought into disrepute by doing what would be considered unjust. It would thus encourage those very practices which it most condemned. If they called upon Bishop Jenner to resign without giving him a fair trial, all quiet, right-thinking men in England would condemn the Synod. The Synod should act as a deliberative assembly, but not as a judicial body; and as they desired to uphold the synodical system, he hoped they would not attempt to condemn Bishop Jenner without a fair, careful and impartial hearing.'

Mr Gifford therefore asked the Synod to 'confirm an existing appointment, unless before a proper tribunal, grounds were alleged and proved why this should not be done.'

Mr W. Carr Young said that at first, before he knew decidedly Bishop Jenner's views, he had felt bound to support him, but on going to England in April 1867, and finding the Bishop taking part in the most extreme ritualistic services, he had at once told the Archbishop of Canterbury that such practices would be distasteful to the majority of church people in Otago, and had requested Bishop Jenner to delay leaving England until he could hear from Dunedin the opinions of church members there. Bishop Jenner had however come out without awaiting the decision of the General Synod, and therefore he must accept his present unpleasant position as the result of his own conduct.

Mr. Ashcroft, while disavowing all sympathy with extreme ritualism, said that the supposed ritualistic practices of Dr Jenner were the sole ground for all the opposition against him. This, however, was not the proper question before the Synod – it was not a question of ritualism versus Protestantism – but of justice or injustice.

'Was not Bishop Jenner expressly consecrated by the Archbishop of Canterbury, who was moved to consecrate him by the late Primate of New Zealand? And did not the Rural Deanery Board – the body whose functions this Synod now possesses, and whose obligations therefore as representing the church are binding upon us – did they not expressly, by the resolution of the 21st February 1867*, accept Bishop Jenner, and by that act condone all previous irregularities?'

[*'The Rev. H. Jenner having been nominated by the Archbishop of Canterbury, and consecrated under Royal Mandate, Bishop of the See of Dunedin, this Board recognises the duty of making preparations for his reception by providing a suitable residence, and completing the requisite endowment.']

'And did they not, on three several subsequent occasions, refuse to rescind this resolution? If so he considered they were bound by every principle of justice and honour to confirm the appointment.',

The Rev Mr Coffey said that Bishop Jenner had promised not to introduce ritualism into the diocese, but they wanted a Bishop who would not only say 'I will not introduce ritualism,' *but also affirm that,* 'I will also prohibit the introduction of ritualism in the diocese over which I preside.'

The Hon. Major Richardson said the whole affair connected with the appointment of Bishop Jenner was irregular. And although there might be a duty to perform towards Bishop Jenner, yet there was a more pressing and more paramount duty to the Christian church in Otago, which the Synod had to perform. On this ground he opposed the nomination of Bishop Jenner, and urged them to begin again.

There was great danger in allowing ritualistic doctrines and practices creeping into the diocese, and they should do all they could to suppress them. If such practices were allowed in the church, the blood of Latimer, Cranmer, and Ridley, and of all their noble army of martyrs would have been shed in vain. He looked upon the ritualists as simply a recruiting party for the Church of Rome.

They were continually referring to the first six centuries in support of their arguments. He cared nothing about the first six centuries. He went at once to the first century and to Scripture.

*It was an aggressive and progressive movement, having for its aim to place
the people under the heel of the priests. They asserted that they had power
to change the elements in the Lord's supper, to create the Deity in short.
One of the most eminent ritualists of the present day says, 'the three great
doctrines on which the Catholic Church has taken her stand are these:- 1.
The real objective presence of our blessed Lord in the Eucharist. 2. The
sacrifice offered by the priest. 3. The adoration due to the presence of our
Lord therein.' These were not the doctrines of the Reformed Protestant
Church of England; but we may expect them to be taught among us if we
admit the upholders of ritualism. Dr Jenner had avowed himself a ritualist
by taking part in extreme ritualistic services. He (Richardson) agreed with
the remark of Mr Gladstone, who had said:*

'I cannot hesitate to say that the deliberate imitation of the professions
and practices of another religious communion in the Church of England,
contrary to the law and spirit of the Church of England, is a grave and
serious evil to which it is quite right that the attention of the public and
of the State should be directed, and which it is desirable to put down by
moral means, if it be possible; but if it is not possible, then, in the last
resort, by the unbending authority of the law.'

*Those were the words of Mr Gladstone, and he contended that those who
did not hold the doctrines of the Church of England had better leave her. Dr
Jenner had told them that the services of the Church of England could not
be too gorgeously rendered, but he had witnessed those services simply
performed in a mud hut in a way to be as acceptable, or more acceptable to
the Deity, than the most gorgeous ceremonial.*

*At a quarter past six o'clock on Friday morning, 9ᵗʰ April, a division was
taken, to vote on the motion before the Synod -*

'That having considered the origin of, and the circumstances connected
with, the appointment of Bishop Jenner to the See of Dunedin, and in
particular, the resolution of the late Rural Deanery Board of Otago and
Southland, passed on the 21ˢᵗ February, 1867, whereby the duty of
receiving Bishop Jenner as the Bishop of Dunedin was solemnly
affirmed by that body, duly representing as it then did, the Church in
this Diocese, this Synod hereby declares and resolves that the good faith

of the Church of England in this Diocese has been distinctly pledged to the acceptance of Bishop Jenner as Bishop of this Diocese, and that therefore his said appointment to the See of Dunedin should, in justice to him, and for the honour of the Church, be duly confirmed. And that therefore this Synod hereby requests the Standing Committees of the several Dioceses to give effect to Bishop Jenner's said appointment shall be brought and duly established within three months from this date by formally sanctioning the same, provided that no charge of being unfaithful to his ordination vows.'

The result was -

Ayes, Clergy, 4 – Laity, 10
Noes, Clergy, 3 – Laity, 15

The motion was therefore lost.

The proceedings of the Synod were terminated by the President pronouncing the apostolic benediction.

One important issue missing from this report that arose in the first part of the meeting concerned regulations to ensure that members in the house of the laity properly represented their church. This was a difficult area in a newly formed church, and the necessity of having received Communion on a regular basis had been used as a rule of thumb on most occasions.

However, as the voting at this meeting was to be of such vital importance this proved a basis for early debate. It was known that at least three of the laity had not had Communion at all, or only once some time ago. The pros and cons of this regulation were hotly debated.

How could a person prove that he had received communion? Did it only have to be once a year, or did it have to be on the three festivals of Christmas, Ash Wednesday and Easter? Did it have to be in the same church each time?

Bishop Harper stated that, yes *'a person who offered himself ought to be a regular communicant. The words of the clause on the subject were:- Any layman, being a communicant of twenty-one years of age, or who shall have signed a declaration.'*

Apparently the matter had been under consideration by the General Synod several times, and it had been found a difficult one to decide, and so it was tacitly laid aside. It was also discovered that there were persons who had no opportunity of being communicants, unless they travelled a distance of perhaps 150 miles to a church, and that was a consideration that weighed with the General Synod.

In the end no decision was made, and if this is put alongside Carr Young's meeting back in January, Jenner's note in his Journal that: *'the lay opposition, elected by the votes of not even nominal churchmen, carried my rejection,'* is a valid point.

April 11. Second Sunday after Easter. We had Matins and Evensong in the house. Mr. Jas. Smith rode over from Dunedin, and stayed three hours. He gave us a full account of the proceedings of the Synod, which are very badly reported. Everybody, including the reporters, was utterly exhausted by the length of the session. Many were asleep.

It was outrageously unfair to our side, and as advantageous to the opposition, to go on sitting till 6 a.m. When Mr. Smith began his reply at 5.15 he was in a state of mental and physical prostration. The members walked home at 6.30 in broad daylight.

Two things seem to have broken down hopelessly at this Synod, the 'English love of fair dealing', and the much vaunted Synodical system of the New Zealand Church. It has been left to the mob, to non-communicants, and even non-churchgoers, to decide one of the most important questions that could be submitted to a Synod. So much for the 'lay element'!

'The much vaunted Synodical system'

Bishop Selwyn had held his first Synod in September 1844, the first Synod to be held in the Anglican Communion since the Convocations were prorogued in 1717. He wanted, he told friends in England:

'to try what the actual system of the Church of England can do, when disencumbered of its earthly load of seats in parliament, Erastian compromises, corruption of patronage, confusion of orders, synodless bishops, and an unorganised clergy.'

It consisted of the Bishop, three Archdeacons, four Priests and two Deacons. At the second Synod held in 1847, Selwyn pressed for the admission of the Laity. Mr. Gladstone (as Colonial Secretary) in 1849 advised the Colonial Churches to 'organise themselves on the basis of voluntary consensual compact which was the basis on which the Church of Christ rested from the first,' and this further stimulated Selwyn's efforts, despite complaints from some quarters in England that the word Synod infringed the Queen's supremacy.

April 14. Mr. Pitt returned at 11, and brought news of the Synod. A strong feeling of indignation against the opposition seems to be setting in. The rejection of a proposed appeal to the Archbishop of Canterbury is viewed with extreme disgust. I sent a letter to Major Richardson asking for his authority for a certain statement of doctrine which he attributed to *Tractarians and Ritualists*, and to Edwards, referring to Bp. Harper's conditional assent to my officiating, and declining to officiate except unconditionally, and also authorising Edwards to propose (1) a trial of my imputed delinquencies before a Tribunal selected by my opponents, and (2) a reference of the whole case to any three English Bishops *they* might choose. With regard to the first , I undertook to offer no defence, even if the charges brought against me were those of Mr. Young, or of the newspaper paragraphs so often repeated, and I pledged myself to resign all pretensions to the Bishopric, if it could be shown that I had done or said anything which entailed penal consequences by any law of the Church, either here or in England. I hope my letter will be read at the Synod and printed on Friday morning.

Letter to Major Richardson

Dear Sir,

I trust you will pardon the liberty I am taking in writing to you. I am extremely anxious for information on a subject touched by you in your speech at the Diocesan Synod on Thursday morning. While by no means holding you responsible for all the incredible nonsense attributed to by the newspaper, on whose accuracy, however, it is impossible, considering the length of the sitting, to bear very hard. I cannot be wrong, I suppose, in assuming the correctness of one sentence, since it is obviously impossible that it could have been invented by the reporters.
You are represented to have said:

'The advanced Ritualist and the Tractarian alike assert that they have the power to create the Deity.'

If these are really your words, may I beg you kindly to inform me, what author or authors have made this piece of profanity the expression of their views on the solemn subject of the Holy Eucharist. We know of course that sacerdos creat Deum *[the priest creates God,] was a saying commonly and irreverently made use of in the 14th and 15th centuries, possibly earlier, but I never myself heard of its having been adopted by any modern writer of our Church. Your more extensive reading may be able to supply the reference which I desiderate. Certainly, the Tractarian or Ritualist, who has committed himself to so objectionable a statement, ought not to be allowed to escape without castigation.*
I remain, &c.,

HENRY LASCELLES JENNER
Bishop.
April 14, 1869

Major Richardson later withdrew the expression, but the inflamatory speech of which this was a part did Jenner a great deal of harm.

April 15, I got letters in the course of the morning from Dunedin. A short one from the Primate wishing to see me before he left for the

South. One from Edwards, and one from Gifford, full of kindness and sympathy. I resolved to go to Dunedin on Monday.

In the afternoon I walked with Mr. Pitt to the Blueskin Hotel and back, to see the day's papers. At the very end of the proceedings in Synod, Bp. Harper had the amazing assurance to declare that that body, in his opinion, fairly represented the mind of the Church! This statement will go home unnoticed, I fear. So then, a majority elected by not even churchgoers, still less communicants, and including at least two non-communicants is a fair representation of the Church in Otago and Southland!!

April 17. A very fine day. Mr. Pitt sent in to Dunedin for my surplice and the Communion plate for the Celebration tomorrow. I was in low spirits all day, by reason of not being able to make up my mind what I ought to do *next.*

If I return home, which is the course I am most inclined to adopt, and which seems to be that which I am *expected* to adopt, the character in which I shall appear before the English Church is that of a repudiated and degraded Bishop (a sort of Colenso in fact,) by no means an agreeable prospect.

On one thing I am determined. That I will not resign my claim to the Bishopric.

This afternoon I took a solitary walk along the beach in a northerly direction, for the purpose of thinking over my sermon for tomorrow. It will seem strange to preach again after so long a silence. The walking was very rough, over rocks and shingle. I came upon an old dug-out canoe which must have been lying on the beach for years.

April 18. 3 Sunday after Easter. A showery morning, but the day improved afterwards. Mrs. Pitt had got ready the kitchen for our service – Matins and Celebration – which was well attended by people from the neighbourhood. Only seven persons communicated. The arrangements were as reverent as circumstances permitted and, with decent altar plate and linen, the celebration was to me and all, I think, very solemn and edifying. Judging from what I have seen, I question whether there have been many more reverent functions in N.Z.

I preached for 20 minutes on the Gospel, and got on better than I had expected. I found that people were much pleased with the whole service. We sang (after a fashion) Hymn 147, to *Dundee*. I started it, and three or four joined in. I wondered what harm would have been done, or what disrespect shown to the General Synod, or any other body, if I had been allowed to do, in other places that I visited, before the inhibition was removed, what I did today. Also what reason for inhibiting me there was before the meeting of the Deanery Synod which does not exist now, for my claim remains the same, unaffected by the Synodical vote. The conclusion is forced upon me, that I was prevented from officiating in order to destroy my chance of acceptance by the people of the Diocese.

In the afternoon Mr. & Mrs. Pitt took me for a delightful walk in a part of the bush that I had not yet visited. The provincial government is making a road through this bush, which will very considerably shorten the distance to Waikouaiti and the north. But it is lamentable to see what a destruction of magnificent trees the undertaking necessitates. They are being demolished wholesale, fire being the principal agent employed. It is a wonderful and almost terrible spectacle. The undergrowth or scrub is first lighted, and the flames speedily climb the resinous trunks of the trees, and leap from branch to branch, till the whole is a mass of fire.

There will be a good deal still to be done, when the vegetation is got rid of, for the line of road is anything but level. It is difficult at first to realise that there are no wild animals in these forests. Their appearance is so entirely that of a jungle, associated in ones mind with tigers and bears, but especially with snakes.

At 9 p.m. we had evensong in the sitting room, which the servants attended.

April 19. I was driven across the bay to the Waitati by a young man now filling the office of ostler at the Waitati Hotel. He, with his father, and other members of his family, had an estate at Wanganui, and had been doing well. But the Maori troubles compelled them to leave their farm and run for their lives, the result being utter ruin. From the Waitati to Dunedin, I travelled in a small express waggon, with a man who had lately come from Tasmania. He told me much about that penal colony. I could not help wondering whether my friend had ever worn the irons.

It was raining hard all the way to Dunedin. The Primate was waiting for me at the Parsonage. We had a conversation which lasted half an hour, and was quite long enough. I got no sort of sympathy from him. He was hard and imperial in tone, evidently wanting to get rid of me as soon as possible. I told him I utterly refused to resign my claim, which he urged me to do. I asked him if he would license me to a charge in the Diocese. He declined! He found great fault with Bp. Selwyn for writing to Edwards upholding my claims.

'*A most ill judged letter,*' he said, '*and likely to do much harm.*'

'*On the contrary,*' I replied, '*it can hardly fail to have a salutary effect, as showing what is demanded by the most ordinary rules of honour and justice.*'
'*In England,*' I continued, '*there will hardly be two opinions among churchmen, as to the utter collapse of the Synodical System of the New Zealand Church, which was to be the model for universal imitation.*'

I spent three hours with the Edwardses and then rode to Green Island on a dreadful horse of Mr. Jones. *Dreadful,* I call him, because it was almost impossible to keep him on his legs. He did not actually fall, but his nose approached too near the ground very many times. The road was in a fearful state, especially after leaving the 'Metal'.

We had a very pleasant evening. Mrs. Rees and Mrs. Boult were at Green Island. The latter sang, after dinner, in a really admirable style.

April 20. I am tired of enlarging on the beauties of the Dunedin scenery, but really the ascent from the valley to Capt. Boyd's cannot be passed over entirely. The road lies through a sort of common, not unlike an English one in effect, only instead of furze there is a dense growth of Manuka scrub, about 6 to 7 feet high, clothing the hillside. The opposite heights are splendid, very bold and steep, and covered with the thick and many tinted foliage of an uncleared bush. And the effect is heightened by the great breadth and flatness of the valley. The road is very rough and not quite safe. The utmost circumspection is required in driving up, and still more, even, in descending, especially with two such fiery animals as 'Lancer' and 'Polka', Mr. Jones's buggy horses.

Capt. Boyd's house is an excellent one and nicely furnished. He showed me an armchair, which my brother, Augustus, gave him 27 years ago. It seemed as if I had seen it before, as indeed was probable, and sat upon it.

At Capt. Boyd's there is a fish hatching and rearing apparatus. It is a little way from the house, in the bush, close to a lovely Fern tree gully. There were a good many young trout swimming about looking very healthy. They are soon to be transferred to the Otago rivers, by Mr. Clifford, the curator.

April 22. I called on the Primate this morning, by appointment, and sat with him an hour. He made strenuous appeals to me to resign my claim to the Bishopric, but I resisted them. I quoted a correspondent of mine to show what people at home thought of the performances at the General Synod, viz, that 'Bishop Selwyn and his son seemed to have done their best for me. Bishop Harper and *his* son their worst!' The Primate became very indignant at the antithesis maintaining that 'Henry' was blamed unjustly, and that he himself only did what he was compelled to do.

He unpacked his 'swag' to get at a copy of the Proceedings of General Synod in order to prove these point, but it was no use. There, in black and white, was the motion of the Bp. of Ch. Ch., *'that the appointment of Bishop Jenner be not confirmed'*, and that of his son*, 'That Bishop Jenner be requested to resign his claim'.*

The Bishop made one highly important admission, viz. that my nomination was the act of the Rural Deanery Board, possessing by his concession the powers of a Diocesan Synod. Therefore, in accordance with the provisions of the Constitution Deed, my nomination was perfectly regular, and ought not to have been submitted to the Diocesan Synod at all.

April 23. I overhauled my books at the Parsonage. They were very damp. There is a capital letter in the *Oamaru Times* from Ashcroft.

At 4.30 a deputation from the S. Paul's vestry came to ask me to take part in the services next Sunday, a request to which I graciously acceded. I ought to have said before, that Bishop Harper earnestly besought me not to avail myself of his permission to officiate. He was certain, he said, that some dreadful scene would take place, people walking out of church, in a body, or something equally distressing!!

I have consented to give a lecture on Church music for the benefit of S. Paul's Church, on May 5. This evening I had a practice with the Choir, which is to give illustrations.

April 24. At the Athenaeum today, Edwards introduced me to Mr. R. B. Martin, one of my principal opponents. We had a few minutes amicable conversation. At 7.30, I had another choir practice.

April 25. S. Mark's Day & 4ᵗʰ S. after Easter. A memorable day.
I preached twice at S. Paul's. In the morning, the congregation was overflowing, about 500 persons, the church being built to hold 400. I preached for 25 minutes on the Sunday gospel. Somebody had told me that S. Paul's was a difficult Church for a preacher to make himself heard in. I found that this was a mistake, as soon as I opened my mouth.

At Evensong, every available square foot of space was occupied. There must have been at least 600 present. 100 of whom *stood* all through the service. I preached on 'Ye are the salt of the earth' with reference to S. Mark. I was 30 minutes. *Dans les pays des aveugles les borgnes sont rois.* [In the land of the blind the one-eyed are kings.] Which must be the reason why everybody seems to have been so hugely delighted. Not a symptom of any irreverent demonstration, such as the Primate dreaded. It is rather amusing to find that people are asking each other now whether nothing can be done to retain me at Dunedin.

Messrs. Young, Watt and Martin, did *not* attend the services. The offerings during the day amounted to £24. The usual average being £8.

April 26. The town today was in a state of wild excitement on account of the expected arrival of the Duke of Edinburgh. [Alfred, Duke of Saxe-Coburg and Gotha – who was the first member of the royal family to visit New Zealand.] Triumphal Arches had been erected in Princes Street and elsewhere, and decorated with a profusion of magnificent ferns, and branches of trees. The Prince landed at Port Chalmers at 2, and came in a coach drawn by eight greys, driven by *Cabbage Tree Ned*, to Dunedin.

[*Ted Devine*, who derived his name from the distinctive headgear he always wore, came to fame as an immensely skilled coach driver in Australia. He arrived in Dunedin at the height of the Otago gold rushes in the mid-sixties, and joined the firm of Hoyt and Co., a subsidiary of Cobb and Co., carrying on the famous firm's business in New Zealand. He was immediately put on the Dunedin-Dunstan run, via Palmerston and the Pigroot, and quickly became a celebrated figure to thousands, his sharp wit, sturdy independence, transparent honesty, and uncanny proficiency with whip and reins making his name a household word along the whole of his 200 mile route.]

I saw the procession from the windows of the Council Chamber, and wonderfully imposing it was. Especially considering the *age* of the settlement. The crowds of people in the streets were quite surprising. Very conspicuous were the mounted constabulary, an extremely fine body of men on grey horses. The red shirted volunteers, also, showed to great advantage. They marched well and evenly. The cortege went to Fern Hill, which has been placed at the Prince's disposal by Miss Jones. (This is a house built in a nice situation on the Caversham road, as a residence for old "Johnny Jones", a great man and early settler at Dunedin, also has died since I have been here.)

In the evening we went out to look at the illuminations, which were, as might have been expected, only moderate. Squibs and crackers were flying about in the streets. I got letters from my darlings today. All well, thank God.

April 27. At 11.30 I went in my robes with Edwards as my Chaplain, to H.R.H's levee. We had the privilege of the entrée and got a private view of the Prince before he appeared in the Council Chamber. This is a fine large room, and it was full of ladies, on this occasion. I tried hard to keep in the background, but they made me take precedence of everybody.

During the presentations, I stood at the Prince's left hand, the ceremony was *not* imposing. The awkward bows of some of the colonial dignitaries, especially the Presbyterian Ministers, who attended in great force, seemed to amuse the ladies immensely. I understood that the said P.Ms, were not a little disgusted at the table of precedence adopted by the Aide de Camp, who called up those who were to be presented. First he shouted, 'Ministers of the Church of England', to which none responded, Edwards and I having been already presented. Then 'Ministers of the Church of Rome', *after* whom were summoned, 'Ministers of the Church of Scotland'. These latter wore black gowns. Some of them walked right past the Prince, not seeing where he was, and then stood still and appeared to be looking for him till they were hustled off by the next comer. At this many of the ladies 'tittered audibly'.

There are more indications today of the feeling, the rise of which I noticed yesterday, in favour of making another effort to keep me here. Mr. Butterworth told us during dinner that he had been conversing with Mr. Power, an influential member of S. Paul's congregation, who said to him, *'You know, Butterworth, that I am not a rich man, but I would give £20 to see that man, righted.* To whom responded Mr. B, *'Ah, many of us would give more than that, if money would do it..*

April 29. At 7 I went with Edwards to dine with the Superintendent *'to meet the Duke of Edinburgh'.* A large party sat down to a miserable meal. The Rev. Mr. Stuart was called upon by the Superintendent to say grace before dinner. This seemed to excite H.R.H's astonishment, for Mr. Stuart is a Presbyterian Minister. He (the Prince) kept looking at me in an unmistakeable manner for two or three minutes after the ceremony. Edwards drew my attention to the circumstance, and inferred the reason.

When dinner was nearly over a messenger came to me, conveying H.R.H's wish that I should 'return thanks'. I resisted, saying that Mr. Stuart had much better finish, as he had begun, but Capt. Fraser told me it was the Prince's particular request that I should officiate, so I could only obey.

My next neighbour was Capt. Montgomerie of the *Blanche.* Opposite was Capt. Pitt, the governor's Aide de Camp, who knew Augustus well, and was greatly excited when he found I was his brother. The governor's great cordiality to me was very gratifying. The Prince was waited upon by his Piper, who after dinner walked up and down the room playing on his bagpipes. There were sundry toasts proposed. H.R.H. spoke fairly.

A rather alarming incident occurred just before we left the table. The Prince being thirsty, sent his Piper for some water. The Piper came and fetched a decanter from just in front of me, supposing it (as I did) to contain water. He filled the Prince's glass, who after swallowing half at least at a gulp, gasped out, *'Why it's Whisky!!'* as indeed it proved to be. He took more than he could carry with any degree of steadiness, and was 'unwell' afterwards, so I heard, during the performances at the theatre.

May 2. Rogation Sunday. I preached twice at All Saints, each time on the Gospel. The church was quite full in the morning; crammed to overflowing at Evensong. In the afternoon I went to S. Paul's, and baptized two grandchildren of Mr. Attwood who was present, and with whom I had some conversation. He knows all East Kent, and a great many residents there.

May 3. (Inv. of Holy) Mr Ashcroft called after breakfast. He and some others appear to be conspiring to keep me here, at all events until next January! What shall I do?! It will be terrible to give up my plans of getting to England in August. A meeting was held this morning at 10.30 and adjourned till tomorrow.

Mr. Mason, who is one of those who are most anxious that I should remain, called, and reported that there will be no sort of difficulty in getting funds for my maintenance, until the meeting of the Synod, to be elected in January, which will probably vote the confirmation of my appointment.

In the afternoon I went to the Athenaeum, and in the evening practised the Choir. I was sitting in the drawing room at the Parsonage this morning, when a message came, begging Mr. Edwards to go and baptise a sick baby of Mrs. Paul's in George Street. Edwards being out, I went.

May 5. This evening my lecture on Church Music was given at S. George's Hall. The attendance was not so good as it would have been had the weather been favourable. My reception was extremely enthusiastic. The Choir sang well and the lecture went without a hitch, and was, apparently, a complete success.

May 6. Ascension Day. The weather is still very disagreeable, and the streets are in a terrible state. There was a Celebration at S. Paul's, at 8 a.m. for which I was very thankful. Edwards wished me to celebrate, but I declined. There were 14 communicants, a very fair number considering the weather.

I went to 11 o'clock Matins at All Saints with Edwards. In the afternoon, I read the paper at the Athenaeum. The Riverton vestry have been presenting an address to the Primate, thanking him for his conduct at the D. Synod, and identifying him with the 'opposition'! The Bishop accepted it all as a matter of course.

At 7.30 there was Evensong at S. Paul's. I preached for 20 minutes on S. Luke XXIV 50.51. In spite of the frightful weather, there were nearly 300 present. After service I went to supper at the Smith's. Preston was of course constantly in my thoughts today, the services at church, and the school children in the orchard, etc.

May 7. First snow today. The hills were quite white in the morning. In the town there was enough snow to make the streets miserable and sloppy, for it thawed almost as soon as it fell. I went to the Athenaeum to read the papers. In the evening I dined at the Smith's, and had an extremely pleasant little party. These good people are kindness itself.

May 8. At 7 started on the coach for Waikouaiti. A most enjoyable drive, the atmosphere being superlatively clear and bright, and the hills looking most lovely, their summits being covered with snow. In the Dunedin valley there was no snow, but it lay pretty thick on the road as we ascended the high ground above Port Chalmers. The Waitati river was very high and there was some difficulty in getting through it, the coach being quite full of passengers. A bridge is being built here, which will be a great advantage. We saw Mr. Fraser, son of the late Vicar of Cheriton, who has a small property here. He was at the King's School, Canterbury, he told me, when I was a Minor Canon. A long letter on the 'situation' came from Gifford today.

May 9. Sunday after Ascension. A moderate congregation at Matins when I preached on Ps. 68 v 18. At Evensong, the church was more than crammed, and I was aware of a considerable audience outside the windows. The church will seat comfortably 75 but there must have been at least 120 inside, besides those without. The night was calm, and still, but the sullen roar of the surf on the adjacent beach was audible during the whole service, and had a peculiarly impressive effect.

May 10. One of the unaccountable days that so frequently occur during a New Zealand winter. The sun was quite hot all day, and the atmosphere clear and calm. After breakfast we had a most delightful ride along the beach to the Maori Kaiki (village) about four miles to the South of Waikouaiti. The canter over the hard sand was most exhilarating. A tremendous surf was breaking on the beach. Near the native village the Waikouaiti river enters the sea. We had to cross this before we could get to the house, and as the tide was rising rapidly it was nearly a swimming matter. On this account we were unable to stay more than a few minutes at the Kaiki. We saw no Maories, and only the outside of the house. This was disappointing, as I had reckoned on being able to buy some specimens of native manufacture.

At dinner we had part of a 'Frost fish', and most excellent it was, the best of all fish, I thought. It is caught at Oamaru chiefly, or rather it catches itself, for, on frosty nights, something impels it to jump out of the water onto the beach, where it is found, if not eaten by gulls, above high water mark. It is a long narrow fish.

I found at the Parsonage a letter from Major Richardson (the second) in which he tries hard to justify the ridiculous statements he made at the Synod.

May 11. Another letter from the gallant Major withdrawing the calumnious words he had used and justified! I telegraphed to Tanner this afternoon, announcing my intended departure for Melbourne on Saturday, and my wish to have a service either at Invercargill or the Bluff on Whitsun-Day.
I went to a Photographers and was 'taken' in various altitudes this morning.

I met Capt. Boyd today. He asked me to baptize his baby, which he proposes to call 'Herbert Lascelles', having got an unaccountable idea into his head that the first was Augustus' name the second was intended to be in honour of me. Capt. B. is an instance out of many an opponent, converted into a most ardent supporter. So warm was he, that, the Dunedin Club having omitted to invite me to a dinner given to the Duke of Edinburgh, Capt. B. declared that he would remove his name from the list of members, unless a satisfactory explanation of the neglect was given. The Committee thereupon professed themselves very sorry, and said that the omission was entirely accidental.

May 12. The photos came, and gave much satisfaction. I stayed indoors most of the day preparing my lecture 'On the Management of Children', which I delivered at the Masonic Hall in the evening, to a large and attentive audience. More than 400 persons were present. In acknowledging the vote of thanks, I remarked, that, although I was on the eve of my departure from the colony, it might be, and I hoped sincerely it would be, God's will that they should see me again. The words had scarcely passed my lips before the most tremendous burst of applause struck the room, and lasted quite a minute. This was altogether unexpected by me.

May 14. A present arrived from Mr. and Mrs. Ward, a lovely water colour drawing of that glorious view on the Blueskin road. Then Mr. Rees gave me an opossum rug of great size and value. And Mr. Wilson, a lawyer, called, with a set of beautiful and large photographs of Dunedin and the neighbourhood.

I went into the town and bought a few things for the voyage, returning by 11, when Capt. Boyd's baby came to be baptized. It was named 'Harry Lascelles'. At 7.30 we had Evensong at S. Paul's, after which I preached a 'farewell sermon' from Acts 1.14. I thought it right to speak very strongly tonight on the imperative duty of patience, urging that we ought to make the most of the privileges already enjoyed, however unpromising things might seem. The congregation numbered at least 300. There was a great proportion of men, but for it being mail night there would have been many more.

After service there was a grand Choir supper at the Parsonage and the S. Paul's Choir presented me with a 'testimonial', in the shape of a pencil case of N. Zealand gold. I was not a little astonished and gratified. There were several speeches, in all of which most warm and sympathetic mention was made of me. Really the kindness of everybody is overpowering. It quite neutralizes all the harshness which has been exhibited by some.

May 15. A very nasty day drizzling rain. *'Dunedin weeping at my departure'* as someone poetically observed. At 1, I quitted the Parsonage, and its most hospitable and warm hearted mistress, with infinite regret. Edwards accompanied me to the jetty, where in spite of the wretched weather, a large number of my friends were collected, all of whom were most cordial in their good wishes.

Mrs. Jas. Smith was there. She introduced me to Capt. McLean of the *Alhambra* (which was to take me to Melbourne), charging him to take care of me, and get me a cabin to myself. Edwards, Howarth, Paultin and Quick went with me to Port Chalmers, and stayed on board the *Alhambra* till the last moment. Much as I longed to get home again, it was a real grief to me to leave Dunedin, and all my kind friends there.

The *Alhambra* sailed at 5, much too late, for it was getting very dark, and the tide was ebbing. The consequence was that halfway between the port and the Heads, she ran aground, the Captain having mistaken the channel, which is not easy to find, even by daylight. There was no getting her off on account of the ebb tide. A most annoying event this. The *Geelong* tug came alongside about 7 and stove in her starboard paddle box in so doing. She tried in vain to tow us off. So here we are for the night at all events.

I turned in early. The Captain has put me into a cabin of his own on the main deck and a delightful one it is. It was not without some gratification that I noticed the demonstrations of regret at my departure today. Poor Edwards completely broke down at the last.

May 16. Whitsun Day. This morning at daybreak we ought to have been nearly entering the Bluff Harbour, whereas the dawn found us still aground in Otago Bay. An attempt was made to move the ship at 5 a.m., but it was unsuccessful. So the Captain went to Port Chalmers for lighters. The cargo must be taken out.

After breakfast I walked up and down the deck, admiring the beautiful scenery of the harbour and wishing I had remained at Dunedin for the services today. At 11 I had Matins and preached a short sermon on the Epistle. A very unsatisfactory way, this, of spending this great festival. If I could have got off and gone ashore, I would have had a service at Port Chalmers, but the ebb tide was running so strong that it would have taken a boat hours to get there. The Maori village at the Heads was plainly visible, and a few settlers' houses scattered about on each side of the bay. I wondered whether I should ever behold this scene again.

One lamentable circumstance in connection with our detention here is, that our chance of catching the English Mail at Melbourne is rapidly diminishing. We shall do it, Capt. McLean says, if we have a fair wind and this preliminary difficulty can be overcome. All the Dunedin Merchants and bankers have written by the *Alhambra*, and I put off writing till the last on the strength of their example, and reckoning on the leisure of the voyage to Melbourne. If we miss the P & O mail steamer, they will get no letter at all at home and will be utterly at a loss to know what my movements are. Besides, I have not quite determined not to go home by the mail route.

At 3.30 a very good dinner was served. While we were at table, a large lighter came alongside, and the crew at once began to move the cargo. This was a very long business and it did not seem to do much good. The tug was again attached and the engines of both vessels went ahead at once, but the *Alhambra* refused to stir from the comfortable bed she had made for herself in the sand. High water approached, and with it our last chance of getting off tonight. At last, just at the turn of the tide, all the passengers got into the lighter alongside, and the men heaving lustily at the warp forward, the ship, to our great joy, began to veer slowly round, and in a minute we were in 30 feet of water. The shouts and cheers that arose were justifiable enough. It was now 7.30 p.m.

We anchored just inside the Heads, and at once proceeded to reship the cargo. This operation was not completed till past midnight and it was 3 a.m. before we put to sea. The confusion on board put an end to all hopes of Evensong. Altogether it was the queerest Whitsun Day I ever passed, corresponding to the Xmas Day in the Bay of Panama. I made the acquaintance of a Mr. and Mrs. Barton, who are on their way to England, from Canterbury (N.Z.) where they have been for two years. Mrs. B. seems to be a good churchwoman, judging from her reverent behaviour at service this morning. I found afterwards that she had been a member of All Saint's, Margaret Street congregation when in London.

May 19. According to the authorities on board we shall easily catch the mail. That is a great comfort. But now comes the serious question. Shall I go home that way or not?
On one side there are the advantages of a rapid passage. 50 days only, and of seeing Ceylon, the Red Sea, Egypt, Alexandria, Malta, etc. and of escaping the dreadful passage round Cape Horn, where the cold at this season will be overpowering.
On the other side are to be taken into account the extra expense £30 at lcast, the S.W. monsoon, the heat of the Red Sea and the desert. I think it will end in my electing the mail route.

May 23. Trinity Sunday. I went on deck before breakfast, when, to my infinite delight, the Captain informed me that I should be able to go home by the P & O steamer, which he expected to meet at Port Phillip Heads.

It will be a very close thing, but I shall not mind that, if I manage it. We had Matins in the saloon at 10.30. The saloon passengers attended in considerable numbers, but I was sorry to see no sailors or 2nd class folk.

At noon we were abreast of Wilson's Promontory, whence the telegraphic cable has just been laid to Tasmania. We coasted along, getting excellent views of the land as we advanced, until we reached Port Phillip Heads. Just before entering there is a piece of broken water, said to be rather dangerous, called (I think) the 'Grip'. [Actually called 'The Rip'.]
The Western Head is called *Port Lonsdale*, the Eastern *Point Nepean*. The latter, in which I naturally took some interest, is a low sandy spit, overhung by the extremity of a range of hills rising to the height of 1,000 feet.
[Jenner's sister Anne had married Rev. Canon Evan Nepean, Canon of Westminster, son of Rt. Hon. Sir Evan Nepean, 1st Bt., after whom this point was named.]

It was arranged that I should go ashore with the mails, and await at Queenscliffe for the arrival of the *Geelong* P & O steamer, which, it appeared, had already started from Melbourne, and was on her way down.

So I went below at 3.30 and ate my dinner with my mind at ease. I had just done, when Capt. McLean came into the saloon rubbing his hands, and exhibiting a countenance beaming with satisfaction.
'*That's all right,*' said he, '*I have got rid of the mails. They've just gone ashore to Queenscliffe.*'
'*And what am I to do?*' said I.
'*Bless me,*' said the Captain, '*I quite forgot you.*'
And off he rushed, to see what could be done to get me ashore. He soon returned with the information that the dinghy belonging to the pilots' boat, would take me to Queenscliffe directly. I got my baggage together and with it went on board a very little boat, pulled by two men, and only just big enough to hold me and my effects.
'*Can you steer, Sir?*' asked one of the men, as soon as we were clear of

the *Alhambra*.

'Yes,' said I, '*if you will show me where you want to go*'.

So they pointed out the jetty, which we reached in half an hour.

The local newspaper for Ballarat included this brief item -

'*Bishop Jenner arrived on Sunday, from New Zealand. His Lordship is on his return to England, where he will probably be speedily appointed to a living. The Bishop landed from the* Alhambra *at Queenscliffe, and spent the few hours he remained in Victoria at the parsonage, and preached at St. Georges's in the evening. He proceeded to England by the* Geelong *on Monday morning, May 24ᵗʰ.*'

[The people of Ballarat had obviously been kept informed about Jenner's visit, but didn't seem to know much about the process of preferment in the Church of England.]

May 28. Lat.36.42 S Long. 127.22 E. Distance 259 miles. The wind having got to N.E. we are making excellent progress. The square canvas was set this morning. Capt. Dundas will not allow the men to sing or shout when they make or shorten sail. Hence the *Geelong* is an unusually quiet ship.

May 31. We anchored in Albany, Western Australia, about 4.30 a.m. It was very pleasant to be at rest, after yesterday's shaking. It was a glorious day, very, yet not too, warm. The climate of W. Australia seems to be perfection.

This is a convict settlement: the consequence is the roads are first rate. The population of Albany is but small, 500. The houses are very scattered, some of them have an old look, which takes one by surprise. They might easily be mistaken for 200 years old. I fancy people know less about Western Australia, than about most other settled parts of this great continent. Yet, under the name of the Swan River settlement, it was a good deal talked about years ago.

The soil of the low ground is principally comprised of the debris of the granite. Perth, the capital, is 200 miles away to the N.E. There is a good road, as wide as Regent Street, all the way.

On landing, we walked through the town, such as it is, a mile or two into the country. One of our objects was to see some of the natives, and in this we were not disappointed. Indeed, we saw only too much of them. They followed us about, begging, and proposing for a consideration to display their skill in throwing the boomerang and spear, and in performing a 'corobbery', which I had always imagined to be something to eat.

The former exhibition was really remarkable. One of the performers was 'King', a most repulsive looking savage, as indeed were all we saw, male and female. Their 'King' was tattooed and painted. He affected a majestic air in his gait, and in the way he carried his kangaroo skin robe, but it was a very poor pretence, and it disappeared entirely when the boomerang throwing began. The 'corobbery' was an extremely tame and uninteresting dance, by a number of natives collected for this purpose, by a resident, who was good enough to act as our guide.

There is a church here, not much of a building. The clergyman, whose acquaintance I made, is Mr. McSorley, a gentleman who once wrote to ask me to give him work in Dunedin ... Mr. McSorley spoke well of the convicts. They give, he says, very little trouble, and their presence is a great advantage to the colony. It is next to impossible for them to escape, the ports being closely watched, and no land communication existing with other parts of the Australian continent.

South Australia is the nearest colony, but the intervening country is a howling wilderness or else an impenetrable bush. The flora of this neighbourhood is most abundant and beautiful. Even in this 'winter' season, the waste ground is covered with flowering shrubs. Most conspicuous were the scarlet blossoms of *Beaufortia sparva* a nuptaceous plant. I noticed also a handsome Proteaceous shrub, not in flower, *Banksia coccinea*.

June 1. We had oysters for lunch, and oyster patties for dinner, a large and coarse kind (the oysters not the patties) found in the Sound. At 6 p.m. our course was altered, and we are now steering straight for Ceylon. The next land we shall see is Point de Galle, and in three days we shall be in the tropics. I am going to write home from Alexandria. The letter will go via Marseilles, and will contain an announcement, which will cause not a little commotion at Preston. Viz. that I shall arrive in five days!

June 7. I had a bath this morning at 7, which I greatly enjoyed. The Indian Ocean does not seem nearly so salty as the Pacific. The Captain has a special bath of extra size (being a fine tall man,) and it is often possible to get it after he has done.

I spent the first part of the night, up to 12, on the skylight on deck. I spread my 'possum rug', and slept comfortably. I had the gratification of seeing some old friends this evening. After a gorgeous sunset, out rushed, to use Coleridge's expression, *Ursa major, Arcturus, Corona Borealis* and *Leo Major.* I had not seen them for six months and they looked quite homelike. The Southern Constellations were very bright tonight. *Crux Australis* was nearly upright. *Canopus* equalled *Sirius* in brilliancy.

June 14. The coast of Ceylon was visible from the scuttle of my cabin when I turned out this morning. We anchored in Galle harbour at 8 a.m. I went on deck as soon as I was dressed, and enjoyed my first Oriental prospect.

One hardly knew what to admire most, or first. I think my eyes rested with the greatest pleasure on the glorious Cocoa nut groves along the Eastern shore of the harbour. About a cable's length from us was moored the *Deccan,* the largest steamer in the P & O service, and a monster she looked. A little further, lay the *Surat* which is to take us to Suez. We had hardly reached our moorings before the ship was surrounded by a multitude of canoes and boats manned by more than half-naked natives, of various shades of brown, several of the Asiatic races being represented. They brought men with all kinds of things for sale, who were very pertinacious traders.

 At 6 p.m. I went on board the *Surat* for the night. The boat that took me off was manned by six Cingalese, who sang the whole way in chorus, the most frightful noise. The *Surat* is a splendid vessel, nearly twice as large as the *Geelong*. Capt. Dundas kept his word, and got me a cabin all to myself on the main deck, a very small one, but there is a fine large port which can be kept open in almost any weather. The *Surat* seems to be built with a view to the heat of these latitudes. Her bulwarks are open, i.e. with network instead of wooden panels, so that the air can enter freely.

June 16. The ship's doctor has a harmonium in his cabin, which he plays during service on Sundays. This evening he and the Captain and I tried some trios for A & T & B (alto, tenor and base,) in the Captain's cabin. The doctor sings rather out of tune, and is a bad timeist, but Capt. Greaves has a capital bass voice and sings fairly. There are no less than six tigers on board, besides other animals and birds.

June 23. 190 miles from Cape Guardafui. The Monsoon is upon us now, without a doubt. It is blowing tremendously, with a sea beyond anything I ever saw. The ship being very 'lively', people are continually spinning about the deck in their chairs.

Scarcely had these last words been written, when a catastrophe befell me, which might have been more serious than it was. I was seated on a chair belonging to Mrs. Mellish, which, by the way, she had herself occupied most of the morning. It was lashed to one of the heavy deck seats, which, in turn, was made fast to the skylight. A heavier lurch than ordinary caused the lashings to part, and the deck seat, chair, and I, bore down together to leeward, wrecking several chairs and wounding several passengers, before we brought up against the lee bulwarks. Here, my leg got jammed between my own chair and that on which another passenger, (a heavy man) was sitting. The result was a severe abrasion and contusion, just below the knee, which I expect will cause lameness for a day or two. What *would* have happened if Mrs. Mellish had been sitting in her chair!

June 25. At 2 we sighted the Arabian coast, my first view of the continent of Asia. Very bold and broken is the coastline. We had no sooner entered the bay at Aden than a number of natives, about 30, swam off to meet us. Directly they came alongside shouts of *backsheesh* arose from the water. Some of the passengers amused themselves by throwing coins to them. It was wonderful to see the whole party disappear under the water, as soon as the money was seen. It was always caught long before it reached the bottom. They would not dive for copper, as I found, on throwing a penny in.

No words can express the utter desolation of the country. It is a wilderness, indeed! The soil is entirely volcanic, and not a plant is to be seen. The road is skirted on the right by a lofty range of rocky heights, very bold and precipitous. At one or two points we noticed the ruins of ancient fortifications, high up on the rocks. We met a great many natives. Most of the women wore the Yashmak over their faces but some were quite unveiled. The men wore nothing in particular, i.e. the lower classes. We passed a respectable looking Parsee riding on a donkey. He had very short stirrups, and the animal being obviously not up to his weight, the pair had a comical look.

June 26. At breakfast we were close to the Straits of Bab-el-Mandeb, through which we entered the Red Sea about 9.30. Unspeakably interesting it is to find one's self in these historical waters. The heat is intense today. Therm. 95° Fahr. in the shade. Not a breath of air. The sea is perfectly calm and smooth, save where a shoal of 'skip-jacks' are dancing about, and gulls trying to catch them.

In the evening we had some music on deck. I found among the passengers a man with a fair bass voice, Mr. Tinne, and we sang *Integer vitae* and other quartettes with some effect.

June 27. 5 S. after Trinity. The therm stands still higher today, 99° at 9 a.m. Matins on the quarterdeck at 10.30. In spite of the heat (during service the glass rose to 105°!) I preached on the Gospel with more comfort than I could have hoped for. The exceeding interest of preaching in the Red Sea carried me away, and made me forgetful of the temperature. A variety of "local allusions" forced themselves upon me as I went on. The re-action when I had finished was terrible. I was completely exhausted and only restored by a small bottle of champagne, for which I claimed the doctor's order. (No one may have champagne except as a 'medicine'.)

In the afternoon, a nice breeze sprang up. We had Evensong in the saloon at 7.30.

July 1. We anchored at Suez about noon but it was nearly 5 before the steamer tender came for the passengers. Suez is a most wretched place. The Canal works seem to be the only objects of interest and of these not much could be seen. We had to wait till 10 p.m. before the train started for Alexandria, the Bombay steamer being after its time. I was standing on the beach, after tea, when a man accosted me by name, and informed me he had known me from my youth. He turned out to be a son of George James of Chislehurst. He is a passenger from India, where he has been at work in his trade, that of a mason.

July 2. I managed after midnight to sleep a little. When I awoke it was just daylight, and the desert was passed. The train stopped at a station close to a village, a wonderful, and, to me, unprecedented scene. The natives were just getting up. A few yards from the train, a dignified gentleman, who had passed the night on the flat roof of his house, brought himself with much deliberation, and in many stages, to an erect posture. Then, after gazing about him for a minute or two, he commenced his 'ablutions' and other devotions, with his face towards Mecca, i.e. in a S.E. direction. I fancy he used sand, not water.

At every station, the carriage windows were beset by crowds of natives, offering for sale fruit and hard-boiled eggs. The people are not bad looking, or would not be but for the frightful disfigurement of ophthalmia, from which so many are suffering. Their colour is very dark. It was difficult to reconcile the idea of a railway and its surroundings with the historic association of this ancient country. The natives, however, seem to take it all as a matter of course. And, indeed, they must have been pretty well accustomed to European peculiarities before the railway was opened, by the constant stream of passengers through Egypt on their way to or from India.

The train entered the station at Alexandria at 8.45. A regular pandemonium, this. The shouting, and wrangling, and general confusion, inside the station, and also in the street outside was intolerable. Here was a confluence of nations, indeed. Representatives of all nations, trying, apparently, to see which could make the most noise. The Southampton steamer is not in yet. If she arrives tonight, we shall leave tomorrow.

July 3. I slept well and, under the protection of mosquito curtains, escaped being bitten. At 7 a.m. I went in a carriage with the Mellishes to the port, which we left in the tender at 8. I got a very good cabin, all to myself, on board the *Delhi*, which is to take us to Southampton. We breakfasted on board, and at 12.30 we weighed anchor and were soon in the Mediterranean.

July 4. 6ᵗʰ S. after Trinity. We had Matins at 11. There was a very large attendance of all classes of passengers, besides seamen. I preached on the Gospel, as usual, for 23 minutes. The congregation were very attentive, with the one exception of the *pursy* purser, (weight 20 stone) who went to sleep. The Captain *would* have singing, for which there had been no preparation, and which proved rather a failure. Miss Smith played the harmonium and we attempted the Canticles and Glorias to *awful* double chants. The effect of these, and of Psalm 24 (Tate & Brady!) to S. Peter's, was almost ludicrous. Scarcely anybody joined. I shall not tolerate this kind of thing again.

We had Evensong at 7.30 in the saloon. I had made arrangements about the singing, and a little practice with Miss Smith, the Captain, and others, made the evening service a decided improvement. Tate & Brady, alas! is the only available hymnal. I chose some single chants for the Canticles. Preached for 25 minutes about David. Prickly heat better.

[*Tate and Brady* refers to the collaboration of the poets Nahum Tate and Nicholas Brady, which produced one famous work, *New Version of the Psalms of David* (1696) which was a metrical version of the Psalms. Still regularly sung today is their version of Psalm 34, 'Through all the changing scenes of life' (which was improved in the second edition of 1698).]

July 10. We anchored in the Bay of Gibraltar about 5 p.m. The Rock is a most striking object, a huge mass, like a lion couchant. The town lies at the base, i.e. under the head of the lion. As soon as we anchored, a party of us went ashore.

I walked about the streets, till dark. The place is not in itself interesting but it is curious to find a town geographically on Spanish territory, and peopled for the most part by Spaniards, in the possession, and under the influence of, England. The streets all bear English names, but comparatively few shops are kept by our countrymen. Jews abound, and I noticed many Moors from the African side walking in the streets. These were men of gigantic stature, of a white complexion, which surprised me. They wore turbans and yellow slippers.

The town is full of soldiers, most of whom, officers as well as men, very respectfully saluted me as I passed. There is a belt of neutral ground outside Gibraltar on which Spanish sentries are stationed. I was told that in each sentry box a notice is posted, enjoining special vigilance 'during the temporary occupation by the British'!

July 11. 7ᵗʰ S. after Trin. Matins on deck at 10.45. I preached on the Gospel for a quarter of an hour, the captain having given me a hint to be short. At 2 we rounded Cape S. Vincent, a bold and striking headland.

We had Evensong in the saloon at 7.45 when I preached for 16 minutes. I carefully followed in my mind, what I conceived would be the course of events today at Preston. I calculated that my letter would arrive there at 7.30. I fancied that there would be a shout through the house, and much running to and fro, as the tidings were published. Then I thought of the walk to Church and the communication of the news to the Slaters, Goodsons, Robinsons and to the Choir in vestry. Then I went with Mary and Herbert to school, and imagined the announcement to Eliza Hunt, and thought that not much work would be done with the children that afternoon. Then Mr. Clarke would come to the service in the evening, and he would have to be told. [None of these events happened, as my letters did not arrive till Thursday morning.] In fact I got into a somewhat fatuous state of mind.

July 13. Tuesday. There was a heavy sea running when I awoke this morning, a sign that we have entered the Bay of Biscay. There is a head wind, and our chance of getting in on Thursday looks rather bad. But it is impossible to grumble. The weather throughout my four voyages, i.e. from Dunedin to Port Phillip, from P. Phillip to Galle, from Galle to Suez, and from Alexandria thus far, has been most favourable. I have nothing to complain of, and much indeed to be thankful for.

In the evening there was a concert in the saloon. Madame Bishop sang several things extremely well. I thought it very obliging of her to consent to accompany herself on the Captain's harmonium, a very poor instrument. She, and the Captain, and I, sang 'Ti prego' (Churchmann) together, I had to take the Alto (faute de mieux) and very hard work it was. Towards night the sea went down a little. It was quite cold all day.

July 15. At 3.30 we got our first view of dear old England, viz. Portland Bill. We got through the Needles by daylight about 8 p.m. Very pretty was the scene on both sides, the village of Yarmouth, Alum Bay, etc. looked lovely, and the smell of newly mown hay was quite strong at one point. As we passed up the Southampton water it became quite dark. There was a fete of some kind going on at Netley. The Abbey was lighted up, and rockets were ascending in rapid succession.

July 16. After breakfast I went ashore, and telegraphed my arrival to Grove Ferry, and posted my letters to N. Zealand. They were just in time. Then I went to see about getting my baggage cleared. This took a long time, and cost far too much money. I got off from Southampton by the 12 (noon) train and caught the 4.38 easily, at Charing Cross. At Grove Ferry the whole family were assembled to meet me. A happy meeting, indeed, it was! As we passed through Preston Street, the 'population' were all out to greet me; and the school children, drawn up outside the school, had nosegays of flowers to present. And so I got safe Home again after my eight months (to a day) wandering.

Laus Deo! pro onmibus beneficiis
Ejus, in me, tam indignum,
Camulatis,
Amen.

(Praise God! for all His favours, on me, who are so unworthy, Amen.)

One of the purposes of this book is to show what a great loss the treatment of Bishop Jenner was to the Church of England. However, this Journal reveals what a great loss his overriding passion for the church must have meant to the study of Music and Natural History. Like the Rev. Gilbert White, Jenner's knowledge of, and fascination for, the world of flora, fauna and astronomy was phenomenal.

*Benmore
Station*

*Bendigo
Station*

It was a scene never to
be forgotten. The view of
the valley, or rather plain,
of the Taieri, was quite
uninterrupted.
1 March

Shag Valley Station (1895)

The Homestead, Shag Valley

Mr. Wayne's house is very superior to any of my former resting places. It is close to the Shag river, or *Waihemo*, a wide, but shallow, stream. Gum trees, which have thriven amazingly, are planted on each side of the house, and give it quite a long established look. *2 March*

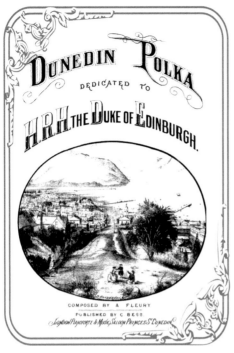

The town today was in a state of wild excitement on account of the expected arrival of the Duke of Edinburgh. Triumphal Arches had been erected in Princes Street, and elsewhere, and decorated with a profusion of magnificent ferns, and branches of trees. I saw the procession from the windows of the Council Chamber, and wonderfully imposing it was, especially considering the *age* of the settlement. The crowds of people in the streets were quite surprising. *26 April*

The Prince landed at Port Chalmers at 2 ... The cortege went to Fern Hill, which has been placed at the Prince's disposal by Miss Jones. (This is a house built in a nice situation on the Caversham road, as a residence for old "Johnny Jones", a great man and early settler at Dunedin. who also has died since I have been here.)

Fern Hill thronging with naval officers and umbrella carrying ladies.(1860s?)

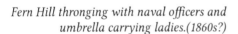

Fernhill today – now owned by the Dunedin Club

I went to a Photographers and was 'taken' in various attitudes this morning ... The photos came, and gave much satisfaction.
11 12 May

On the back of the photo

Photograph by J. W. Allen of Moray Place, Dunedin

St. Luke's, Oamaru, 1865

At Oamaru all day. In the forenoon Mr. Ashcroft, a very pleasent man called. We had a long conversation and he lent me his horse, on which I rode for a couple of hours with Gifford. The day was magnificent. The town and bay looked extremely pretty from a headland which forms the southern extremity of the bay. "First Rocky Point"* it is called on the maps. There is a tremendous surf here sometimes. We went into the Church, which I suppose must be called good for New Zealand, this of the white Oamaru stone, an excellent material. *16 Feb*

It is not known what maps he saw as, from the early 1800s, it has always been called 'Cape Wanbrow'.

The Rev. Algernon Gifford, the Vicar of St. Luke's, Oamaru, and family

We reached Invercargill at 12. A most forlorn place, this, the most southern town in the world.

It is built on a vast plain. The area of the "town" is immense, the streets being as wide as Regent Street, but the early promise of the place has never been fulfilled.

7 March

ASAB BAY, STRAITS OF BAB-EL-MANDEB — THE FIRST ITALIAN SETTLEMENT IN AFRICA

At breakfast we were close to the Straits of Bab-el-Mandeb, through which we entered the Red Sea about 9.30. Unspeakably interesting it is to find one's self in these historical waters. *26 June*

Thanks to fair winds and good navigation Jenner found himself able to travel home through Suez and Alexandra, rather than around the Cape of Good Hope. The Suez Canal was nearing completion, but didn't officially open until 17 November 1869, so on the first three days of July that year he took the railway between the two ports. Designed by Robert Stevenson it was the first railway to be built in Africa.

Suez Station 1890

SUEZ. - The Raelway Station
SUEZ. - La Gar.

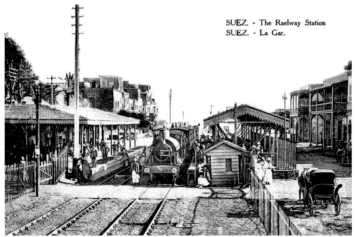

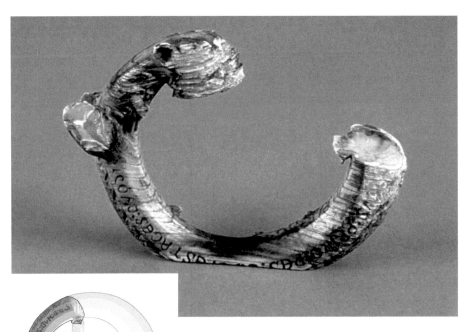

This fragment of the 12th century crozier that is held in the Hunt Museum can be seen to bear a striking similarity to Burges' design.

Bishop Jenner in the end of term photo of the Preston Council School in 1898, a few weeks before his death.

Grove Ferry Railway Station

The Jenner Family Grave and the east window of the south chapel at St. Mildred's, Preston-next-Wingham

The Sufferings of a 'See-less' bishop

In comparison to our present age, when the rich and powerful can fly at great speed around the world; from international conference to summit of world leaders, to global gathering in some exotic resort – or from London to the Midlands for a quick photo opportunity in a day-glow jacket – and lesser mortals can travel at unearthly hours to holidays on seasides in the sun, Henry Jenner's return to Preston must have been an incredibly emotional and transforming experience. Here he was, having travelled all around the world, clutching his encrusted crozier and opossum rug, to be met off the local steam train at nearby Grove Ferry station.

In his journal and his speeches Jenner had often mentioned the thoughts and the great affection that he had for the little parish of Preston and its inhabitants, and he must have felt an immense tear between that much loved place and the land where he could have been a bishop. For, despite everything, he still believed that he was called to be the Bishop of Dunedin – or, if not of Dunedin, then at least of somewhere.

But Preston and St Mildred's church were to be his home and his place of ministry for the rest of his life, and there is a certain sadness and understandable anger and frustration to be found in the account of how he kept badgering the church hierarchy to give some practical and spiritual meaning to their consecration of him back in Canterbury Cathedral on St Bartholomew's Day in 1866. He too had thought that, 'on his return to England he would probably be speedily appointed to a living.'

A week after his return Bishop Jenner wrote to the Archbishop of Canterbury:

My dear Lord Archbishop,
I beg to announce my arrival in England, and resumption of the duties of
my parish. If your Grace will kindly grant me an interview, I will take an
early opportunity of waiting upon you. It is hardly necessary to say that

I am by no means satisfied with my present position. I have no means of knowing what view your Grace takes of the 'situation', but I am quite sure that I may reckon on your sympathy. The injury that I have suffered is probably without parallel. I wish I could think that any good to the Church was likely to result from my being sacrificed, as I have been, to the demands of a noisy minority.

I remain
Your Grace's faithful servant
Henry Lascelles Jenner

There then follows a more homey postscript.

'P.S. It has just occurred to me that, as I am to be in London on Monday to assist at the wedding of one of my nieces at Westminster Abbey, I might ask your Grace, if quite convenient, to see me on that afternoon.

In a reply worthy of Reggie Perrin's 'CJ', Tait offers Thursday as being more convenient.

My Dear Bishop,
I have this morning received your letter of the 23rd on my return from work at Herne Bay.
I am truly glad that you have returned in health to your family and parish. Your trial has been a great one, and I sympathise sincerely with you in your many anxieties.
As matters stand I suppose there is no course open but a return to your ordinary duties at home.
I shall be in town till Thursday. On that day I shall be at the Ecclesiastical Commission, Whitehall Place at 11, and at 3. Deans Yard at 2.

Yours sincerely
A. C. Cantuar

The meeting went well, as it left the Archbishop with the belief that Bishop Jenner had a just claim to be considered the Bishop of Dunedin. But in order to be sure of his ground he sent for Bishop Selwyn and questioned him closely. Bishop Selwyn's account of the controversy tallied so exactly with Bishop Jenner's that the Archbishop felt that he had to take some action. So he produced a 'Judgement'.

JUDGMENT OF THE ARCHBISHOP OF CANTERBURY

Addington,
20th October 1870.

I must premise that the following judgment is founded only on a partial statement of the case; and I am necessarily in ignorance how far it might be my duty to modify it, if I were in possession of such statements as the Churchmen resident in New Zealand might wish to forward, if they had the opportunity.
Having carefully considered the various statements which I have received from the Bishop of Lichfield and Bishop Jenner, with reference to the appointment of a Bishop to the See of Dunedin ...
[He goes through the history of the affair, and comes to this summary.]
On the whole, considering the unsettled state of the constitution of the Church of New Zealand, in respect of the absence from its code of any distinct regulations respecting the establishment of new Sees, and the mode of election or nomination of Bishops thereto, and believing that the other Sees in New Zealand were originally constituted much in the same way as that of Dunedin, I am of opinion that Bishop Jenner, having been selected by the Archbishop of Canterbury on the request of the Metropolitan of New Zealand and consecrated under Royal License to act as 'a Bishop in the Colony of New Zealand', and having afterwards been accepted by the Rural Deanery Board of Otago and Southland, i.e. the whole of the Diocese of Dunedin, has an equitable claim to be considered Bishop of Dunedin, and I think it probable that a Court of Law would establish his right to the interest of the moneys collected on his behalf. But, as I can scarcely suppose that he is prepared to force himself upon a body which is now unwilling to receive him, my advice is the same as that of the General Synod of New Zealand,

viz., that he should forego his claim. Yet I can scarcely think it equitable that he should not receive payment from the moneys at present in hand, for the expenses which he has incurred, owing to the painful position in which he has been placed.

(Signed) A. C. CANTUAR

This judgment was sent to the Primate of New Zealand by Bishop Jenner, together with a letter of protest that he should be officiating in the See of Dunedin.

The letter and the judgment were laid before the Fifth General Synod held at Dunedin on 1 February 1871. Bishop Abraham, the only person in the whole controversy who seems to have kept his head, had returned to England as assistant to Bishop Selwyn at Lichfield. His throne was now occupied by the former Archdeacon Hadfield who rose to say that: *'He had no doubt that a few hours after the document was penned the writer regretted it'!*
As John Pearce wrote, *'What could you do with men who made statements of this kind without the slightest foundation?'*

The Synod went on to record:
That whereas the last General Synod of the Branch of the United Church of England and Ireland in New Zealand took into consideration all the circumstances of the nomination and consecration of Bishop Jenner, and did thereupon formally request that he should withdraw his claim to the position of Bishop of Dunedin, for the sake of the peace of the Church, to which request Bishop Jenner has declined to accede; and whereas the law of the Church requires the sanction of the General Synod to the nomination of a Bishop to any See in New Zealand.
Resolved, that this Synod does hereby refuse to sanction the nomination of Bishop Jenner to the See of Dunedin, whether that nomination were in due form or otherwise. But, at the same time, this Synod begs to express its sympathy, with Bishop Jenner in the painful position in which he has been placed.

That last sentence at least acknowledges a little concern for, and an acceptance of, Bishop Jenner being the victim in this situation - *'has been placed'* and not *'has placed himself'* – and not that the situation was his fault, (which was a view adopted by later episcopal correspondence).

Meanwhile, back in Kent, Bishop Jenner is getting confused by the two different responses that he seems to be getting from Archbishop Tait. On the one hand his Grace is saying how sympathetic and understanding he is of Jenner's position over Dunedin, and on the other he goes on to recommend that he resigns from the whole affair. He tries to get in touch with his Grace to clarify the matter.

Preston Vicarage, Sandwich
28 February 1871

My dear Lord Archbishop,
Not having received any reply to a letter I ventured to address to your Grace more than three weeks ago, I must conclude that the letter miscarried. It was addressed 'San Remo, Italy'. But Mr. Sandford* has very kindly answered the question to which I had begged a reply from your Grace.
He is certain that the opinion expressed (about my treatment in Dunedin,) and the advice given (to resign my claim,) were intended by your Grace to be equally binding ...
I do not pretend to be satisfied with this view of the matter, for your Grace may recall that in stating the case I only undertook to resign my claim in the event of your Grace pronouncing it neither legally nor morally tenable. But after all that Mr. Sandford has said I shall not contest the matter any further.
I have already intimated to the Bishop of Lichfield and by the next mail I shall inform the Primate of New Zealand, that I withdraw from the struggle I have so long carried on, although with a bitter sense of the dishonourable and unjust treatment which I have experienced, and a painful feeling of having been 'left in the lurch' by those to whom I had a right to look for protection, by whose antipathy I was placed in the humiliating position I now occupy.

Believe me my dear Lord,
Your most faithful servant,
H J Jenner

[*The Rev. Charles Waldegrave Sandford was Commissary to the Archbishop of Canterbury and acted as his secretary.]

Tait's mail forwarding staff were on the ball this time as his reply came the following month, from the grand palace of *Chateau Eléonore, Cannes,* - built by the late Lord Henry Brougham, journalist, barrister, MP, and peer, who helped end the slave trade, and 'invent' Cannes as the playground of the rich - and now having writing paper bearing Tait's crest.

My Dear Bishop,
I have now got the letter of Feb. 28ᵗʰ, and not having heard from you again
I presume you have read my reply to my former letter which had not
reached you when you last wrote. I cannot but approve of the course which
you have decided to adopt in resigning the Bishopric of Dunedin.
You may feel assured that I sympathise with you in the unpleasant position
in which untoward circumstances have placed you.
A C Cantuar

Jenner's decision to 'withdraw from the struggle' seems to have produced a great sigh of relief from those who had been in power during the affair. A typical letter of the time is this from Archbishop Tait to the Bishop of Waiapu (William Williams).

Stonehouse,
St. Peter's,
Isle of Thanet
May 20 1871

My dear Bishop,

I beg to ask of your letter of Feb 25ᵗʰ 1871 respecting what I must still
consider as the strange circumstances connected with Bishop Jenner's

appointment to the See of Dunedin. I presume that there is now no
necessity for entering further into the matter, as Bp. Jenner in a letter to me
of Feb. 28ᵗʰ 1871 tells me that he has withdrawn his claims. It strikes me, as
I am at present advised, that some fresh and more definite rules are
required in the Constitution of the Church of New Zealand with regard to
the formation of a new Diocese and the appointment of Bishops thereto.
Believe me to be ..."

Jenner sent letters announcing his resignation on June 15ᵗʰ 1871 to
Selwyn – *'for transmission to New Zealand'*, and to Archbishop Tait.

On 21 June George Selwyn (now the Bishop of Lichfield) wrote to the
Archbishop:

I think that your Grace will not be sorry to hear that Bishop Jenner has
placed in my hands his written resignation of all claims to the Bishopric of
Dunedin. I have paid to him two hundred pounds (£200) on account of
interest which has accrued upon the Endowment Fund collected by me. His
last letter, herewith enclosed, will show that he is not quite satisfied with
our opinion, but I do not think that we could have done more.

As I paid him two hundred pounds (£200) before, on my own account, I
hope that the sum of £400 which he has now received in all, will have
covered his expenses; and we may consider that your Grace's written
opinion upon his case has been carried out.

While this went on, and before his resignation, Jenner had been trying
to get support for his situation. Without the opportunity for balanced
and sensitively argued debate now available to us through the media of
social networking, the great and the good of the mid 1800s conveyed
their thoughts and feelings through professionally printed and bound
pamphlets. Several of these were produced during the Dunedin Affair,
on both sides of the conflict, and at this point Bishop Jenner used the
device to publicise his claim.

THE CASE OF THE RIGHT REV. H. L. JENNER DD
CONSECRATED FOR THE SEE OF DUNEDIN, NEW ZEALAND.

Humbly submitted to the Upper House of the Convocation of the Province of Canterbury.

Printed by Charles Cull, Houghton Street, Strand, V.C.

Price Sixpence

[1871]

It began ...

It is intended in the following pages to set forth, as concisely as possible, the grounds on which Bishop Jenner claims the See of Dunedin.

The question, being one which intimately concerns the whole Anglican Communion, is respectfully submitted to the consideration of the Bishops, in Convocation assembled, in the earnest hope that their Lordships will be able to see their way to an investigation of the case, and to an expression of opinion on its merits. On a former occasion, when the case of Bishop Colenso was under review, the Upper House of Convocation was able after careful consideration to arrive at a definite conclusion on the grave questions submitted to it; and in the present instance, which is not wanting in analogy to that, it is hard to believe that there will be any more serious difficulty in proceeding to the discussion and examination of the facts and arguments by which Bishop Jenner's claims are supported. As in the Natal so in the Dunedin case, the real question to be decided is whether the See of the Bishop is vacant – spiritually and ecclesiastically – or not.

The circumstances under which Bishop Jenner was first nominated and subsequently consecrated by the late Archbishop of Canterbury, are detailed in a 'Statement' published in July 1868 ...

Jenner then describes, over sixteen pages, his experiences and treatment whilst in Dunedin, and the arguments for and against his being their new Bishop – seen, of course, from his perspective. He ends with a statement that perhaps could have been better put, and which may well have had a detrimental effect on the bishops perception of him.

May God in His mercy grant that out of this painful controversy, out of all the evil – the heart-burnings, the bitterness, the misunderstandings, the misconstructions – with which it has teemed from the first, some good at least may issue; so that God's glory be promoted and the true interests of His Church advanced, even by circumstances which, in man's judgement, seem fraught with consequences of a very opposite kind.

Their Lordships were able to see their way to an investigation of the case, and to an expression of opinion on its merits, and this was published in June 1871:

We the undersigned Bishops of the Province of Canterbury, having no authority to pronounce any judgement on the conduct of the Bishops and Synod of the province of New Zealand, can express no opinion thereon. But being asked for Our Brotherly counsel by the Right Reverend Henry Lascelles Jenner, DD do advise him under all the difficulties of this case to resign all right and title to the Bishoprick of Dunedin.

Signed by

The Archbishop of Canterbury

The Bishops of London, Llandaff, Norwich, Bangor, Gloucester and Bristol, Lichfield, Hereford, Peterborough, Lincoln, Chichester, Exeter, Oxford, Salisbury, Bath and Wells, Saint Albans, Rochester and Ely.

To which Jenner replied:

My dear Lord Archbishop,

I cannot pretend to be satisfied with the document which has this day reached me, signed by Your Grace, and seventeen Bishops of the Province of Canterbury.
On the contrary, I cannot but feel that I have been sacrificed to a mere point of etiquette. It may be quite true that the Bishops have 'no authority

to pronounce any judgement on the conduct of the Bishop and Synod of the Province of New Zealand', but I really cannot see that they are hereby precluded from expressing an opinion on my claim to the Bishop of Dunedin.

However, another issue was to arise that provided an opportunity for the English Bishops to more forcibly express their opinion of Henry Jenner's claim.

After the financial debacle of failing to raise an Endowment for Jenner, the church authorities in Dunedin were keen to appoint someone who had his own source of funds, and preferably someone without what they saw as being 'ritualistic tendencies'. As mentioned in the chapter on the Endowment, the Rev. Samuel Tarratt Nevill, on a trip to visit his wealthy wife's brothers in New Zealand, and recommended by Selwyn, was an ideal choice, and he was duly elected as Bishop on the 1 March, and consecrated on Trinity Sunday 4 June 1871.

On 8 June 1871 the Rt Rev H C Harper, Bishop of Christchurch wrote to Archbishop Tait:

In pursuance of the directions of the General Synod of the Church of England and Ireland in New Zealand, I have the honour to notify to your Grace that the section of the Province of Otago and Southland, which has hitherto been included in the Diocese of Christchurch, has now been made into the separate Diocese of Dunedin, and that there has followed the choice and consecration of the Reverend Samuel Tarratt Nevill MA of Magdalen College, Cambridge, and Rector of Shelton, Staffordshire, to be the Bishop thereof.

At the next meeting of bishops in Lambeth Palace the Archbishop passed on the news of Nevill's consecration and they produced the following Resolution, kindly agreeing to recognise the event, but with a subtle spin at the end:

RESOLUTION OF THE ARCHBISHOPS AND BISHOPS
Lambeth Palace, Feb 5th 1872

The Archbishop of Canterbury, having announced to the Bishops assembled that he had received from the Bishop of Christchurch notification of the Rev. Samuel Tarratt Nevill having been elected and consecrated to the see of Dunedin the Province of New Zealand; and Bishop Jenner having signified to the Archbishop of Canterbury his resignation of the see, it was resolved to inform the Bishop of Christchurch that the Archbishop and Bishops assembled are ready to recognise the Rev. Samuel Tarratt Nevill as second Bishop of Dunedin, taking, however, for granted, that his Grace will receive some more formal announcement of the consecration.

This, eventually, produced the following reply:

Letter from the Bishop of Christchurch to the Archbishop of Canterbury,

Christchurch, New Zealand
June 4ᵗʰ 1872

My Lord Archbishop

There has been some delay in the transmission of the mail from England via San Francisco since January last, and consequently I did not receive until the end of last month your Grace's letter of Feb. 20ᵗʰ, and the copy of the resolution of the Archbishops and Bishops assembled at Lambeth, dated Feb. 5ᵗʰ relative to the consecration of the Reverend Samuel Nevill as Bishop of Dunedin.

The notification of his consecration, which I sent to your Grace on the 8ᵗʰ June 1871, was forwarded in accordance with the following directions of the General Synod of the Church in this province, vis:-

'The Primate shall notify the erection of any new Bishopric, and the choice and consecration of the first Bishop thereof to all Archbishops and Metropolitans, and all presiding Bishops of the Anglican Communion.'

A similar notification was forwarded to the Archbishops of York, Armagh, and Dublin, to the Primate of the Church in Scotland, to the Metropolitans of the Indian, Canadian, Australian and South African Churches, and to the Presiding Bishop of the Church in the United States of America. I now send copies of the following documents.

He then includes the relevant mandates, minutes, resignations and certificates connected with the consecration.

And I forward these documents, not as claiming to represent in so doing the Church and Episcopate of the Church in New Zealand, nor as admitting that the consecration and appointment of Bishop Nevill as Bishop of Dunedin, required any more formal announcement than that which I was instructed to give in the case of every newly erected Diocese, and the consecration of its first Bishop, but as desiring to show all respect for your Grace and the Bishops of the Church of England, and in the hope that the more detailed information on the matters in question, which these documents supply, may tend to prevent any interruption of that loyal attachment to the Church of England which is entertained by the members of the New Zealand Church, which, I trust, will always be maintained.

It is due, however, to myself and the Church in New Zealand, that I should not leave unnoticed what is implied, if not directly stated, in the resolution of the assembled Archbishops and Bishops, viz., that their proposed recognition of Bishop Nevill, as Bishop of Dunedin, is based on the assumption, to be admitted by the New Zealand Church, that Bishop Jenner was the first Bishop of Dunedin.

I am persuaded that the New Zealand Church will not consent to this, nor could such consent be reconciled with what she believes to be the real facts of the case, nor be given without a virtual surrender of her just rights and that liberty of action which belongs to her, as a duly constituted branch of the Catholic Church; and moreover, she will be able to maintain, and with no slight degree of truth, that the Archbishops and Bishops have arrived at a decision respecting Bishop Jenner's claims, on information wholly insufficient to enable them to have formed an impartial judgement on the validity of those claims, inasmuch as the information on which they have acted, so far as it has hitherto been necessarily limited to letters and documents, which require the presence of some person representing the views of that Church, if their bearing on the matters in dispute is to be fully understood.

[Sir Humphrey Appleby couldn't have done better.]

Given the communication problems between England and New Zealand it is not surprising that there was an unfortunate clash of dates. Jenner had formally resigned from his struggle to be the Bishop of Dunedin on 15 June – several days after Nevill had taken on the job. This meant that, as he believed and argued, his position as First Bishop of Dunedin had been usurped by Nevill without any communication between them at all. This, inevitably, acted like a red chasuble to a bull for Jenner who, as far as he was concerned, was still the First Bishop of Dunedin.

Now was the time for him to write another pamphlet in his defence. This was published in June 1872 by J T Hayes of Eaton Square, London, and titled,

THE SEE OF DUNEDIN, N. Z:
THE TITLE OF THE RIGHT REV. H. L. JENNER, DD
TO BE ACCOUNTED THE FIRST BISHOP
BRIEFLY VINDICATED.

It began ...

The question on which the Church in New Zealand and myself are now at issue is simply this: Who is to be accounted the First Bishop of Dunedin? My own claim is disputed in the interest of Bishop Nevill, the schismatic intruder into my as yet unvacated see; who apparently clings to the notion of my never having been Bishop of the see for which I was consecrated, as the only means of justifying his own most unhappy position. In the following pages I shall confine myself to the confutation of the assumptions and sophistries – I cannot call them arguments – with which Bishop Nevill, and the Bishop of Wellington, (who comes to the rescue) vainly endeavour to prop up their tottering cases.

To defend that which is utterly indefensible – to justify conduct which has already fatally discredited a much vaunted Synodical system in the estimation of all who prefer Truth and Justice to Falsehood and Wrong –

such is the task to which these two Christian Bishops have addressed themselves; with what success I hope to show in the following pages.

He ends ...

It now therefore only remains for me to declare, that, while disclaiming all wish to interfere in any way with Bishop Nevill, his work, or his position, nothing short of the award of such an arbitration as I have proposed shall induce me to desist from pressing my claim to have been the lawful occupant of the See of Dunedin, from August 24th 1866 until June 16th 1871 at least.

This issue was taken up by the Bishops in England, and a letter subsequently sent to the Bishop of Christchurch, who replied to it, and then asked for the dialogue to be published in the *Guardian*.

From his Grace the Archbishop of Canterbury to the Most Rev. the Primate of New Zealand.
Addington Park, Croydon

20th Jan 1875

My dear Bishop, I enclose a copy of the letter which the Bishop of London, in conjunction with the Bishops of Winchester and Lichfield, submitted to me on the subject of the Dunedin bishopric. The letter was laid before the bishops at our meeting last week, and was by them approved.

From the Bishop of London to his Grace the Archbishop of Canterbury,

London House, St. James's Square, S.W.
May 20th 1874

My Lord Archbishop,

The Bishops of Winchester and Lichfield and myself, who were appointed at a meeting of bishops held at Lambeth in February 1873, to consider and draft an answer to the Bishop of Christchurch on the matter of Bishop Jenner and the Dunedin bishopric, have had before us the various documents relating to the whole transaction, and beg to submit it to your Grace's judgement as an opinion that a reply should be returned to the

Primate of New Zealand in the tenor following: - Seeing that Dr. Jenner was selected by the Archbishop of Canterbury (Dr. Longley), with consent of the Crown, to be Bishop of Dunedin, and was consecrated at the request of the Primate of New Zealand for the bishopric of Dunedin; that he was recognised, as appears by the letters before us, as the Bishop of Dunedin both by the Bishop of Christchurch and by the Ruridecanal Board of Otago; that he made to the Archbishop of Canterbury the declaration required by the synod; that that declaration was received without remonstrance or objection by the standing commission of the General Synod; that an endowment fund of nearly £1,300 was raised in his name and for his use as Bishop of Dunedin in the colony itself, and that the interest of the endowment fund was paid to Bishop Jenner from the time of his consecration to the time of his resignation of the see of Dunedin; the bishops of the Church of England do not see how they can, consistently with the facts of the case, refuse to recognise Bishop Jenner as the first Bishop of Dunedin.

The Bishop of London

Meanwhile in New Zealand their General Synod was meeting in Wellington and a report of a select committee, [what would the Anglican Church do without select committees?] appointed to draw up a statement of the grounds on which the General Synod had acted in reference to the bishopric of Dunedin, was laid before the synod, and the following resolution adopted:

That, it having been brought to the notice of this synod that the Archbishop of Canterbury and certain bishops of England have formally recognised Dr. Jenner as the first bishop of the see of Dunedin, apparently in disregard of the judgements of the synod formally pronounced on Dr. Jenner's claims – this synod, in exercise of its undoubted authority, having carefully examined the circumstances under which Dr. Jenner claims to be regarded as having been the first bishop of the see of Dunedin, declares that Dr. Jenner, not having been apponted to the see of Dunedin in accordance with the laws of the Church in New Zealand, ought not to be recognised as having been such first bishop; and this synod doth recognise the Right Rev. Samuel Tarratt Nevill, D.D. as the present and first Bishop of Dunedin.

That this resolution seemed to have been ignored by the English side produced a critical response from Bishop Harper.

As no reference is made to this report and resolution in your grace's letter to myself, or in the letter which obtained the approval of the bishops of the Church of England, there is some reason to fear that these documents did not come under their consideration at their meeting in January last.

The Church of this colony will, at all events, be reluctant to believe that no importance was attached by their lordships to the statements contained in the report, or to the decision of the General Synod, as expressed in the resolution.

It is obvious, however, to remark that the bishops have approved of a letter which apparently ignores the authority of the General Synod in the appointment of bishops within the province of New Zealand, though some such authority is attributed to the standing commission, which derives all its powers by delegation from the General Synod.

As the Church of New Zealand has now, in three successive sessions of her synod, refused to admit the validity of the claims of Bishop Jenner to the bishopric of Dunedin, all further comment of mine upon the letter would be out of place. I have only, therefore, to add that I have communicated the letter to the bishops of this province, and I am assured from their replies that they will concur with me in upholding the judgement of the General Synod in the matter in question, and in accepting the responsibility incurred thereby by the Church of New Zealand.

I have the honour to be, my Lord Archbishop, your grace's very obedient servant in Christ.

H. J. C. Christchurch
Primate of the Province of New Zealand

Although Dunedin didn't want him, he was still a bishop, and Jenner, having the beliefs about the church that lay behind the Catholic renewal, had a very high regard for the role for which he had been consecrated. For him a bishop wasn't just the ecclesiastical equivalent of a Chief Executive Officer or an Area Manager. His consecration had been about being empowered by the Holy Spirit for the sacred task of enabling the church to keep alive the rumour of God.

So, he lived in hope that the Archbishop would offer him another chance to carry his crozier, in England, or some other land.

The *Church Review* published a verbatim report of a conversation on 28 September 28 1871, between Bishop Jenner and Bishop Wilberforce (then the Bishop of Winchester,) as to what the Bishops at Lambeth had said with regard to the Dunedin affair.

Bishop Jenner. I suppose that business of mine did not take long to settle, when you discussed it at Lambeth, five minutes at the utmost.
Bishop Wilberforce. On the contrary we all felt how important were the issues raised; and considered the matter most carefully.
J. Well, I confess I could not feel satisfied with the decision you came to, if decision it can be called.
W. No, so I gathered from your letter. But what could we do? To have done what you wanted i.e. to have declared you in the right and the N.Z. Church in the wrong, would have been a challenge to the N.Z. Bishops who would certainly have sent an answer to which we must have replied and a hopeless controversy must have resulted. But I hope you understood the import of the phraseology we employed. The first draft of the resolution, I forget by what Bishop proposed, contained the words *'We advise him under the difficulties of the case to resign his claim to the Bishopric'* on which I observed that a claim might be rightful or wrongful and that it was hardly fair to use so indefinite an expression on such an occasion. So I proposed the substitution of the words *'All right and title'* an amendment which was unanimously accepted as expressing the true state of the case, and thus altered the resolution was carried nem con.
J. Then you meant, I presume, in advising me to resign all right and title to the See of Dunedin to express your opinion that I had such *'right and title'.*
W. Unquestionably: how could we ask you to resign that which we did not believe you to possess?
J. Well, I hoped and trusted that was your intention only I desiderated a more outspoken pronouncement. But now that you assure me that you deliberately used words which recognised my title to the See I am quite satisfied.

W. My dear fellow, you had as much right and title to your See as any of us have to ours; and I am sure we all felt that.

J. It is a great comfort to me to hear you say so.

W. I still think that if you had ignored the opposition and taken possession of your Diocese as if nothing had happened you would soon have established yourself in your rightful position.

J. Possibly, but remember, I should have had to fight all the N.Z. Bishops.

W. Well, you would have been victorious and I should have done so. Yet I can't blame you for choosing peace in preference to war.

J. My successor, Bishop Nevill has come to England. In what light is he to be regarded? If my view of the situation is correct, and you English Bishops have confirmed it, his position is a very awkward one. For he was consecrated before my resignation.

W. I was not aware of that. It was very wrong if it was so. They ought to have waited.

J. And since they did not Bp. Nevill's consecration was a schismatical proceeding?

W. I don't say as much as that. Sad things have happened in the Church before now, and have been condoned *Factum valet* [the fact is worth it], you see, though *fieri non elebuit* [it was not easy to be done.] If I were you I should now condone this irregularity.

J. Certainly, if it rested with me, although I cannot but feel that Bp. Nevill's consecration was a deliberate aggression on my rights, but then there comes the question, Who is to go down to posterity as the *first* Bishop of Dunedin?

W. You are most certainly. Nevill is your successor.

J. So I contend. But the N.Z. Bishops and Boards ignore me altogether denying that I ever *was* Bp. of Dunedin.

W. They never will be able to maintain that.

J. They will try. But what I wish you and the other bishops to understand is this, that although I am quite willing that Nevill should be received and recognised as Bp. of Dunedin I never can allow that he is so except in succession to myself, and I trust you will all support me in this. The fact is Nevill is not so much to be blamed as those who have placed him in the false position he occupies. I consider Bishop Harper the first culprit.

W. Bye the Bye. What was the reason of Harper's behaviour towards you? I never could make it out.

J. There was more than one motive, but you can trace throughout the dogged obstinacy of one of the weakest of men.

W. Yes, he is weak, as I have reason to know for he was in my diocese before he went to N. Zealand.

J. What do you think of his inhibiting me from officiating in my own Diocese directly I arrived in N.Z.?

W. You don't mean to say that! This is the first I have heard of it. Nothing could excuse such a step. What did you do?

J. Oh I obeyed; and was three months in the colony without ministering in public.

W. There I think you were wrong. I should certainly have resisted such a monstrous order.

J. Yes, I can see now that I ought to have done false steps. But you see, I had no one to advise me and had to act on the spur of the moment on almost every occasion. No wonder I made mistakes now and then.

W. Well there can be no doubt that you have been most shamefully, infamously, iniquitously dealt with. As far as I can see, the matter has been mismanaged from the beginning and you have been made the victim. But now tell me. You made a remark at breakfast this morning that troubled me. Referring to words of mine last night you said I had set you dreaming of Honolulu. Now the Archbishop and I have just offered that See to Willis of Chatham who has accepted it. It never struck me that you would have taken it, otherwise I feel sure you might have had it.

J. Oh no, I never had any thought of that and I am extremely glad that Willis is to go. It is an excellent appointment. I do not know a better man in every sense of the word. What I desire is the refusal of the vacant see of Mauritius.

W. I heartily wish you may have it. If I knew the Colonial Secretary well enough I would write and suggest it, as I certainly should do *vive voce* if I met him in society.

J. Thanks, I have no right to expect your interference, yet the extremely anomalous position in which I find myself at present is perhaps not altogether undeserving of sympathy from the English Episcopacy at large. I have one qualification for Mauritius which may not always be easy to find, a familiarity with the French language (the vernacular of the island) from childhood. Also my robust health may be considered some recommendation. I am most anxious, as you may understand, to obtain Episcopal work of some kind.

W. Of course you are and I only hope and trust you may be successful.

For some reason Jenner never saw himself as being a bishop in England, and in this conversation he mentions two colonial dioceses that were vacant and that he would like to have been offered.

The position of the Bishop of Honolulu had become vacant the previous year when Bishop Thomas Staley had decided to retire, having found the political struggle between the British and the American churches over who should have control over the church in the islands very painful. He had been consecrated on 15 December 1861, at the suggestion of Samuel Wilberforce and Queen Victoria, as the church's first bishop of the Kingdom of Hawaii, and had arrived there in 1862. Although keeping political neutrality his background meant he was seen by the American's, including Mark Twain, as being an agent for Britain. On his retirement he had hoped to be replaced by an American bishop, but was replaced, as Wilberforce says, by Alfred Willis, Vicar of St Mark's, New Brompton, Chatham. The territorial jurisdiction of the Episcopal Diocese of Honolulu was given up to American Episcopalians in 1893.

Why Jenner should want to be the Bishop of Mauritius is unclear. Sometimes he doesn't seem to have done enough research into what the different dioceses were like. The Anglican church established itself on the island after the defeat of the French, with oversite being given to a Civil Chaplain in 1812. The first Bishop of Mauritius wasn't consecrated until 1854, and the second one – Thomas Hatchard, son of the publisher – died of cholera within a year of his arrival in 1869. The man who got the job Jenner had his eye on – Henry Huxtable – died in 1871 at the age of 45.

Because of its missionary roots the diocese had always been of a low-church, evangelical persuasion, not at all what Jenner would have wanted. This seems to have continued – as ecclesiastical preferences tend to do – with Wikipedia stating that, '*The Church of the Province of the Indian Ocean [of which Mauritius is part,] is a member of the Global South and the Global Anglican Future Conference (GAFCON), and has been involved in the* Anglican realignment.'

This interest in Mauritius comes up again in a letter from the Bishop of Dover to the Archbishop of Canterbury of 9 October 1870:

My Dear Lord,

Jenner has been with me. He would like Mauritius and says he can speak and preach in French. How this may be I know not, but I think he has behaved like a Christian and a gentleman in a very difficult position.
He is no doubt a Ritualistically inclined High Churchman. But I presume that, if appointed to Mauritius, he would take the advice of his friend the Bishop of Winchester, and obey the law as regards postures and vestments. It would also be necessary to extract a guarantee that he would not leave England in debt.
I am sorry I did not see him before I came to Addington, as we might have had a word about him in the intervals of the Archdeacon and Canon Bateman: uproarious conversation without being overheard!
I would have preferred for Jenner a backwood Diocese, where he could help his flock to cut down trees and look after sheep, but I am not sure that it is right to...?..P. Under the circumstances he is stranded as he is.
He and I differ widely, but in all relations to me he has behaved as well as I think he has about Dunedin.
Yours truly,
        E. Parry
          Bishop of Dover.

From the flippant comment about '*uproarious conversation without being overheard!*' it would not be surprising to discover that Parry and Tait were pretty well lifelong friends. Parry had been at Rugby when Tait had been its Headmaster, he became his domestic chaplain when Tait became the Bishop of London, and he was appointed archdeacon and canon of Canterbury when Tait succeeded to the primacy. When Tait began to find the responsibilities of being Archbishop getting very heavy, what with all the problems involving the new Colonial Provinces and stuff, he consecrated Parry as the first Suffragan Bishop of Dover since 1597.

[The concept of a suffragan bishop in the Church of England was formalised by the *Suffragan Bishops Act* 1534, the last Tudor suffragan bishop being the Bishop of Colchester, who died in post in 1607/8. No more suffragans were appointed for more than 250 years, until the consecration of the Bishop of Nottingham on 2 February 1870, and Parry on 25 March 1870, (only the fourth Suffragan Bishop of Dover since 1536).]

In an undated letter of about this time the Archbishop writes to Jenner concerning his future in the Church of England. It must have been very difficult for Jenner to read as it seems that his time in Dunedin would forever blight his career in the church – even though it was not his fault.

Dear Bishop,
You may feel sure that not only I, but all my Brethren, have felt much for the painful position in which you find yourself. But, even though they entered on the consideration of the case in the most kindly spirit, they were not able to devise any plan by which your wishes could be complied with.
It was not unnatural that they should call to view all the circumstances which have contributed to your present difficulties. Your rejection by the Church in New Zealand, however it arose, placed you in a very unpleasant position, and naturally raises enquiries as to what was the cause of you not going out to your Diocese when first appointed, and what circumstances had arisen in the interval between your consecration and departure from this country of a nature to give rise to so strong a feeling in the Diocese of Dunedin against you being placed at its head.
Again, since your return to England an unfortunate impression has prevailed amongst the English Bishops that your presence and officiating in their Dioceses was likely to minister to strife and confusion, and they have

*also been pained to remark that your living has been under some strain
and that many pecuniary difficulties have impeded your usefulness.
Unfortunately the impression generally produced by these various
circumstances has been such that, when any position in the Colonies to
which you might have been eligible has been vacant, and I have been
requested to nominate a Bishop, I have gathered that, were I to nominate
you, the very same scenes may again be enacted which took place in
Dunedin, and I am sure you would not wish for the repetition of anything
so painful.*

*The unfortunate result is that you find yourself with no sphere of action
beyond that of a parish priest, and it is perhaps fortunate that you had not
resigned your parish before you left. As disagreeable as it may be for you to
realise the fact, I fear there is nothing for you but to determine to find as
much occasion as you can for your energies in the sphere which He
assigned to you, remembering after all that it is by no means inconsistent
with the Canons of the Church that a Bishop who has in any way lost his
diocese should confine himself to the work of the priesthood.*

In August 1873 Jenner writes from Preston Vicarage a letter which
seems to be in response to this, and which looks to a non-Colonial
solution:

*I see now – what I do not think I fully realised before – the difficulties with
which your Grace would have to contend in recommending me to a
Colonial See. I can do nothing therefore but accept what seems inevitable.
With regard to Paris, I cannot say that I feel disposed to abandon my
intention of migrating thither. In fact it seems the only thing left for me to
do, for I <u>cannot</u> remain here, and an exchange, unless it be a very
advantageous one, is too expensive to be thought of … At Paris I conceive I
should be autocephalous, as I presume was Bishop Luscombe in former
days.*

[In 1824, Archbishop Canning had appointed Matthew Luscombe
embassy chaplain in Paris, and also general superintendent of the
Anglican congregations on the continent. The following year he was
consecrated to a continental bishopric.]

I do not deny that domestic reasons, such as educational advantages for my daughters, have had some influence on my choice of Paris for a residence, but my chief object is to place myself in a position less unsuited to the Episcopal Character than my present one.

He goes on to argue for the need of a third Anglican chapel in Paris. There is no indication anywhere of why there should be a vacancy in Paris at that time.

Bishop Jenner's name being associated with an overseas see was not always due to his own involvement. For example, this fascinating article about the Diocese of Bombay appeared in the *Holloway Press* of 2 October 1875:

The Cowley Fathers, who went out from Oxford to evangelise India, seem to have given still further offence by setting up the confessional in their church at Bombay. The Rev. Luke Rivington, who had served at All Saint's, Margaret Street, announced from the pulpit his intention to do this. All this time Bombay remains without a chief pastor. Poor Bishop Douglas is understood to have resigned his Bishopric several weeks ago; and there was a rumour that Bishop Jenner, who was sent back from Dunedin, and who is the head of the Confraternity of the Blessed Sacrament, had been appointed, but this report has not yet been confirmed.

And this in the *Bath Chronicle and Weekly Gazette* a month earlier:

The Right Rev. Dr. Douglas having formally resigned the Bishopric of Bombay, urgent representations have been made to the Secretary of State for India to nominate to it the Rev. Dr. Jenner, the first Bishop of Dunedin, New Zealand.

Perhaps Jenner's last shot at an overseas bishopric was in 1879, when the See of Jamaica became vacant. In May of that year he wrote to Archbishop Tait, with a self-made copy of a letter of recommendation from John Mitchinson, Bishop of Barbados. Before his consecration Mitchinson had been Headmaster of the Kings's School, Canterbury for fourteen years and knew Jenner well. Jenner admits that the letter is not the original, having lost it, but is confident that it expresses Mitchinson's views, as they had known each other very well and, 'as a near neighbour over the years he had had ample opportunities of judging my fitness for the Bishopric, the qualifications for which must be about the same as for his own diocese.'

The copy read -

I have been urging your claims hard on the Jamaica folk, and have told them, not only that in robust vigour of physique you would be well suited for the laborious work of that diocese, and that you are a just and courteous man, able to appreciate and encourage good work, wherever you found it, even though it should not happen to run in the theological groove which you yourself adopt.

I do hope they will choose you, and that you will make no difficulty in coming out if they should do so. Most gladly should I welcome you as a welcome addition to our new West Indian Province.

Jenner was also supported in his request for the See of Jamaica by George Dowker, a Fellow of the Geological Society. Dowker lived in a village adjacent to Preston in *Stourmouth House,* a delightful property owned by his family since being built in the sixteenth century, and was a leading geologist, archaeologist and botanist in Kent. He writes that he has known Bishop Jenner intimately for upward of twenty five years. In an appropriately glowing song of praise he wrote:

Your Lordship is aware of his great learning and ability. You also know that he has had the courage to uphold his own convictions. But you may not know so well as I do of his great liberality (taken in its widest meaning,) and during the many years I have known him I have never heard him speak one word against those who disagreed with his opinion. Though in a small village where his learning and ability are not half appreciated he has drawn many to Christ by his earnest preaching and teaching.

He then goes on to talk of how an episcopal appointment would offer an opportunity to repair the cruel injustice of the Dunedin affair.

The Diocese of Jamaica was another one with short term bishop problems. [It may have been that news of Colonial dioceses with bishop problems led Jenner to think he stood a better chance with them than the more established episcopacies.] Jamaica's third bishop, Bishop Courtenay, had resigned in 1879, and the Synod failed to elect a new one. The English Committee of Reference - composed of the Archbishops of Canterbury and York and the Bishop of London - selected Bishop William Tozer. who had resigned his appointment as Missionary Bishop of Central Africa because of ill heath. He arrived in Jamaica in October 1879 but resigned and left the country in April 1880. However, the bishop who did get the job, the Rev. Enos Nuttall, lasted for thirty six years.

Jenner was very keen to be able to exercise his episcopal role in any way he could, and in 1885 there occurred an incident that got him into hot water with Frederick Temple, the Bishop of London.

He had taken on the role of Visitor to a large boarding school in Bruges called St Laurence's, whose Principal was an English priest and whose pupils were all sons of English churchgoers. They had invited Jenner to take the Confirmation Service in their private chapel in March of that year, which of course he was delighted to do. The problem arose because, at that time, it was the Bishop of London who had responsibility for Anglicans in Europe, and he kicked up a stink about it, arguing that Jenner had no right to, as he wrote, 'invade his jurisdiction'. He went on:

It is out of the question that the Bishop of London should continue to add this heavy burden to his other duties if he is to deal not only with the ordinary matters coming before a Bishop for decisions, but also with the confusion that must arise if other Bishops claim and exercise the right of interference.

Jenner argued that there was no Canon or any other law which gave the Bishop of London that particular jurisdiction, (which was true, but like many things in the CofE, it had been like that for a very long time, and 'to upset this doctrine would be to introduce utter confusion.') He also pointed out that there wasn't a Bishop of London in place when he took the Confirmation, there being a gap between the death of John Jackson on the 6 January and the translation of Temple on the 24 March. Inevitably Jenner's view was not thought worthy of discussion and nothing more seems to have happened.

In January 1882 Jenner had printed another pamphlet:

A Letter addressed to His grace the Archbishop of Canterbury and the Bishops of the Church of England by The Right Rev Henry Lascelles Jenner D.D. Formrly Bishop of Dunedin, N.Z.
Printed in Canterbury by M. J. Goulden

It began ...

My Lord Archbishop,

If I make no apology for addressing your Grace, and, through you, the Bishops of the Anglican Communion, it is because what I am about to write relates to a matter which concerns not myself only, but the whole Church of England. For the strange spectacle of a Bishop in full enjoyment of almost exceptional strength, yet condemned from the beginning of his Episcopate to a life of inaction as regards the office to which he has been called, can hardly, one would suppose, be a matter of indifference to the Church at large.

He goes on to list the events of the Dunedin Affair and then describes ways in which his Bishopness could be used in its present state.

1. It very frequently happens that the nomination of a Bishop to a Colonial See is left to your Grace, and two or three other Bishops. Is it presumptious to suggest, that on such occasions my claims need not always be overlooked?

2. At the present time, as your Grace is aware, the expediency of placing the English Chaplaincies in Northern Europe under regular Episcopal superintendence, is again being discussed. Probably the time has not come for the consecration of a Bishop for that sphere of labour. But, supposing a see-less Bishop, like myself, were willing, if only as a temporary arrangement, to accept such a post, there might, perhaps, be no overwhelming reasons for refusing his services. As for myself, I can only say that that particular work has special attractions for me.

3. Again, how often does it happen that the services of a 'spare' Bishop might be utilised in relieving a Diocesan of the labour of Confirmations and other duties, which are apt to press heavily on the latter, when in ill health or advanced years. Need I say how gladly I would take any such work, whether pro re nata *for any Bishop who might require assistance; or, and of course preferably, as recognised coadjutor in a particular Diocese?*

The same year an opportunity arose for Jenner to be properly accepted as a bishop and for him to exercise his episcopal skills. Unfortunately it was not within the Church of England but the *Église Gallicane* in Paris.

Just as he and other 'ritualists' were working for a more Catholic aspect to the Church of England, so, in the Roman Catholic Church there were some who were not happy with the way that their own denomantion was going, particularly over the issue of Papal Infallability and the teachings that came out of the First Vatican Council. In Germany and Holland such groups took the form of the Old Catholic Church, and in France they found a spiritual leader in Père Hyacinthe Loyson, a Discalced Carmelite who built his reputation as the most effective orator of his day, preaching in Lyon and Bordeaux and subsequently gaining fame for his sermons and orations at the Eglise de la Madeleine and at Notre Dame de Paris.

In June 1869, Loyson had delivered an address before the Ligue internationale de la paix, in which he spoke of the Jewish religion, the Catholic religion, and the Protestant religion, as being the three great religions of civilized peoples. In 1869, he protested against the manner in which the First Vatican Council was convened.

He was ordered to retract, but he refused and broke with his order in an open letter of 20 September 1869, addressed to the General of the Discalced Carmelites, but evidently intended for the governing powers of the Church. In it he protested against the sacrilegious perversion of the Gospel, and went on to say:

'It is my profound conviction that if France in particular and the Latin races in general, are given up to social, moral, and religious anarchy, the principal cause is not Catholicism itself, but the manner in which Catholicism has for a long time been understood and practised.'

He was subsequently excommunicated.

His foundation of the *Église Gallicane* was seen by many Protestant groups as introducing a powerful tool to bring about Catholic reform. In Britain he had the support of Arthur Stanley, the Dean of Westminster; Archbishop Tait; the Bishop of Winchester; the Bishop of Edinburgh; and William Gladstone. In July 1876 Father Hyacinthe addressed three meetings in London, chaired by the Bishop of Winchester, the Duke of Argyle, and William Gladstone. At his meeting Gladstone announced:

My first and agreeable duty is to make an announcement on the part of His Grace the Archbishop of Canterbury, that had it not been for a peculiar and special engagement connected with the discharge of his high office he had earnestly hoped and intended to be present on this occasion.

Under Tait's influence a committee was appointed by the Lambeth Conference of 1878 to confer with the Old Catholic congregations in France and elsewhere, and to supply such congregations, if they needed it, with Episcopal ministrations. The *Association for making known upon the Continent the Principles of the Anglican Church,* (latterly the Anglo-Continental Society or ACS,) agreed to finance any such appointments.

This led to the authorising of Robert Eden, Primus of the Scottish Episcopal Church, to be the first '*evĕque provisiore*', of *Église Gallicane*. In 1882 Jenner offered his assistance to Père Hyacinthe Loyson, and in 1883 he was duly installed as Eden's successor. He retired from the role in 1887 and, in a letter to the then Archbishop of Canterbury, Edward Benson, telling him of his resignation, he explained that the American Episcopal Church were keen to be involved with Catholic Reform in France and had appointed a committee, under the Presidency of the Bishop of Western New York, Arthur Coxe to look into it. Jenner felt that the *Église Gallicane* would do better under American administration.

[Benson didn't want to be told about the resignation as he was unaware that Jenner had even been Bishop of the *Église Gallicane*, and didn't really seem to know much about it.]

Coxe was duly appointed as Presiding Bishop, and lasted until 1893 when Loyson passed the church over to the Old Catholic Archdiocese of Utrecht.

In February 1884 Bishop Jenner wrote a long letter to the Archbishop of Canterbury thanking him for allowing him to take a Confirmation service for his own people in St Mildred's church. He included a list of the numbers of different kinds of people being confirmed, their ages, and their backgrounds, and ends the letter with this triumphant paragraph:

Preston is a small and not very important place, but it has been in several respects a pioneer, as regards Church worth, in the part of your Grace's Diocese. And although it may have been outstripped in the race by many parishes which once lapped far behind it, I am confident that, with regard to the reverence and heartiness of its services, the number of communions annually made, and the evident devotion of the Communicants, there is still cause for thankfulness if not for absolute satisfaction.

Tucked into the envelope with it was another sheet of paper with the title *P.S. Confidential,* in which Jenner gives what was probably the real reason for the Confirmation letter being written:

There are two things that I wish to mention to your Grace, and which I may perhaps be allowed to make the subject of this Postscript.

1. I informed your Grace some months ago that I was anxious to remove from this parish. In the absence of any apparent prospect of a permanent change I shall venture to ask your Grace to give me leave of non-residence for a year from (probably) the 1ˢᵗ of May next.

2. Judging from a reply given by Mr. Gladstone [now Prime Minister] *on Thursday to enquiries respecting the Bishopric of Natal, it seems probable that a Bishop will be required to provide, temporarily, episcopal ministrations in that Diocese. As it is not to be supposed that anyone will be especially consecrated for this work, I venture to say that I would myself willingly go out to Natal and do what was required, only for a twelve-*

month – working, I need hardly add, on the lines of the present South African Episcopate. I make this offer, presuming that your Grace will probably be consulted in the matter."

The following was the advice concerning Jenner's request given to Benson by Randall Davidson. Davidson had been Tait's chaplain and secretary and had stayed on at Lambeth with Benson until being made Dean of Windsor in 1883. This letter was dated 28 February 1884, and shows how he remained close to Benson before Temple became Archbishop in 1896.

Bishop Jenner requires most careful handling. He will hearafter bring up – quite probably – anything you may say as justifying his quest for a permanent Episcopal Charge! You know how carefully he has <u>not</u> been asked to confirm anywhere out of his own parish.

I don't think a full explanation to him about South Africa would be desirable. No saying what use might be made of it. I would have thought a few kind lines saying you were glad to hear about his Confirmation would do, with a separate P.S. saying that you venture to think he scarcely realises (as he clearly doesn't,) the state of affairs in South Africa.

RTD

[In South Africa John Colenso had remained as the Bishop of Natal - despite having been 'excommunicated' by Robert Gray, Bishop of Cape Town in 1866 - retaining both his stipend from the Colonial Bishoprics Fund, and his control over church property in Natal. The declaration had been made that the diocese of Natal was vacant, with the predictable consequence that Colenso – as was his legal right – continued in office, and was shadowed by a Bishop of Maritzburg, consecrated by a frustrated Gray to administer much the same territory. The anomalous situation continued until Colenso's death in 1883, at which point it took a further decade before the warring constituencies in Natal were more or less reconciled.]

There is another trivial example of Davidson giving advice concerning Bishop Jenner. In March 1887 John Puckle, Vicar of St Mary's, Dover, wrote to the Archbishop expressing concern about the 'creeping

Ritualistic practices' he had recently come across, the most troubling being a photograph in his local photographic shop of '*my neighbour Bishop Jenner in full Pontificals from Mitre to hem of Dalmatique. He has at times officiated in this Deanery, and I could but think whether, if he did so again, it would be in this dress. Now I do not want to bring a needless trouble but ...*' and inevitably does just that by suggesting that he keep a watch out for these new practices, and sending the Archbishop regular updates.

Davidson sends this advice:

There can, I imagine be, in any case, no harm in Puckle keeping you privately informed. But really, this Jennerian Mitre is rather strong! Perhaps it was only for the photographers?

RTD

This seems to relate to Jenner's concerns about his status as a bishop. In 1875 he had written to Tait to seek his guidance on the wearing of episcopal vestments, and had pointed out that, as a result of the recently passed Public Worship Regulations Act, (implemented by Tait to limit what he saw as the growing ritualism in the Church of England,) he was now in the odd position of facing prosecution for wearing bishop's robes, whilst at the same time being obliged by the ornaments rubric in the 1662 Prayer Book to wear a cope or vestments, and to carry a pastoral staff. Apparently the canons of 1604 stated that he must, as a bishop, wear a cope if celebrating in cathedrals and collegiate churches. Jenner pointed out that at least two diocesan bishops were now wearing copes when celebrating in their own cathedrals.

Three years later, just down the road in Folkestone, the Vicar of St Peter's, Fr Ridsdale, was to become the first Anglican clergyman to be prosecuted under the Public Worship Regulations Act and, like Jenner, objected to abandoning vestments contrary to his interpretation of the Ornaments Rubric of the Book of Common Prayer. Fortunately he was treated leniently because of this, and, unlike four other parish priests, did not end up serving time in prison.

A Punch cartoon commenting on the Public Worship Regulations Act drawn by John Tenniel.

The Dunedin Crozier

There is something both richly symbolic and immensely sad about this tangible remnant of Jenner's status as a bishop. It was a loving gift, paid for by friends and colleagues, designed by one of the greatest of the Victorian art-architects, and based on the fragment of a crozier from the twelfth century. It was carried, hopefully and expectantly, around the world by Jenner, to the South Island of New Zealand, and then – like Jenner's hope's and expectations of an episcopacy – brought back home again, sadly superfluous to the needs of the Church of England.

Contrary to other accounts, the crozier was not commissioned by Jenner himself, and he did not travel the country raising money for its purchase. As mentioned elsewhere, Jenner had been part of the *Ecclesiological Society* since his student days, when he was a member of the Cambridge Camden Society, and over the years had been both a contributor and its secretary. It was therefore not surprising that in 1866 *The Ecclesiologist* should include the following:

The accompanying illustration represents the pastoral staff (to be executed in silver and ivory) designed by Mr. Burges, which is to be the gift of his colleagues on the Ecclesiological Committee to the Rev. H. L. Jenner, Bishop designate of Dunedin. Those gentlemen who have not forwarded their contributions are requested to send them to the Rev. B. Webb, 3 Chandos Street, Cavendish Square. W.

With hindsight it can be seen that the money raised would have been better sent to New Zealand to be part of the future bishop's Endowment, as the lack of funds needed to house and support him in that country would prove to be one of the many reasons why Jenner was unable to be more than a 'bishop designate'.

The designer of the crozier **William Burges** was also a member of the *Ecclesiological Society,* as well as being   "a wide-ranging scholar, an

268

intrepid traveller, a coruscating lecturer, a brilliant decorative designer and an architect of genius" (J. Mordaunt Crook). Along with nineteenth-century architects George Edmund Street, William Butterfield and George Gilbert Scott, he is recognized as one of the major figures of the Gothic Revival in Britain – in particular of that phase of stylistic eclecticism and formal experimentation known as High Victorian Gothic (circa 1850-1870). His work echoed that of the Pre-Raphaelites, and heralded that of the Arts and Crafts movement.

He won his first major commission for *Saint Fin Barre's Cathedral* in Cork in 1863, (visited by Jenner on his journey to New Zealand,) when he was 35, and he died, in 1881, at his Kensington home, *The Tower House* (now home of Jimmy Page of *Led Zeppelin,*) aged only 53. His architectural output was small but varied. Working with a long-standing team of craftsmen, he built churches, a cathedral, a warehouse, a university, a school, houses and castles, and designed furniture and jewellery...and a crozier.

Burges was known to have a passing addiction to opium (which may have enhanced his already dreamy nature), and was friendly with all the Pre-Raphaelites. On his deathbed his last visitors were Oscar Wilde and James McNeill Whistler. He was known to be "eccentric, unpredictable, overindulgent and flamboyant" as well as very near-sighted – he once mistook a peacock for a man. He was also child-like by all accounts. Dante Gabriel Rossetti wrote:

> *"There's a babyish party called Burges,*
> *Who from childhood hardly emerges.*
> *If you hadn't been told,*
> *He's disgracefully old,*
> *You would offer a bull's-eye to Burges."*

In 1875 he published the crozier design in a French magazine as being a thirteenth century original of a curiosity, and in his Velum Sketchbook he put a note by the design, *"the staff of the Lord bishop of the isles where they eat one another"*. Similarly inventive were his designs for fish plates for Lord Bute, in which a service of eighteen plates is decorated with punning illustrations, such as a skating skate, and a winged perch seated on the branch of a tree.

In his study *Life in costume: the architectural fictions and anachronisms of William Burges* (McGill University, Montreal 2011,) Nicholas Roquet wrote this very whimsical description of the meanings within the crozier's design (illustrated on the front cover).

The ambiguities of Burges's imaginative process in the Vellum Sketchbook appear most clearly in the Jenner Crozier, which Burges designed and had manufactured for the Anglican bishop of Dunedin in 1866-7. Though the carved figurines on the crozier's ivory handle are clearly meant to "tell a story," that story's content remains always elusive. At first hand, the figurines seem to represent the legend of England's patron Saint George slaying a dragon: thus the crozier symbolises the colony's inclusion in the British Empire and the Church of England's evangelical mission among its native population. But the figures of knight, dragon, and lady might also be a representation in Gothic dress of the Greek myth of Perseus and Andromeda. Viewed this way, the crozier also embodies Burges's belief in the similarities between Gothic and classical Greek architecture. Furthermore, the imagery on the crozier relates to a constellation of more private meanings, which played out simultaneously in Burges's interior in Buckingham Street. The dragon may be an iteration of the allegorical monsters – Contract, Arbitration, Law, etc. - painted on the cabinet in his study (c. 1858); if so, then the bound female figure might symbolise art threatened by the conditions of contemporary practice.

That may be so, but it was unlikely to have been in the mind of the twelfth century designer who created the crozier on which Burges's design is based.

In the *Hunt Museum* in Limerick, Ireland, is part of an eleventh or twelfth century ivory crozier head. It was recently dated by John Cherry of the *British Museum* who described the design as being a dragon's head and ear, and that it was of walrus ivory. He also identified the script on the object as rounded Lombardic from the twelfth century, and transcribed what can be read of the inscription:

[qvia]: non est : nb col[vcato] adversus : c[arn]em : e[t] : s[anguinem] : s[ed] adver]svs : principes : [et pot]estates : mvndi

This can be compared to that on the Dunedin crozier;

quia non est nbscollvcato advesvs : carnem : et sangvinem sed : adversus : principes : et potestates : mvndi rectores

(*For we wrestle not against flesh and blood, but against principalities, against powers, against the rulers of the darkness of this world, against spiritual wickedness in high places.* Ephesians 6:12 KJV)

This striking similarity, along with parallels in the shape of the animals head, the widely splayed jaws, the position of the animals feet, and the disposition of the head, feet, and sword pommel, suggests that Burges's design is based heavily on that in the Hunt museum.

In 1867 the *Oamaru Times* reproduced this article from the *Church Times*:

The pastoral staff of the Bishop of Dunedin, recently completed, is one of the most beautiful modern specimens of Gothic art. It was designed by Mr. W. Burges for the Ecclesiastical Society, and is in every respect perfect. The crook represents, carved in ivory, St. George and the Dragon. In the crockets there are jewels of great size and richness. The staff itself is of ebony, with bands of silver gilt. The beaten work of the knob and crook is most exquisitely done, and the whole may be regarded as a work of real excellence. The Bishop's episcopal ring is of pure gold, with onyx stone.

The work bears the London hallmarks of 1866, and was executed by the Danish and German silversmiths Barkentin & Krall who did a lot of work for Burges.

There is an interesting picture of Jenner holding the crozier, taken by the distinguished photographer Robert Mason of 28 Old Bond Street London in 1867. He is standing by a Glastonbury chair in front of an elaborately decorated wall, wearing surplice and scarf and posed as if giving a blessing. The same chair appears in the photographs that Mason took of over twenty five other Anglican bishops, an Archdeacon and a Dean, (but interestingly not in his many photographs of Charles Dickens). In all of these they are sitting in the same chair in front of the same wall. None of them is robed and none of them carries a crozier. They were probably all taken during the first ever Lambeth Conference held that year – of which Mason took group photographs – which would explain the long suffering chair. It becomes clearer from this to see why Jenner never succeeded as a Bishop. If he had sat in the chair, as the others did, Anglican episcopacy might well have rubbed off on him.

That the photograph shows Jenner holding a crozier and with one hand raised in blessing would not be remarkable today. However, when it was taken its impact would have been both contentious and divisive. According to Owen Chadwick:

Bishop Hamilton of Salisbury used a pastoral staff. He was the first of the Tractarian bishops, and therefore the use caused comment. But about 1867 at least three bishops accepted gifts of such staffs, Lonsdale of Lichfield (ruefully, for he was not fond of ceremony), Claughton of Rochester, and Wilberforce of Oxford who was in trouble for the usage. The laity liked the symbol. They desired that their bishops should carry such an instrument of office when performing duty in church, and gave them to more and more bishops. A bishop was hesitant to accept lest he give offence, but usually preferred not to refuse lest he give offence. Lightfoot of Durham refused a staff at first and accepted it later. The laity found it a historic and meaningful symbol. Such little changes, such as purple cassocks and pastoral staffs, are typical of the way in which the usages became more elaborate, because they felt appropriate to the aesthetic judgment of many lay worshippers. A majority of bishops were not eager to carry staffs, but a majority of bishops ended up carrying them.

(Chadwick, *The Victorian Church*, 1970).

In 1871 Jenner very kindly – considering his opinion of the consecration of his successor – offered the crozier to the Rt. Rev.

Samuel Nevill, who had been consecrated Bishop of Dunedin that year, asking if it would be possible for Nevill to acknowledge him as the first bishop of the diocese. Nevill declined to accept it, saying in a speech in 1889 that he thought the offer had been a 'bit of a bribe', although that was not how Jenner had intended it.

Jenner kept the crozier for the rest of his life, and in 1900 his son Henry exchanged a series of letters with the Bishop of Dover to establish a 'deed of gift' so that it could be offered to him, which it was. The following report of an interesting act of telekinesis appeared in the *Guardian* of 12 June 1900:

A Pastoral Staff in ebony and ivory has been presented by the late Bishop Jenner to the Archbishop of Canterbury, to be held by him in trust for the use of the Bishop Suffragan at Dover. The staff was originally presented to the late Bishop Jenner on his nomination to the See of Dunedin, N.Z. by the Cambridge Ecclesiological Society, of which he had been for many years the honorary secretary.

The staff was used by the then Bishop of Dover Rt. Rev. William Walsh on the occasion of the Rev. A. N. Armstrong becoming curate-in-charge of the new church of St Michael's and All Angels in July 1900.

It has been used, on occasion, by his successors ever since, being kept in Canterbury Cathedral Treasury for the rest of the time. It will perhaps stay there a lot more since the present Bishop of Dover, the Rt. Rev. Rose Josephine Hudson-Wilkin, was given her own personal crozier, made of Blue Mahoe, the national tree of Jamaica, the country of her birth.

The Jenner Chapel

In the church where Henry Jenner spent most of his ministry the south chapel, (or Chapel of St Nicholas,) has been re-designed as a memorial to him. It was rededicated in 2004 – after an oil painting of the Bishop was discovered hidden under a rather mildewed photograph of him, and then restored – and renamed as the 'Jenner Chapel'. The picture was hung in the Canterbury Cathedral Archives, and for a while its copy hung in the south chapel, along with a chair purporting to be his.

On the south wall is a framed notice which reads:

This Chapel of St. Nicholas
was restored for the offering
of the Holy Sacrifice in
October 1938 by Friends and
relations of Bishop Jenner.
It was re-opened on December 1st
1938 by the Right Reverend
the Lord Bishop of Dover.
At the same service the
Bishop dedicated the new
Altar, the Memorial Window
and other gifts in this Church.

The date of 1938 gives rise to a couple of questions, however. Both dates are written in a rather different style to the rest of the document, giving the impression of having been added later. If they are correct, then the friends would have been quite old, it being forty years after Jenner's death.

The other question concerns the date of the Memorial Window. In the bottom right hand corner of that widow is a piece of glass with the names *Curtis, Ward and Hughes*. This was the Soho based company that made the window and whose work was regularly praised in the *Ecclesiologist*. As this firm had finished production by the 1920s the window would have been put in many years before the dedication.

The **Memorial Window,** (illustrated on the back cover,) itself is a glorious tribute to Henry Jenner, both in design and colour, and in what it celebrates about him.

It consists of two lancet windows, each with a saintly figure.
On the right is *Saint Augustine*, or so the Latin lettering on his halo says:

𝔖t. 𝔄ugustinius 𝔈𝔘𝔖

A closer look, however, shows him to have the finely portrayed face of Henry Jenner. With that great beard, and those sad but loving eyes, it couldn't be anyone else. He is even holding the *Dunedin crozier*, although the design is simpler than that of the original, with no bound woman, and St George replaced with a smiling girl, apparently scratching the dragon on its nose. All are looked upon by two young angels. The Bishop is carrying a large shiny orange ... or it could represent a heart.

Below the Bishop is a small picture of St Augustine, standing in a garden looking upwards, with his hands raised in surprise at hearing the words 'Tolle Lege' (Latin for the command "take up and read" and written on scrolls on either side of the picture,) that he heard from a mysterious voice during his conversion to Christianity.

Sitting behind him on a bench and holding a book on his lap is another saint, whilst on the ground is an open book with SAINT PAUL written in large letters across the open pages, which Augustine takes to be what he should take up and read.

In the bottom right hand corner of the window is a coat of arms with a mitre on the top. The mitre traditionally meant that this was the shield of a bishop, but nowadays tends to relate to a whole diocese.

On the top left is a fragment containing three white stars against a blue background, representing the Southern Cross and appearing on most of the New Zealand Diocesan arms. The rest of this half contains a saint holding a white Saltire against a red background. This is the design for the Diocese of Dunedin in 1894. [See *A Treatise on Ecclesiastical Heraldry* by Rev John Woodward.]

On the right hand side of the shield are three covered cups, between two swords chevronwise, with hilts and pommels, on an azure background. This is the arms of the Jenner family, and was granted to Sir Thomas Jenner in 1684. [See *A genealogical and heraldic history of the landed gentry of Great Britain & Ireland* (1879) Sir Bernard Burke.]

In the left lancet is the figure of *Saint Gregory*, or that is what it says on his halo:

St. Gregorious + Magn [Great]

But again, the face is not that of the sacred pope but of a fairly pale and sketchy looking chap, (in comparison with Jenner's,) described by a recent church leaflet as "the then Archbishop of Canterbury". As with so much concerning Jenner, his life seems to have been damaged by the misuse of the written word. What does 'then' mean? At the time of the window's creation? That would make it Cosmo Gordon Lang (1928–1942), but it doesn't look like him, and besides, he had nothing to do with Jenner. The next Archbishop who did have dealings with our Bishop was Archibald Tait (1868-1882), and it could possibly be him. But probably the Archbishop who was chosen to stand beside Jenner in that Memorial Window was Charles Longley (1862-1868), the man who had been headmaster at Harrow when Jenner was a student, who had chosen him to be the first Bishop of Dunedin, who had consecrated him as such in Canterbury Cathedral ... and then somehow quite lost the plot, and became a source of pain and despair for our hero. The sketch bears a likeness.

He is portrayed wearing a rather simple Papal Tiara and carrying a Papal Staff, and in his right hand he holds a parchment on which is written Psalm 84 in Latin set to Jenner's tune *Quam dilecta tabernacula tua.*

Beneath him is a picture of Pope Gregory telling his famous Gregorian pun when he first encountered pale-skinned English boys at a slave market, sparking his dispatch of St. Augustine of Canterbury to England to convert the English - *'Not angles but angels'.*

At the lower edge of the window is written:

To the Glory of God and in loving memory of Henry Lascelles Jenner first Bishop of Dunedin, New Zealand and for 44 years Vicar of this Parish who entered into his rest Sept 18th 1898

In the *Whitstable Times and Herne Bay Herald* of Saturday 19 August 1905 is an article which solves the dating of the memorial window.

PRESTON-NEXT-WINGHAM DEDICATION OF THE BISHOP JENNER MEMORIAL ...
... It was decided that the appropriate form would the filling of a two-light window at the eastern end of the south aisle with some beautiful painted glass, and that no better choice be made as regards figures than the two eminent churchmen. St. Gregory and St. Augustine of Hippo. The figures are surmounted by canopies of the perpendicular order of white and gold upon ruby backgrounds, and beneath are bases of the sama character, containing small subjects illustrating events in the lives of the saints. One inscription under the window is :—

'To the glory of God, and in loving memory of Henry Lascelles Jenner, D.D., first Bishop of Dunedin, New Zealand, for 44 years vicar of this parish, who entered his rest September 18th, 1898.' *The design of the window has been arranged by Mr. Henry Jenner, F.S.A., son of the Bishop, and the window was executed under his superintendence by Mr. T. F. Curtis (of Messrs. Ward and Hughes), Frith Street, Soho Square.*

The final mystery about the chapel is, why is it dedicated to St Nicholas?

We love the place, O God ...

In an article about Jenner entitled *'A Bishop without a See'*, by Robert Douglas in *Bygone Kent* (Volume 24) , there is a delightful picture of the great man standing in the back row of a photograph of the boys of Preston Council School. He appears just like he did in the group photograph of the First Lambeth Conference, tall, bald, and bearded, with that kindly, thoughtful expression that could perhaps be attributed to his bushy eyebrows – or more likely to his true nature. It was taken at the end of the Summer Term of 1898, a few weeks before he died.

The *Canterbury Press* for 24 September 1898 recorded the event in this oddly inaccurate article:

We regret to record the death on Sunday last [18ᵗʰ September,] of the Right Rev. Henry Lascelles Jenner, first Bishop of Dunedin, New Zealand, at Preston Vicarage, Wingham. The health of the venerable prelate had been satisfactory until within a very brief period of his demise. He had been actively engaged in his duties as vicar of the parish, occupied with business in London on Thursday; on Friday he visited several sick parishioners – travelling about on his tricycle – his chief method of locomotion – with all his accustomed vigour. Saturday found him indisposed but not apparently to any serious extent. He was not able to conduct services on Sunday, but it was not until that evening that there was any cause for alarm. Dangerous symptoms then developed, and at 9.30 p.m. he breathed his last, succumbing to syncope or failure of the heart's action.
Mrs. Jenner and her three unmarried daughters were with the Bishop at the time of his decease, but the married members of the family – Mr Jenner of the British Museum and Mrs Edgell of Teddington – did not reach Preston until the following day, there having been no apparent reason to summon them until Sunday evening.

On the same day the *Canterbury Journal, Kentish Times and Farmers' Gazette* had a slightly different, and perhaps more accurate account:

We regret to record the death of Bishop Jenner, vicar of Preston-next-Wingham, which occurred suddenly at the Vicarage at nine o'clock on

Sunday night. He had been slightly indisposed for two or three days, but there was not considered to be any cause for alarm, his condition being attributed to the excessive heat. Shortly before nine o'clock on Sunday evening he had a seizure of some kind, and before his medical attendant could reach the Vicarage the Bishop had expired. It appears that on the previous Thursday, the 15th, the deceased rode on his tricycle from Preston to Grove Ferry, [past the farmhouse that years later was to be the scene of sea scouts celebrating soccer,] *where he took the train to London. He returned the same evening, and tricycled back from Grove Ferry to the Vicarage. He appeared none the worse for his journey, nor for the excessively hot weather. On Friday, however, he complained of a drowsy feeling, but felt well enough to be able to attend his church. He continued to complain of drowsiness, but it appeared to be passing off. He stayed indoors the whole of Saturday and Sunday, and it was hoped that he would be about again as usual on the following day.*

In 1866 he was appointed, on the recommendation of Archbishop Longley, to the See of Dunedin, but he practically never occupied it, the Scottish population taking alarm at his advanced Church views. The circumstances are too long and intricate to attempt a summary here – there being prolonged discussions among the home bishops and those in New Zealand – but it may be mentioned that the matter was gone into at length in the Church Review *on the occasion of his golden wedding last year, and that Bishop Wilberforce said that he had been 'shamefully, infamously, iniquitously dealt with.'*
He would say pathetically that, except once for the Bishop of Ely, he had hardly ever performed episcopal functions in England – save confirming his own parishioners – but for some time he acted as Bishop of the Eglise Catholique Gallicaine at Paris.
A man of notable presence, genial manners, and considerable ability, he was a conspicuous figure at all Canterbury functions, and at meetings of the English Church Union, of which he was a warm supporter.
Few men were more disappointed in life, but few bore their troubless with greater dignity.

A broader account was in the national *Morning Post* of 27 September.

The death of Henry Lascelles Jenner, first Bishop of Dunedin, New Zealand, removes a familiar figure from High Church gatherings. As a matter of fact Dr. Jenner was never really in possession of the newly-formed Diocese. He was, in a somewhat hurried manner, selected and consecrated for Dunedin by Archbishop Lomgley in 1866, and was accepted by the Synod of Otago in the following year. Subsequently opposition to the appointment was aroused in New Zealand, and when Bishop Jenner visited Dunedin his flock refused to accept him as their shepherd. He did not formally resign for five years, and the appointment of another Bishop to succeed him before the resignation had been actually made aroused considerable feeling at the time.

Dr. Jenner was an accomplished musician and hymn-writer, and expert ecclesiologist, and a man of many accomplishments. His tall and venerable figure and purple soutane were especially conspicuous at gatherings in Canterbury Cathedral. He was very widely esteemed for his amiable qualities, but for some reason or other his brother Bishops at home treated him with cold neglect, and he was seldom allowed to exercise his Episcopal office. The late Bishop Wilberforce declared in vigorous terms that Bishop Jenner was shamefully treated.

It was fitting that the hymn 'We love the place, O God wherein thine honour dwells,' sung to *Quam Dilecta*, should be set at the beginning of Henry Jenner's burial service. Not just because he had composed the tune, but also because it reflected his deep and lasting belief in the nature of the Church. As befitting a man who had given much of his life in the service of choirs (both with and without surplices,) and singing of all kinds, it was appropriate that it was a full choral service. Indeed, many different choirs from all over the place turned up, which, along with his many parishioners and friends and admirers, rather packed out the small church of St Mildred's. The local paper mentioned the names of various senior clergy present (no fellow bishops) and the other hymns sung (the usual suspects) and concluded:

The sorrowful groups of friends and mourners withdrew, leaving the beloved pastor and faithful priest resting under the shadow of the church and scene of his long and devoted ministrations.

Bishop Jenner was replaced as Vicar of Preston by the Rev. Walter Delmar Lindley, who was also Rector of the neighbouring parish of Elmstone. He was the son of the previous Rector of Elmstone, the Rev. William Baldock Delmar - the Delmar family owning the Manor of Elmstone Court, which held the patronage of the church. William Baldock had been Rector of Elmstone for 58 years (compared with Jenner's 44), but had also been Rector of St Clement's, Knowlton, and Vicar of Holy Trinity, West Marsh during the same period. The wealth of the Delmar's came directly from their famous ancestor William Baldock, smuggler, property tycoon and gentleman, who, in the space of just sixty years from 1749, had risen from smuggling on the Seasalter Marshes to amassing an estate said to be worth £1.1m.

It is difffficult to understand why Henry Lascelles Jenner should have spent such a large part of his life in the situation that he did. Not just as a See-less, 'spare' bishop, but in a position that made a mockery of his wide and intellectual gifts and abilities, and which failed to provide him with an adequate income, social status, and mental stimulus.

Unlike his colleague in Elmstone he had only one small parish to serve, of a population of about 500 people and an income of about £400 a year. It is clear from refernces in various letters concerning his future that his pecuniary circumstances were not good, as does this section of a letter written by him to Archbishop Tait on 14 Sept 1869:

It seems ridiculous for one who is presumably competent to govern a diocese to settle down as a Vicar of a small agricultural parish. My robust state of health makes the absurdity the more glaring. How long my bodily health will hold out against the depression of spirits to which I have been subject since my return (a most unusual complaint with me) is another question ...

If I am to remain Vicar of Preston for the rest of my life – God's will be done. I shall try to go on doing His work as well as I can, here, if He denies me a more extended field of labour. I shall then have to rid myself, in outward appearance, at all events, of (what will then be) the terrible encumbrance of the Episcopal Character. And it will be necessary for me to take pupils, or adopt some other means of adding to my means of support – the expenses to which I have been put since my Consecration having well nigh ruined me.

There are perhaps three groups of people who could have helped Henry Jenner to widen his experiences of life and find a situation that made use of his gifts and abilities.

The first was his family, that great world-wide tribe of worthy Jenners in their positions of power and influence. They could, presumably, have lent him a quid or two, or given him a regular top-up to his stipend from the Bank of Mum and Dad. After all, as Pearce wrote in his account of the consecration:

They were doing well in their chosen professions - the Law, the Navy, the Army and the Civil Service. His sister Charlotte was there with her husband Francis Hart Dyke, Queen's Proctor and Registrar of the Province. Anne was also present with her husband Evan Nepean, Canon of Westminster.

But there is, at the same time, something haunting about his earlier remark - which for some reason appears in most of the accounts of Jenner's consecration - that s*ix of Bishop Jenner's brothers were present, and all were over six feet and particularly broad and handsome.*

It is not uncommon for one member of such a successful set of siblings to find it a difficult place to be themselves. But what do we know? Certainly his place in history was to be somewhat overshadowed by two very close fellow Jenners.

His father, Herbert - King's Advocate, knighted, sworn of the Privy Council, Vicar-General of the Province of Canterbury, Dean of Arches and Judge of the Prerogative Court of Canterbury, and Master of his old college, Trinity Hall, Cambridge.

And his son, Henry - a clerk in the Probate Division of the High Court, nominated by the Primate at Canterbury for a post in the Department of Ancient Manuscripts in the British Museum and a scholar of the Celtic languages, a Cornish cultural activist, and the chief originator of the Cornish language revival.

The second group of failing friends were the fellow members of the Ecclesiological Society, and all those who travelled the same 'theological groove', and shared his passion for Catholic renewal in the life of the church. Pearce writes that:

The catholic movement had itself gone on and left him standing. He suffered by being in his younger days before his times, in his latter by being behind them.

Given the many ways in which he overtly supported the Anglo-Catholic movement, and how this led to his rejection by the Diocese of Dunedin, it is hard to see why its members seem to have ignored him when offering preferments or positions in their various organisations.

And then there were the English bishops.

On the whole, except for Wilberforce, they come out very badly from the whole Dunedin affair. They seem to take his side and say that he should have been appointed Bishop of Dunedin, and they are good at signing documents which begin 'it's no business of ours but ... ', but in the end they, who were in the best position to give Jenner's consecration some practical meaning, just let him decay in the wilderness of rural Kent.

They even seem to take a slightly mocking attitude towards him, as in the letters of the Bishop of Dover and Randall Davidson. Archbishop Tait even implies that they had no respect for him, and that they regarded his treatment in Dunedin and his financial difficulties as being *his fault.*

Still, bishops are bishops, and their behaviour here is not much different from that in other generations. Having said that, it's tough on Bishops. They are meant to be 'Fathers and Mothers in God', implying that they are loving, caring, motherly and fatherly-like figures who you could share a friendly coffee or a pint with, or have a chat about your latest crisis. But the job is actually more like a cross between being the Chief Executive and head of human resources, a person with power who you have to be toady-ish towards if you are to climb the greasy pole of promotion. That must be tough to juggle. And tough too to hold together the beliefs that you declare at General Synod and in the *Telegraph*, but which are markedly different from the ones you live by, and know to be true.

At the time of writing the *Church Times* has two articles, printed on opposite pages, concerning the appalling treatment by the Church of England hierarchy of two different priests, both accused of paedophilia.

One was about a privileged, high ranking barrister, friend of the royal family, and the unquestioned charismatic leader of an evangelical community. He was a child molester, but his behaviour was overlooked, accepted, ignored, and made light of, by those in authority around him until he died.
[At the time of going to press several other such cases have arisen, particularly that of the saintly founder of 'Soul Survivor Youth Movement ' in Watford.]

The second concerned an Anglo-Catholic priest who had a PhD in Classical Languages, Greek, Latin, Art, Linguistics and History, and was lecturer in Classics and Senior Warden of the Duryard Halls, and Honorary University Chaplain at the University of Exeter. As an Anglican priest he had been Rector of St Andrew by the Wardrobe and St James Garlickhythe, and Chaplain to the Lord Mayor of London. The ordination of women moved him to become a Roman Catholic, and it was in this role in his retirement that the Diocese of London, without any evidence, accused him of paedophilia. As he was completely innocent of such offences, and being an excellent and caring priest, he found it hard to have his life's ministry denigrated in this way, and so he committed suicide.

He was not alone, the Chancellor of Lincoln Cathedral spent two years suspended from his living falsely accused of "a crime of a serious nature".

The list is endless. Jenner's treatment was typical of an institution that so hides behind its pomp and power that it fails to see where its real strengths and weaknesses lie. It sometimes seems as if, were the CofE to make a pitch for itself, it would need to use the opposite of that advert that says, **"It does what it says on the tin"**.

SOURCES

Seeking a See - A Journal of the Right Reverend Henry Lascelles
Jenner D.D. on his visit to Dunedin, New Zealand in 1868-1869
Edited by Rev. John Pearce M.B.E
The Standing Committee of the Diocese of Dunedin 1984

Southern See
John H. Evans MA
The Standing Committee of the Diocese of Dunedin 1968

Henry Lascelles Jenner: the first Bishop of Dunedin?
Dr Tony Fitchett
August 2018

Dioceses of New Zealand (Colonial Church Histories)
Very Rev. H. Jacobs
SPCK 1887

A History of the English Church in New Zealand
Rev. H. T. Purchas
Sampson Low and Co. Ltd., London 1914

TROVE – holds freely available online copies of documents
about New Zealand that are held by the Lambeth Palace Library (as
filmed by the Australian Joint Copying Project).

Lambeth Palace Library – Holds vast amounts of stuff about
Bishops etc. which can be seen in their reading room.
15 Lambeth Palace Road,
London, SE1 7JT
Email: *archives@churchofengland.org*

Papers Past
A freely available collection of early New Zealand newspapers.
Email: *paperspast@natlib.govt.nz*

The British Newspaper Archive
A collection of early British newspapers.
https://www.britishnewspaperarchive.co.uk/

Bob Simmonds has a degree in Theology, a Diploma in Careers Guidance, and has been an Anglican priest for the past forty-three years. As well as being a Vicar he has been the founder and manager of an Oxfam bookshop, a provider of guidance and support for Volunteers working in the NHS, and a crew member of a dirty British coaster with a salt-caked smoke stack ... but not all at the same time. He has also written the following books.

The Small Happy Family of Broadstairs ISBN 101 905 477 395

Footpaths of Thanet ISBN 1 905 477 732

Broadstairs Harbour ISBN 1 905 477 686

The Petrified Haystack of Broadstairs ISBN 1 905 477 287

'Weather Here, Wish You Were Lovely!' A History of Holidaying in Ramsgate ISBN 1 905 477 635

Ramsgate From the Ground: An Alternative Look at the Town and its History ISBN 1 905 477 473

Ramsgate's Answer To Turner and Tracey: Famous People Who Have Lived and Loved Ramsgate ISBN 1 905 477 465

Hidden Scenes in Kent: by Sir Frank Short RA and JMW Turner ISBN 9 781 789 726 589

Priest & Sow Corner ... and other Swalecliffe mysteries ISBN 9 781 788 081 160

Pubs, Skateboards and a Slender Spire ISBN 9 781 788 081 566

Bricks Planes and Camping Sites ... a quirky look at the Life and Times of Swalecliffe - the 'East End' of Whitstable ISBN 9 781 788 081 153

He can be contacted at
writerbobsimmonds@gmail.com